Horton Foote's
Three Trips to Bountiful

Also from
Southern Methodist University Press

Selected One-Act Plays of Horton Foote

Horton Foote

Horton Foote's
Three Trips to Bountiful

⋅⋅⋅ Edited by ⋅⋅⋅

Barbara Moore *and* David G. Yellin

Southern Methodist University Press
Dallas

Library of Congress Cataloging-in-Publication Data

Foote, Horton.
    [Trip to Bountiful]
    Horton Foote's three trips to Bountiful / edited by Barbara Moore and David G. Yellin.
       p.   cm.
    Includes the scripts of Foote's play, television play, and screenplay of The trip to Bountiful.
    Includes bibliographical references.
    ISBN 0-87074-326-0 : — ISBN 0-87074-327-9 (pbk.) :
    1. Foote, Horton—Film and video adaptations. I. Moore, Barbara.
II. Yellin, David G. III. Title. IV. Title: Three trips to Bountiful. V. Title: 3 trips to Bountiful.
PS3511.0344T7 1993
812'.54—dc20   91-52779

Designed by Whitehead & Whitehead

For Horton Foote
  —B.M. and D.G.Y.

Contents

Acknowledgments

WE'D like to thank all of the people who allowed us to interview them and who helped us secure photographs. For help in preparing the manuscript, we are grateful to Paul Alatorre and Kathy Biggar and for her editing, Kathryn Lang. Suzanne Comer's enthusiasm for the project was a source of inspiration. Also helpful were Len Maniace, Barbara Monteiro, and Susan Sandack. A faculty research grant from the University of Tennessee, Knoxville, provided support for a summer's work.

B.M. and D.G.Y.

Horton Foote's
Three Trips to Bountiful

Introduction

ABOUT sixty-five years ago in the small town of Wharton, Texas, a young boy sat on his front porch and listened to his relatives talk. Horton Foote heard the story of a young man and woman who were deeply in love but were not allowed to marry each other. They married other people, but he continued to walk by her house on his way to work every day just to see her. This tale of frustrated love and ruined lives amid the routine of everyday small town life must have made an impression on Foote because he alluded to it in several of his works.

One day he began to think about the life of the woman. What would she be like when her love was barely a memory? In 1953 he wrote *The Trip to Bountiful* for the "Philco/ Goodyear Television Playhouse," a live hour of drama presented weekly.[1] (These presentations, with varying casts, characters, settings, and plot lines, dominated the TV screen in the early days of the new medium. Today the predominant television form is the serial with a continuing story from week to week.)

Bountiful starred Lillian Gish and won high praise from viewers. Eight months later, Foote expanded the television script into a play that ran on Broadway for a few weeks. Lillian Gish again played the lead, and Jo Van Fleet played Jessie Mae, a performance that earned her a Tony Award for best supporting actress. Thirty-one years later, the story was reincarnated as a film starring Geraldine Page, who won an Oscar for best performance by an actress in her role as Carrie Watts.

1

The plot centers around a sixty-year-old widow who shares a cramped apartment in Houston with her son Ludie and his wife Jessie Mae. Carrie Watts yearns to return to her hometown of Bountiful and finally manages to catch a bus to the Texas countryside where she grew up. On the trip, she meets Thelma, a newlywed, who sympathizes with her, and a sheriff, who helps Mrs. Watts reach her goal. The story ends with her arrival at the old homestead, which has fallen into disrepair. After a tentative reconciliation with her son, who has followed her to Bountiful to bring her back to Houston, Carrie Watts is resigned to returning to the city.

Bountiful shares many characteristics with other plays by Foote. Of primary importance is the fact that he borrows from his past. Details of his own childhood are woven into the fabric of his story, giving *Bountiful* its quality of authenticity and its evocative power. Jessie Mae talks of going to three movies in one day in Houston, and Mrs. Watts describes how her father protected the birds on his land. These incidents and others are derived from Foote's own Texas memories. However, his script does more than create a sense of nostalgia; it depicts with merciless accuracy the people and times of both urban and rural America in the late forties and early fifties.

One critic comments that Foote "redesigns real stories so that they take the shape and nature of myth. He crafts them into tales of going away and coming home, grief and rebirth, despair and healing—tales for all places and times."[2] Foote belongs in the same category as Flannery O'Connor, William Faulkner, and Eudora Welty—writers with a strong sense of place who believe that environment and past generations are powerful forces in shaping character and fate.

In his plays, Foote also displays a strong sense of music, as in his use of hymns in *Bountiful*. The rhythm of hymns underlies some of Foote's dialogue, and his narrative moves with the dignity, simplicity, and quiet power of a hymn. Foote explains, "I have a strong childhood memory of hearing music, either Mexican dances or music of the blacks or the church music of white dances. It permeated everything; if you went out on the porch, you could always hear something."[3] He admires the music of Charles Ives with its folk themes and has worked with choreographer Martha Graham. Author Reynolds Price, a friend of Foote, calls him "the supreme musician among our great American playwrights."[4]

The dialogue of *Bountiful* is shaped by the dialect of the Texas Gulf Coast, a combination of southern gentility and western stoicism. According to writer Stark Young, "The speech [of that region] tended to be alive, unselfconscious and rural. As for Horton Foote's dialogue, there is everywhere present a kind of elusive and glowing accuracy. And there is never any sense of arch intention or any sign of the playwright's coquetting with quaintness."[5] Or as another writer notes, "Foote's words offer a private kind of pleasure, much like the scrubby, flat landscape of Wharton in winter; ordinary to the itinerant eye, but oddly beautiful for one who lingers."[6] The dialogue is as plain as the people who inhabit Foote's fictional world. The problems of the Watts family are as commonplace as their lives. The mother and son suffer heartbreaks too ordinary to be labeled tragic, and they respond by surviving quietly and hiding their despair. They don't allow themselves the luxury of long, tear-stained speeches; they don't rage at God, and they don't commit suicide. They gather what is left of their dignity and go on living.

At the end of *Bountiful* Mrs. Watts allows herself a short bout of bitter crying. She asks her son what's happened to them: "Why have we come to this?" But immediately she comforts herself with the sights and smells of her home and with her memories. She and the other characters, however, are not mere symbols for Everyman. They have the "peculiarities and eccentricities" that make ordinary people human.[7]

The emotions of Carrie and Ludie Watts seem as faded as their everyday clothes. They accept their suffering as they accept the weather. When the sheriff tells Mrs. Watts she cannot go to Bountiful, she says, "Suffering I don't mind. Suffering I understand. I didn't protest once. Though my heart was broken when those babies died." When the characters discuss their pain, their language is not suddenly elevated in tone; it remains simple, plain, colloquial. It is significant that Foote's scripts offer few directions on the way lines are to be performed by actors. As a former actor himself, Foote prefers to allow actors latitude to interpret his words as they see the character. If his lines are read as they are written, much of the emotion is inherently clear.

The quiet tone and even pacing of *The Trip to Bountiful* are monotonous in the opinion of some critics; others admire the dignity and spareness of the work, like that of Shaker furniture. "For [Foote's characters] emotion is to be understood, to be mastered and channeled, not imposed upon those who do not share it. It is . . . the Jessie Maes who tell everyone always what they feel because nothing they can admit to feeling is worth being reticent about."[8]

While the style is understated and the characters' problems at first glance seem trivial, the underlying questions Foote examines in *The Trip to Bountiful* are serious. One question he has spent most of his career as a writer asking is, How can the human spirit survive, not in the face of tragedy, but in a world of ceaseless disappointments?[9] Foote offers no definitive answers. "But that is because he writes to discover, not to preach. Rather than lecture to his readers, he investigates with them the 'great mystery' of courage and personhood."[10]

The American dream is based on the hope that each generation's life will be better than that of the preceding generation. Ludie's grandfather was wealthy, well-respected, prominent, and Ludie expected that he would exceed his grandfather's accomplishments or at least equal them; yet the circumstances of life dictated otherwise. The family wealth was lost, and the family name lost its respectability.

Ludie cannot justify the downward spiral. Even if the blame for the financial and social failure doesn't lie with him, the shame does. He finds it difficult to cope with the continual presence of failure. Ludie admits he cannot provide a real home for his wife and mother; he is dependent on his mother's social security checks; he has been unable to sire a child to carry on the family name. While Mrs.

Watts's memories of the past bring her solace, her son feels only the disappointment of promises not kept, promises he made, like naming a son after his grandfather, and promises he believes life made to him. At their decaying family homestead in Bountiful, he tells his mother he wants to stop remembering, that "it doesn't do any good remembering."

Ludie and his mother have small dreams and fear they will never accomplish even their limited goals. They don't want to rule the world; they don't dream of curing society's ills; they don't wish for the consummation of a passionate love affair. They want the comfort that somehow, in some way, their life will be better, and they have to face the knowledge that their lot will probably not improve. What makes Foote's characters so appealing is that they survive with some measure of dignity and with some ability to feel joy and compassion. Foote concentrates not on the pain, but on their reconciliation with life.

Because Foote writes about simple people with simple problems, some critics have described his work as sentimental. But if *Bountiful* were merely a sentimental drama, the plot would have provided Mrs. Watts an easy escape from her suffering and a triumph over her enemies. She might have reconciled with her penitent daughter-in-law, or found a home with her friend on the bus, or died in the arms of her son on the front lawn of the homestead with a noble speech guaranteed to bring tears to the audience's eyes. But people don't change their personalities abruptly; strangers rarely rescue us from our problems, and we seldom die at convenient moments. Instead, Foote searches for the truth. The language is too muted, the author has too much respect for his characters, and he is too realistic about the choices society offers them for the manipulation of sentiment.

For some, the ending of *Bountiful* is unsatisfactory. Jessie Mae remains unchanged, unaware of her own insensitivity and shallowness. She is not punished for her crimes of selfishness, pettiness, and meanness. In the film, we can see the surprise on her face when Mrs. Watts responds to her list of demands with a kiss and a generous hug. Ludie finally finds the strength to insist that the women stop bickering, and together the two women shade their eyes against the glare of the sun; they seem almost to salute him. The film leaves us feeling that life will be more bearable for Mrs. Watts, even though Jessie Mae has shown no remorse.

Mrs. Watts faces her future with composure and an acceptance of her fate. Seeing her home and the land of Bountiful has been a source of comfort for her. And Mrs. Watts seems buoyed by feeling that she has proved she is not a helpless old woman imprisoned in a small apartment with a daughter-in-law who torments her. Instead, she sees herself as a woman capable of plotting and carrying out a successful escape. She boasts to Thelma about having fooled her watchful relatives. She has dealt with the complications of purchasing a ticket to a town that no longer exists. She has found friends who listened to her and helped her on her way. She has accomplished her goal of reaching Bountiful despite all sorts of obstacles, including ill health, and she must take some pride in her achievement, even if the goal has been illusory.

Carrie Watts broke off a relationship with the man she loved and married a man she didn't love to please her father. She lost two children to death. She was at the mercy of the weather and the soil while she was farming. She left the land for the sake of her son's future. Throughout her life, she has been a victim, one who sacrificed. Her trip to Bountiful is her declaration of independence, an act of rebellion, a signal that she has taken control of her life. Her explanation to her son for running away is simply that she had to, and as she tells Jessie Mae, "I've had my trip. That's more than enough to keep me happy the rest of my life." Visiting her home seems to provide her with some magical strength and a will to survive, but it is the strength of her character, her determination, that has gotten her to Bountiful.

For a short while, Mrs. Watts manages to defeat the present with the past. Her visit reassures her that once life did have some measure of beauty and grace. Her parents, her home, the land—all existed. Even Ludie cannot deny the past any longer. Through her courage, he is forced to recall a better time, a better life. She understands that people like themselves can't be free of their history until they confront it directly. For Ludie and his mother, reconciliation with the past is a necessary aspect of facing reality. They are now free to live in the present and maybe the future.

Mrs. Watts learns that her home in Bountiful will not provide her with a refuge from city life and Jessie Mae. At the end of the story, she reconciles herself to the fact that she has no escape. "Suffering (to the point of devastation) is the central human condition and our most unavoidable mystery. Yet we can survive it and sing in its face."[11] Mrs. Watts sings hymns, but not only as an act of defiance. The hymns also express her hope for the future, they console her, and they remind her of a community of believers from the past. The pain is inescapable, but it is bearable.

A message of comfort and an affirmation of life come in *Bountiful* when Mrs. Watts comments on how the land has been cleared, planted, and allowed to degenerate. People abandon it, and trees, thorns, and wildflowers reclaim it. Later, other people, she says, will clear it again as the cycle continues. Her own family's downward spiral may come to an end, if not in Ludie's generation, then in another, and if there are no more members of her line, then someone else's family will join the cycle and carry it on to the next phase. Her hometown of Bountiful in some form will endure; Bountiful will live up to its name again. Mrs. Watts's view of life as a circular process is part of the reason she finds the homestead at Bountiful a refuge. It reminds her that her life was once better, that her entrapment in the apartment is just temporary, perhaps even that a better home awaits her in heaven, as her hymns suggest.

With Mrs. Watts, Foote portrays death as a gradual process. The outline of that process is sketched in the television script, and some of the details are filled in with the other two versions. She has uprooted herself from home. Her parents have died and their generation has disappeared. Her search for some confirmation of identity is lonely. She and the ticket man at the bus station go over a list of people she has known in Harrison, but all are dead or forgotten. She alone remembers how she looked and sounded as a little girl. The only evidence of the central event of her life, her first and only love, is the locket she wears. The only evidence of the existence of her parents and her deceased children is gravestones. The house has deteriorated, and the land has returned to weeds and scrub brush. Ludie has denied his past and, therefore, hers. Callie Davis, her childhood friend, her last link to her youth, has died. Mrs. Watts is the only remaining witness; she has to accept the fact that one day she too will be only a memory.

On her old front porch, she says to Ludie, "Pretty soon all this will be gone. Ten years. Twenty. This house. Me. You." When the owners of the memory die, what trace of her will be left behind? She decides the land of Bountiful will endure and will have to serve as her monument. "Foote's people endlessly pursue healing ties to the land, their families, loved ones, even work. Finally they are faced with the terrible reality that each must live and die, to some degree, alone."[12]

Nostalgia does not bring comfort to all of the characters. Ludie finds only pain in a return to the past, and Jessie Mae is genuinely puzzled that anyone could be interested in or touched by a reality that is old-fashioned, inconvenient, and unglamorous. She complains about her shoes getting scratched, worries about the quality of the water at the farm in Bountiful, and looks forward to stopping at a drugstore for a Coke.

To Jessie Mae, the past is irrelevant and unimportant. Her dreams are of the present, not the past. She wants to go to Hollywood, not a dilapidated farmhouse. The radio, the movie theater, and the gossip magazines form the basis of her present dreams and future hopes. Her freedom from the past makes Jessie Mae the most shallow of the characters, but it also makes her the best survivor. Although her lack of sensitivity prevents her from sharing the warmth of Ludie's and Mrs. Watts's reconciliation, it protects her from the pain they feel. Ludie, Mrs. Watts, and Thelma all admit to worrying too much, but they say they can't help it. Jessie Mae's attitude is "Worry? What for?"

Some have seen the story as a tale of the fate of rural Americans in an industrialized, urbanized economy.[13] The Wattses have left the land they owned for a city where they crowd together in a small apartment. With these external changes have come a new set of values, personified by Jessie Mae. Ludie has tried hard to succeed in this situation, but a nervous breakdown has been the result. He seems unable to meet the demands of the new urban America. He wants to belong, but lacks some ingredient to propel him into success. Hard work, promptness, and neatness are not enough. His choice of reading material—*How to Be an Executive*—is a telling detail in Foote's portrait. The economy, the landscape, and the values of America have been transformed by powers outside the Wattses' control, and they must learn to accept these changes.

To Foote, a sense of continuity with the past is necessary, if not for survival, then for sanity, at least for some people. Not everyone in Foote's world needs this hint of eternity, but those who do must fight for it or be worn out by the confusing, abrupt changes of the modern world that seem to have no causes and to be controlled by no one. "Going away from home and coming home again are both powerful needs, mythic patterns of attachment and freedom. Both rely on a set of assumptions and shared values that order human experience. When 'home'—that grounding force larger than the individual and more enduring, whether religion, the family, work or whatever—is stripped away, identity itself is threatened."[14] *The Trip to Bountiful* is a tale of a search for home.

Differences in the Three Media

It is interesting to see how Foote adapted his own work for the three different media. The traditional approach to adaptation emphasizes the importance of changing the material to fit the aesthetic strengths and the practical limitations of each art form. Foote chose to make relatively minimal changes, most of which were dictated by differences in the nature of the media. Some of the factors that must be considered in the process of adaptation are concrete and easily identified.

A teleplay is presented in the home on a television screen. Viewers are comfortable, watching the performance either alone or with friends and/or family members. Distractions of all sorts—telephone calls, conversations, eating—exist. If they are bored, viewers can change channels easily. The medium has no admission charge and is generally a source of relaxation rather than of intellectual challenge. A live theater audience usually must dress up and travel to attend a performance. The performance is shared with a large group of other people, many of whom are above average in income and educational level. They pay to attend and expect an emotional and, perhaps, an intellectual experience. Members of a movie audience share the performance with other people who have paid to see the film and who usually come for entertainment.

The structure of a drama and the nature of the viewing experience change from medium to medium. Television programs, regularly interrupted for commercials, need small climaxes before advertising breaks to hold the attention of the audience until the program resumes. Live theatrical performances generally are divided into acts with intermissions. Like live television drama, the end of each act in a stageplay usually has its own climax to keep viewers interested during the interval between the acts. Movies, however, usually have no interruptions; the film experience flows seamlessly for an audience.

Each medium also has a standard length for a performance. Live television plays usually run sixty minutes, minus commercials; stageplays usually run ninety minutes to two hours, and films generally run ninety minutes. As a result, a teleplay has less dialogue than a stageplay, and a stageplay more than a screenplay. The first act of the stage version of *Bountiful* expands on a few lines in the opening of the television play; in the teleplay we don't even meet Ludie until the scene at the bus terminal. In the two later versions, the relationships among the two women and Ludie are fleshed out. We are given more insight into the minor miseries of their lives. The stageplay's longer first act offers more information about the characters: we find out that Ludie has been an accountant and that the couple cannot afford a doctor to diagnose the reasons for their childlessness. The longer time frame allows the author more room for characterization and plot complications.

One result of this expansion of *Bountiful* is that the structure of the work is changed. In the television version, Thelma and the sheriff are given almost as much prominence as Ludie and Jessie Mae; Mrs. Watts is clearly the lead character tying the others together with her mission. In the stageplay and the film, Jessie Mae, especially, and Ludie become more vivid and important: for the first third of the drama, all three characters are equally involved in the action. With Mrs. Watts's departure on the bus, Jessie Mae and Ludie almost disappear, and two new characters—Thelma and the sheriff—are introduced. At the climax, the Watts family is reunited, and the other two characters have left. By building up the roles of Jessie Mae and Ludie in the stageplay and the film, the author runs the risk that the audience will miss their presence during the journey portion of the drama.

Some differences among the media seem obvious, but their impact on an audience is significant. A prime example is the difference in the way the three media deal with time. Live television, like a stageplay, takes place in real time. If an actor takes three seconds to walk across a room, the audience experiences all three seconds. A recorded medium like film allows the writer and director to play with time. An actor can cross the room in a fraction of a second or an hour, depending on the way the film is shot and edited. (For example, the film version of *Bountiful* showed the bus ride from Houston in a few minutes with selected shots of the changing scenery. Without difficulty the audience interprets those seconds of footage as a trip of several hours.) Flashbacks and flashforwards are much easier to accomplish in the medium of film.

The factor of "live-ness" functions in other ways also. As they watch either a stageplay or a live teleplay, audience members know that actors are reacting to one another and to their surroundings. Furthermore, members of a stageplay audience know the performers can also react to them. The perils of live theater are great; if a mistake occurs, an actor must deal with it at that moment, and the change, for that performance, is irrevocable. But the interaction between live actors and a live audience in real time can add electricity to a performance. The recorded nature of film allows perfection of a sort. Mistakes can be discarded on the editing room floor, and the dialogue can be recorded again and again. The result is that an audience loses the sense of the unpredictable. Each live performance is different from every other, a unique creation for one audience, but the film is always the same.

Live television and film can take advantage of special effects, ranging from the sophisticated to the very simple. In the television version of *Bountiful,* dissolves (the technique in which one frame seems to melt into another) signal that time has passed. Mrs. Watts walks into her home and a few seconds later walks out, the dissolve indicating to viewers that she has been in there long enough for a tour of the place.

Another technique used in film is crosscutting, in which scenes are intercut with each other to indicate events happening simultaneously in different places. For example, in the movie version of *Bountiful,* Mrs. Watts's escape is depicted in more detail than in the other two versions. Crosscutting between the beginning of her adventure and Jessie Mae's errand-running adds suspense. Mrs. Watts's efforts to hide in the bus station are more vivid in the film version since we can see her actions as well as those of her pursuers.

Unlike live drama on television or on the stage, film can be edited. A film's director, therefore, has much more power over the final product. The pace of a film, for instance, is influenced more by the way it is edited than by the way it is acted. Movies are shot in small segments, not necessarily in the order laid out in the script. On film, one actor can have a romantic conversation with another across a dinner table, while in reality footage of each could have been shot months and miles apart. Actors don't have to be on the set at the same time unless the audience is to see them together simultaneously on camera. For live drama, however, actors must be physically present during a flirtation and must interact with each other.

Performers must adjust to the various media in other ways. With its small screen, television depends heavily on the close-up. An actor's face must register subtle changes to express emotion. Reaction is more important than action. A stageplay requires an actor's whole body to convey feeling, with the voice being especially important. The large movie screen magnifies even the slightest movement; therefore an actor must know how to suggest emotion without elaborate gestures or facial expressions.

In both television and film, the director, through the camera, can control where the audience looks. A close-up of a face eliminates our ability to see the setting; we can see events from an actor's point of view with the camera; we can be in two places at once, or whatever the director wishes. For live television, the director is limited by technical considerations. With only a small space in which to work, and a limited number of sets, productions have to be simple, although basic camera techniques are possible. A director of a stageplay, like a magician, has to direct an audience's attention through "tricks of the trade." (While Ludie and Jessie Mae talk in their bedroom, the director could show Mrs. Watts hiding her check in the living room by spotlighting her, leaving Jessie Mae and Ludie's bedroom in low, diffuse lighting, and having Mrs. Watts bustle around at the front of the stage while Jessie Mae and Ludie sit immobile on the dimly lit bed at the rear.)

The concept of space is also different for each medium. Live television seldom takes an audience out of two or three small rooms, but viewers must feel that beyond those rooms are other rooms. A stageplay requires more imagination from its audience. An audience usually views artificial sets through a proscenium arch. Actors must function in that designated space. A film can take an audience anywhere a camera can go. Studio executives assume that an audience wants movement and sweep. When material is adapted from stage to film, the usual executive dictum is to "open it up," that is, to create a wide variety of visually interesting scenes, often outdoors, and to add motion.

A critical debate has arisen over whether the traditional wisdom of "opening up" a scene is always appropriate. (In his interview for this book, Horton Foote says this maxim is a myth.) In all three *Bountiful*s, we can feel the small apartment in Houston closing in on us as it does on the Watts family, but in the film we also see an external shot of the neighborhood, with its mature trees and well-manicured lawns. The overall impression is that of a pleasant, old-fashioned blue-collar suburb. In the live television and the Broadway stage versions of *Bountiful,* chairs and cardboard represented the bus, and the audience had to imagine Mrs. Watts's journey. In the film, we can see the landscape change from urban to rural and the beauty of the land and the decay of the towns as the bus rolls by. It can be argued either that seeing the countryside as Mrs. Watts does in the film helps us appreciate her longing to return, or that the vision we create in our own imagination as we see the scene on the stage is more compelling because it reflects our personal dreams. Perhaps the film's ability to go where the other two media cannot is most effective in three scenes from the film version of *Bountiful:* Mrs. Watts's tour of the interior of the house, the opening frames with the mother and son running through the blue flowers, and the closing image of the car driving off into the horizon.

It is generally considered to be true that the verbal element is more important for live theater and the visual for the movie screen. Well-written dialogue, elevated in diction and structure, is most effective in the context of the theater. Action is more effective than words for a film. Three pages of explanation declaimed from a stage can be replaced by one picture on the screen. Live dramatic television is more like theater in its emphasis on dialogue since the cameras are limited to a small stage area.

Most of the changes in the three versions of *Bountiful* are small. Whole sections of dialogue are transferred intact from medium to medium, although minor deletions and additions create subtle differences in characterization. In the television version, we're introduced to the most shrewish Jessie Mae and the most pitiful Mrs. Watts. Jessie Mae orders her mother-in-law to get her a soft drink and to fix dinner, threatens to call the police if Mrs. Watts tries to go back to Bountiful, and nags about the hymn singing and the pouting. Mrs. Watts responds by screaming when Jessie Mae leaves the room and later cries out, "And what about me? What about me? Sitting here cooped up in these two rooms. Me. A woman that was active all her young life, working the land . . ."

In the playscript, Foote's directions describe Jessie Mae as "hard, driven, nervous and hysterical." She whines more about Mrs. Watts's presence restricting their freedom and says her mother-in-law is losing her memory. Jessie Mae's obsession with Hollywood is clearer. She chatters about fan magazines and her favorite movie stars. Mrs. Watts is still treated like a maid in this version; cooking, cleaning, and sewing are her regular duties. Jessie Mae seems more spiteful, but less evil, and Mrs. Watts is feistier. In the stageplay she says of Jessie Mae, "I know why she wants me back. It's for my government check. She takes it from me to buy herself Cokes and movie magazines." Jessie Mae sums up her feelings for her mother-in-law when she complains that Mrs. Watts will "get to Bountiful and die from excitement and then we'll have all kinds of expenses bringing her body back here."

In the film, some of the harsher aspects of Jessie Mae are downplayed. She becomes more human and less hateful. She no longer tells Thelma she could wring her mother-in-law's neck.

Another difference between the stageplay and the film is the relationship between Jessie Mae and Ludie: in the play, she is prudish about his seeing her undressed, but in the film she seems interested in a sexual relationship with her husband despite the presence in the next room of a wakeful, hymn-singing mother-in-law. (The interviews at the end of the book indicate that this interpretation came from the director and the actress who played Jessie Mae.)

As Foote rewrote the scripts for the various media, he pared away some of the more obviously emotional scenes, replacing them with scenes of a more stoical quality. This tendency is especially clear in the final scene. In the television version, an impassioned Mrs. Watts tears her social security check into little pieces, Jessie Mae calls her a "spiteful old thing," and Ludie cries. Foote substitutes a quieter scene in the later versions, in which Ludie demands that the two women stop arguing and Jessie Mae allows Mrs. Watts to keep the check and, with it, some of her dignity.

In all three versions, Mrs. Watts's friendship with Thelma and the sheriff is an axis, although at first glance the two seem to be the most expendable characters. Thelma, unlike Mrs. Watts, married the man she loves, a man of whom her parents approve. She can move in with her family while her husband is overseas, and we know her situation will be much more peaceful than Mrs. Watts's. In Thelma, Carrie Watts can see what her life might have been. The sheriff provides a contrast to Ludie. Although the sheriff is a stranger, he is willing (as Ludie has not been) to help Mrs. Watts achieve her heart's desire. The characters of Thelma and the sheriff, though secondary, are as intrinsic to the author's purpose as Jessie Mae and Ludie.

The film has an added scene that at first seems unnecessary. At a gas station in the small town of Gerard, passengers wait for the bus. A brief exchange of dialogue hints at some interesting themes in the work. When a black woman is told the hour-long interruption in the trip can't be helped, she responds, "We have to take what comes." The woman, who seems to be close in age and income level to Mrs. Watts, says she is going to Corpus Christi, Texas, and the stationmaster explains that the Spanish name means "body of Christ." When he asks a Hispanic passenger for confirmation, the passenger indicates that he doesn't understand English. The Latin origin of the words, their religious significance, and the history of the city have all been forgotten. To Foote, the words may suggest another time when a religious ceremony like communion could bind generations of believers together and bring a sense of community to the faithful everywhere. To the travelers in the film, the name "Corpus Christi" merely means another American town, another destination on the highway. The bus arrives, and the passengers, from different backgrounds and on different missions, resume their journeys.

This scene reminds the viewer that many people undergo a journey of some sort. Foote seems to say that we can find a brief moment of companionship and a word of wisdom, but then the travelers must separate, each to follow a different road to a different destination. This scene in the film serves as a transition between Houston and Harrison, the nearest town to Bountiful, and perhaps as a bridge between the older religious certainties of Mrs. Watts and the modern world's loss of faith. To Mrs. Watts, the Gerard bus station is a sort of purgatory where she waits with other souls before she embarks on a journey to her heaven.

Some of the differences in the three versions of *Bountiful* are related to the fact that each medium operates under different economic imperatives. Each medium has its own organizational principles and traditions that guide decision making. There are also legal considerations. The television medium is more strictly regulated, giving the writer less artistic freedom than in either a stageplay or a film. For example, the Federal Communications Commission forbids the use of indecent language during hours when children are likely to be watching television. Film and theatrical productions are not regulated by the FCC.

The nature of the creative team in a particular production can also result in varying interpretations of a work. For example, critics' response to the Broadway version of *Bountiful* indicates that they considered Jessie Mae as played by Jo Van Fleet to be a comic character. Carlin Glynn's Jessie Mae in the film is played less as a caricature and more as a shallow but not unsympathetic character.[15] Vincent Donehue directed a contemporary piece in the first two *Bountiful*s; Peter Masterson's film thirty-five years later is a period piece.

While some of the changes in *Bountiful* stem from differences among the media, some of the changes are the result of the writer's having given each new script a little more polish. Some changes may also be attributable to the length of time that had elapsed between the second and third versions. The author may view the world differently after thirty-five years.

In adapting a work from one medium to another, an artist is faced with a fundamental choice—to preserve the integrity of the original concept or to make changes dictated by the new medium, the cliches of media aesthetics, or market forces. Horton Foote is clearly a preservationist. The changes in the transformed *Bountiful* scripts are minimal, made mostly to conform to the restrictions of time and technology of each medium. All three versions are grounded in Foote's experience and observation; they are the product of his style, the bearers of the same message.

One of the reasons the film was not produced for three and one-half decades after the story's conception was that Foote wanted to retain control over his original vision. He wanted to find a director and coproducer willing to carry out his vision, performers who would play the roles as he had written them, and financial backers who would allow him the right to the final edit. The result is a cinematic conversion that articulates the author's original truth.

The Trip to Bountiful is a story of journeys—over land, over time, to self-realization—and of survival with dignity. This book traces the extended journey of the work from an NBC television studio in Radio City to a Broadway stage and then to theater screens and home videocassettes. The scripts for television, theater, and film are included here, each with a brief introduction describing the circumstances of the original production of each version. The film script has been edited to reflect the actual scenes in the released version.[16] The three scripts are presented in chronological order to allow the reader to see how the structure and the dialogue changed over time.

Interviews with some members of the creative team from the film follow the scripts. The coproducer, the writer, the director, and an actress share their experiences in making the movie. (Unfortunately, Geraldine Page, who played Mrs. Watts, died before the editors started research on the book. An effort was made to reach some of the people involved in earlier versions of *Bountiful,* but many were deceased, some had forgotten most of the details of production from the middle 1950s, and others did not choose to cooperate.) These interviews will give the reader an idea of the functions of various members of the creative team in the making of the film.

In telling the story of *Bountiful,* we hope to illuminate each medium, highlighting the similarities and differences among them. We make no judgment as to which version is "better"; rather we think that each should be considered on its own terms. A good story about believable and compelling people, presented with integrity and devotion, can work well in any of the three forms. Such a work is Horton Foote's thrice-told tale, *The Trip to Bountiful.*

Barbara Moore and David G. Yellin

Notes

1. "Philco Television Playhouse" began on NBC in the fall of 1948. In 1951, Goodyear signed on to sponsor alternate weeks of the program as "Goodyear Television Playhouse." The two are usually referred to together as the "Philco/ Goodyear Television Playhouse" since they shared the same production team and the same time slot, an arrangement that lasted until the fall of 1955 (Tim Brooks and Earle Marsh, *The Complete Directory to Prime Time Network TV Shows, 1946–Present,* 4th ed. [New York: Ballantine Books, 1988], 623, 307).

2. Gerald C. Wood, "Introduction," in *Selected One-Act Plays of Horton Foote* (Dallas: Southern Methodist University Press, 1989), xviii.

3. "Dialogue on Film: Horton Foote," *American Film* 12 (Oct. 1986): 14.

4. Reynolds Price, "Introduction," in *Courtship, Valentine's Day, 1918* by Horton Foote (New York: Grove Press, 1986), xi.

5. Stark Young, "Introduction," in *The Traveling Lady* by Horton Foote (New York: Dramatists Play Service Inc., 1955), 6.

6. Samuel G. Freedman, "From the Heart of Texas," *New York Times Magazine,* Feb. 9, 1986, 50.

7. Gerald C. Wood and Terry Barr, "A Certain Kind of Writer: An Interview with Horton Foote," *Literature/Film Quarterly* 14 (1986): 234.

8. Marian Burkhart, "Horton Foote's Many Roads Home," *Commonweal* (Feb. 1988): 111.

9. George Terry Barr, "The Ordinary World of Horton Foote," (Ph.D. diss., University of Tennessee, 1986), 15.

10. Wood, xix.

11. Price, xii.

12. Wood, xix.

13. Gerald Weales, *American Drama since World War II* (New York: Harcourt, Brace & World, 1962), 66.

14. Wood, 345.

15. One critic wrote: "Miss Van Fleet's diction is like the twittering of an exhausted bird, intermittently punctuated by screeches of rapture or despair; her little trills of laughter are terribly unnerving, having no remotest connection with amusement; her habitual expression is as vacant as the moon but somehow smouldering; her gestures are profuse, abrupt, and almost completely meaningless; her carriage is languorous but at the same time industrious, in the sense that all the separate parts of her body are deeply involved in getting her slowly from place to place. Altogether it is one of the funniest and most awe-inspiring comments on Southern womanhood I have ever seen" (Woolcott Gibbs, "The Theatre," *New Yorker,* Nov. 14, 1953, 76).

16. Normally, a screenplay goes through several versions with scenes being added, subtracted, and rewritten. The writer eventually turns over a script to the director, who usually does not follow it exactly as he or she shoots the film. In the editing process, more scenes may be deleted or rearranged. The final film released to movie theaters may be noticeably different from the original screenplay. For the script printed here, we transcribed the feature film, using Horton Foote's shooting script as a basis.

I

The Teleplay

Vincent J. Donehue (director), Horton Foote, Lillian Gish
(© *Eileen Darby*)

The Teleplay

URING the early fifties, while he worked on plays for Broadway, Horton Foote also earned money writing television scripts on a freelance basis. In 1953 he became a regular contributor to the "Philco/Goodyear Television Playhouse," one of the most prestigious of the weekly live television drama programs. Vincent Donehue, a director with whom Foote had worked, introduced him to Fred Coe, producer of the "Playhouse." Foote did many scripts for the program; his third was *The Trip to Bountiful*, directed by Donehue.

Foote has commented that writing for television "was more like [writing for] theater. In other words, you couldn't stop the performance; you rehearsed . . . then did the show. So, really what I did mostly was use all the one-act plays I'd been storing up inside of me. Oh, I learned about fade-out and dissolve and all that, but we didn't have much of that in those days."[1] The programs were produced in New York City using actors with theatrical training and were performed in real time like plays. But despite its similarities to the stage, the new electronic medium had its own strictures of time, technology, art, commerce, and audience.

Television's live dramas usually had a maximum of four sets arranged around the perimeter of a studio. Three or more bulky studio cameras captured the images and fed them to a control room, where a director selected the shots that went over the air. Actors moved from one set to the other while the camera was turned away from them. Creative ways of allowing characters to exit had to be designed, and costume changes had to be minimal. Because of the small size of the sets and the limited focusing capability of the camera lens, showing more than four people on the screen at a time was difficult. As a result, teleplays had tight structures and few subplots, if any. The hour drama, because of commercials and credits, had to tell its story in no more than fifty-three minutes, sometimes even less. The writer had to craft the narrative to allow breaks for commercials, whether the interruptions were organic to the plot or not.

Given the technical and aesthetic limitations of the small-screen medium, dramas about simple people in ordinary settings were a logical development for live television. Writers were forced to deal with small spaces and to focus on human problems. Action scenes, panoramic shots, and intricate, fast-moving slapstick were difficult. Live teleplays had to probe the intimate life of a character's relationships with only a few people. The taboos of the 1950s prohibited anything overtly sexual, and the threat of advertisers' displeasure led to an avoidance of politically controversial issues. The central conflict, therefore, usually was concerned with the psychology of a character or questions of personal ethics. The dimensions of this conflict had to be presented in simple terms, easily comprehensible to the audience at home. The result became known as "kitchen sink" drama since the setting was frequently the kitchen of a blue-collar family, and the topics were their small family crises.

In the early days of television, programs could be allowed the luxury of exploring small problems quietly. Television sets in 1951 were most often found in the homes of the affluent and well educated. The medium was novel enough to command an audience's attention; television programming had not yet become a background activity. Ratings were less important than they are today when millions of dollars of advertising revenue are determined by the variations of a few percentage points. *The Trip to Bountiful,* for example, was judged a success because more people than usual called NBC to praise the program.

The usual first step in writing a teleplay for the "Philco/ Goodyear Playhouse" was to present the idea in outline form to producer Fred Coe; Coe would then discuss the project with the sponsor's advertising agency and would notify the writer if the idea was approved. Foote's approach, however, was different: "I may be superstitious, but I felt if I told someone beforehand [about my concept], it would kill it for me. So I wrote *Bountiful*, and I told Coe I was thinking about writing a story about an old lady who wanted to go back to her hometown. He said, 'Okay.' And I handed in the play—which I'd already finished—two days later."[2]

Many of the dramatic writers in the early fifties were hampered by interference from sponsors. If, for example, a program was sponsored by a cigarette manufacturer, the hero had to smoke on screen; controversy had to be avoided, and happy endings were preferred. The "Philco/Goodyear Playhouse" was unusual because Coe's experience and expertise had earned him the respect of agency executives and sponsors. More than any other producer of his time, he protected and prized his writers. Foote noted that no one ever interfered with his scripts while he was writing for the "Philco/Goodyear Playhouse": "Fred Coe always fought the battle. I was never asked not to do anything. I was never censored."[3]

The financial structure of the television industry, in which programming was paid for by advertisers whose primary concern was to sell viewers their products, led creative people to tread softly on social commentary, to pursue middle-class values, and to resolve conflicts with upbeat endings. Horton Foote and Fred Coe were exceptions. According to Foote, "I am not prone to write sensationally. I don't know how anybody could disapprove of what I choose to write about unless they think it's too depressing or not commercial. That I'm sure [Coe] had plenty of flak about, but I don't go in for nudity or extremely vulgar language so I never really had any problems. I'm not *per se* a social writer. In other words, I'm not out to overthrow anybody or anything. Really I'm trying to report on the human condition as I see it."[4]

According to Foote, Coe could not afford to pay high salaries. The usual fee he paid writers for one-hour live dramas was twelve hundred to twenty-five hundred dollars. But Coe more than any other producer emphasized the writer.

Foote said, "We were the ones he featured very aggressively so that it became an hour for the writer. The writer was really a kind of kingpin, not just me, but the whole group of writers. . . . We were encouraged as writers not to find formulas that would please many people, but just to very deeply please ourselves. So that was an enormous lesson for me and a great gift."[5]

At the insistence of Fred Coe, the writers for the "Philco/ Goodyear Playhouse" were involved in casting and other aspects of production, an unusual privilege by television standards. Although Coe suggested Lillian Gish as the star of *Bountiful*, he didn't sign her until Foote agreed. Director Vincent Donehue and Foote called on Gish to offer her the role of Mrs. Watts. Eva Marie Saint played Thelma, Eileen Heckart was Jessie Mae, and John Beal played Ludie. "It was a happy company," Foote remembers. "I think we had ten days of rehearsal. And a couple of those days were really for technical runthroughs; so we really only had about eight actual days of rehearsal for the actors."[6]

The "Playhouse" had a regular group of directors. Foote commented that they were "very talented—Vincent Donehue, Delbert Mann, and Arthur Penn; so it was a wonderful time in that sense—very gifted, talented people to work with. And we got wonderful actors because there was a lot of young talent coming up and marvelous people like Lillian Gish always interested in experimenting with new forms."[7] The program also had talented writers, some of whom later became famous, including Paddy Chayefsky, Tad Mosel, Robert Alan Aurthur, Gore Vidal, and J. P. Miller.

Foote's scripts for the "Philco/Goodyear Playhouse" influenced other writers, including Chayefsky, who had started out doing adaptations from Broadway plays and novels. "One night I saw . . . ["Philco/Goodyear Playhouse"'s] *The Trip to Bountiful*, a lovely simple play laid in the South, and it hit me right away. I thought to myself, 'Boy, that's how to do television'—and after that first [adaptation] for Coe, I started trying to do stories of my own."[8]

In the late 1950s, the Golden Age of Television, with its live dramatic anthologies, faded away. Live drama was replaced by filmed—and later videotaped—series with continuing characters. Chayefsky, author of many of the medium's live classics, said of this short-lived television genre, "What we did was to dramatize the lives of the people out there in the audience, and we contributed what any artist is supposed to contribute, some sort of understanding. It's the job of the artist to let his audience have some insight into its otherwise meaningless pattern of life. . . . That's why that drama was important and significant—and why it produced a crop of such first-rate writers."[9] Foote's *The Trip to Bountiful* was the first teleplay to be included in the Museum of Modern Art's collection of television drama.

Notes

1. Ronald L. Davis, "Roots in Parched Ground: An Interview with Horton Foote," *Southwest Review* 73 (Summer 1988): 306.

2. Max Wilk, *The Golden Age of Television: Notes from the Survivors* (New York: Delacorte Press, 1976), 132.

3. Horton Foote, personal interview with Barbara Moore, New York City, July 1987.

4. Foote interview.

5. Gary Edgerton, "A Visit to the Imaginary Landscape of Harrison, Texas: Sketching the Film Career of Horton Foote," *Literature/Film Quarterly* 17 (1989): 5.

6. Foote interview.

7. Foote interview.

8. Wilk, 129.

9. Wilk, 136.

The Trip to Bountiful

Goodyear Television Playhouse
March 1, 1953

Director: Vincent Donehue
Producer: Fred Coe
Associate Producer: Gordon Duff

Cast

MRS. WATTS: Lillian Gish
JESSIE MAE WATTS: Eileen Heckart
TICKET MAN (*railroad station*): Dennis Cross
THELMA: Eva Marie Saint
TICKET MAN (*bus station*): Will Hare
LUDIE WATTS: John Beal
BUS DRIVER: Charles Sladen
ATTENDANT: Larry Bolton
TICKET MAN (*second bus station*): William Hansen
SHERIFF: Frank Overton

Act I

The living room of a small apartment in Houston. It is furnished in the most ordinary manner. Sitting in a chair by a window is an old woman, MRS. WATTS. *She is tall and thin and holds herself very straight. The hands in her lap are gnarled and twisted, but there is the feeling of great strength about them. She is constantly opening and closing the hands, nervously, as if to test their power. Putting on makeup in a corner of the room is* JESSIE MAE WATTS, MRS. WATTS'*s daughter-in-law.* JESSIE MAE *is in her early forties. An obviously vain woman, she is also hard and self-centered and domineering.* MRS. WATTS *hums to herself snatches of a hymn from time to time.*

JESSIE MAE: Mother Watts, look out that window and tell me what time it is by the drugstore clock.

(MRS. WATTS *does so.*)

MRS. WATTS: Three forty-five, Jessie Mae.

JESSIE MAE: Oh, I better get a move on. I want you to remind Ludie tonight to get our clock fixed.

MRS. WATTS: Yes, ma'am.

(JESSIE MAE *hurries into the bedroom.* MRS. WATTS *continues rocking and singing her hymn, her hands nervously working back and forth.* JESSIE MAE *hurries in carrying a hat.*)

JESSIE MAE: Mother Watts. Please stop that hymn singing. You want me to jump right out of my skin? You know what hymns do to my nerves. (MRS. WATTS *doesn't answer but stops. She rocks in silence.*) And don't pout. I can't stand pouting.

MRS. WATTS: I didn't mean to pout, Jessie Mae. I only meant to be silent.

(*A pause.* JESSIE MAE *gives her makeup one last going over.*)

JESSIE MAE: Skip in the kitchen and get me a Coke. I'll drink it while I'm putting my hat on.

MRS. WATTS: All right.

(*She goes and comes back with a Coke. She hands it to* JESSIE MAE. JESSIE MAE *takes the Coke and begins to drink it while putting on her hat.*)

JESSIE MAE: Did your old-age pension check come today?

MRS. WATTS: No, ma'am. You asked me that twice before and I told you it hadn't.

JESSIE MAE: Well, it should be here. Today's the day.

MRS. WATTS: It didn't arrive.

JESSIE MAE: All right. *(She takes a swig from her Coke.)* That movie magazine I got last night is running a contest. First prize is a free trip to Hollywood. I'd enter it if I thought I could win. But I wouldn't win. I don't have that kind of luck. I'm gonna make Ludie take me to Hollywood one of these days. I want to visit Hollywood as bad as you want to visit Bountiful. *(*MRS. WATTS *is singing again.)* Mother Watts, I asked you not to sing. I'm nervous. *(*MRS. WATTS *stops.* JESSIE MAE *has her hat on now.)* I'm ready. I'm gonna be home at seven. You get supper started. *(She starts out the door. She stops.)* And I want you to promise me you won't put a foot out of this house and start that Bountiful business again. You'll kill Ludie if he has to chase all over Houston again looking for you. And I'm warning you. The next time I'm calling the police. I don't care what Ludie says.

(She goes out slamming the door. MRS. WATTS *sits quiet for a moment. Suddenly she jumps up. She screams.)*

MRS. WATTS: And what about me? What about me? Sitting here cooped up in these two rooms. Me. A woman that was active all her young life, working the land . . .

*(*MRS. WATTS *stands for a moment . . . Then she runs to the window and looks out. She thinks* JESSIE MAE *has gone. She puts her hand in her dress and brings out a check. She runs to the desk and endorses the back of it . . . She hears someone at the door. She pushes the check back inside her dress.* JESSIE MAE *comes inside.)*

JESSIE MAE: I forgot my movie magazine. I've read all the ones at the beauty parlor. *(She picks up a magazine and starts out the door. She pauses.)* Just in case you're trying to put something over on me with that pension check, I've told Mr. Reynolds at the grocery store he's never to cash anything for you.

(She goes out. MRS. WATTS *runs to the door and stands listening. Then she runs to the window and looks out. Again she is satisfied* JESSIE MAE *is gone and runs to the bedroom and comes back with a suitcase. She starts to pack it.)*

DISSOLVE TO: A ticket booth in a railroad station.

There are several people in line waiting for tickets. MRS. WATTS *comes running in. She keeps nervously looking back to see if she is being followed. She is humming the hymn softly to herself. She gets behind the line. A man finishes buying his ticket. She steps up to the window.*

MRS. WATTS: I want a ticket to Bountiful, please.

TICKET MAN: Where?

MRS. WATTS: Bountiful.

TICKET MAN: Just a minute, let me look it up. *(He steps away from the window and begins looking the town up in a book.)* What's it near?

MRS. WATTS: Between Harrison and Cotton.

(He looks through the book again.)

TICKET MAN: Here's Harrison. But I don't see no Bountiful.

MRS. WATTS: Oh. Does the train stop at Harrison?

TICKET MAN: No. You take a train to Richmond. And from there you'd have to take a bus to Harrison.

MRS. WATTS: I see. What time does the train leave?

TICKET MAN: Six o'clock tomorrow morning.

MRS. WATTS: Six o'clock? I have to leave before that.

TICKET MAN: Then you better try taking a bus. There might be one leaving earlier.

MRS. WATTS: Yes sir. *(She hurries out.)*

DISSOLVE TO: The ticket window at the bus station.

A young girl is buying a ticket there. She is very pretty.

TICKET MAN: Yes?

THELMA: I want a ticket to Old Gulf.

TICKET MAN: Yes, ma'am. *(He reaches for a ticket.)* Here you are. Change buses at Harrison.

THELMA: I know. How much please?

TICKET MAN: Four eighty.

THELMA: Yes, sir.

(She gives him four eighty and steps out of line. A man steps up to the window.)

MAN: Ticket to Leighton.

TICKET MAN: Leighton? Yes, indeed. *(He gets a ticket.)* Be seven sixty, please.

(MRS. WATTS *has come in with her bag. She is standing behind the man. She looks around the bus station nervously. She is humming snatches of her hymn. The man moves away. Two people have come behind* MRS. WATTS. *She is oblivious to the fact that the next turn is hers.*)

TICKET MAN: *(Calling.)* Lady. *(She is so busy watching the door to the bus station she doesn't hear him.)* Lady . . .

MRS. WATTS: Oh, yes. Excuse me. I'd like a ticket to Bountiful, please.

TICKET MAN: Where?

MRS. WATTS: Bountiful.

TICKET MAN: What's it near?

MRS. WATTS: It's between Harrison and Cotton.

TICKET MAN: Just a minute. *(He looks in a book.)* I can sell you a ticket to Harrison or Cotton. But there's no Bountiful . . .

MRS. WATTS: Oh, yes, there is. It's between . . .

TICKET MAN: I'm sorry, lady. You say there is, but the book says there isn't. And the book don't lie . . .

MRS. WATTS: But . . . I . . .

TICKET MAN: Make up your mind, lady. Cotton or Harrison. There are others waiting.

MRS. WATTS: Well . . . Let me see . . . How much is a ticket to Harrison?

TICKET MAN: Three fifty.

MRS. WATTS: Cotton?

TICKET MAN: Four twenty.

MRS. WATTS: Oh, I see, thank you. I'll have the one to Harrison, please.

TICKET MAN: All right. That'll be three fifty, please.

MRS. WATTS: Yes, sir. *(She reaches in her bag and takes out a check.)* Can you cash a pension check? You see I decided to come at the last minute and I didn't have time to stop by the grocery store.

TICKET MAN: I'm sorry. I can't cash any checks.

MRS. WATTS: It's perfectly good.

TICKET MAN: I'm sorry, it's against the rules to cash checks.

MRS. WATTS: Oh, is that so? I understand. How much was that again?

TICKET MAN: Three fifty.

MRS. WATTS: Oh, yes. I've got it all here in nickels and dimes and quarters. *(She takes out a handkerchief from her purse and puts it on the counter. She unties it and begins to take out coins. She talks as she counts.)* Here, I think this is three fifty.

TICKET MAN: Thank you.

MRS. WATTS: That's quite all right. I'm sorry to have taken up so much of your time. *(She picks up her bag and starts away.)*

TICKET MAN: Here, lady. Don't forget your ticket.

MRS. WATTS: Oh, my heavens. Yes. I'd forget my head if it wasn't on my neck. *(She takes the ticket.)* Thank you.

(She starts away. The others step up into line to get their tickets. MRS. WATTS crosses to a row of benches where the girl we saw earlier is seated. There is an empty seat next to her. MRS. WATTS stops in front of the empty seat.)

MRS. WATTS: Good evening.

THELMA: Good evening.

MRS. WATTS: Is this seat taken?

THELMA: No, ma'am.

MRS. WATTS: Are you expecting anyone?

THELMA: No, ma'am.

MRS. WATTS: May I sit here then?

THELMA: Yes'm. Are you going on a trip?

MRS. WATTS: Yes, I am. I'm trying to get to a town nobody ever heard of around here.

THELMA: What town is that?

MRS. WATTS: Bountiful.

THELMA: Oh.

MRS. WATTS: Did you ever hear of it?

THELMA: No.

MRS. WATTS: You see? Nobody has. Well, it's not much of a town now, I guess. I haven't seen it myself in thirty years. But it used to be quite prosperous. All they have left is a post office and a filling station and a general store. At least they did when I left.

THELMA: Do your people live there?

MRS. WATTS: No. My people are all dead except my son and his wife, Jessie Mae. They live here in the city. I'm hurrying to get to see Bountiful once before I die. I had a sinking spell this morning. I had to climb up on the bed and rest for an hour. It was my heart.

THELMA: Do you have a bad heart?

MRS. WATTS: Well, it's not what you call a good one. Doctor says it would last as long as I needed it if I could cut worrying out. But seems I can't do that lately. *(She suddenly jumps up out of her seat.)* Excuse me. Would you watch my suitcase?

THELMA: Certainly.

(MRS. WATTS hurries off in the direction of the door. THELMA picks up her book and reads. MRS. WATTS comes hurrying back. She sits on the edge of the seat looking in the direction of the door.)

THELMA: Lady, is there anything wrong?

MRS. WATTS: No, honey. I'm a little nervous, that's all. *(She jumps up again. THELMA watches her go. When she gets out of sight, THELMA again starts to read her book. MRS. WATTS comes running in and grabs her suitcase. In her confusion she drops a small white handkerchief. Neither she nor THELMA sees it.)* Say a prayer for me, honey. Good luck.

THELMA: Good luck to you.

(She is gone. A man comes in. He is LUDIE WATTS. He is in his early forties. He looks shabby and beaten. His face was once sensitive, but is now covered with bitterness and defeat. He stands in front of THELMA. She has gone back to reading her book. JESSIE MAE comes in.)

LUDIE: You want to sit down, Jessie Mae?

JESSIE MAE: Yes. Go and get yourself a Coke if you want to. I'll wait.

LUDIE: All right. Want me to buy you a movie magazine?

JESSIE MAE: Yes. *(LUDIE goes off to get her a movie magazine. JESSIE MAE takes out a cigarette. JESSIE MAE searches for a match. She can't find one. She turns to THELMA.)* Excuse me. Do you have a match?

THELMA: Yes, I do. *(She reaches in her coat and gets one. She hands it to JESSIE MAE.)*

JESSIE MAE: Thank you. I hope you're lucky enough not to have to fool with any in-laws. I've got a mother-in-law about to drive me crazy. Once a month we have to spend the evening in the depot to try and keep her from getting on a train to go back to her home town. Oh, she's so stubborn. I could just wring her neck. Her son spoils her, that's the whole trouble. She's just spoiled rotten. Do you live with your in-laws?

THELMA: No.

JESSIE MAE: Well, you're lucky. They're all stubborn. My husband is as stubborn as she is. We should be over at the depot right now instead of sitting here. She always tries to take the train. But no. We wait at the depot for five minutes and because she isn't there, right then, he drags me over here. I'm just worn out. I've had my fourth Coca-Cola to keep my spirits up. People ask me why I don't have any children. Why? I say. I've got Ludie and Mother Watts. That's all the children I need. Of course, I can tell when she's gonna sneak out. Something said to me when I went to the beauty parlor this afternoon . . . She'll be gone when you get back. And she was. (LUDIE *comes back in. He has a movie magazine in his hand.*) What did you bring me? (*He shows it to her.*) Oh, I've seen that one.

LUDIE: Have you seen Mama?

JESSIE MAE: No, you goose. Do you think I'd be sitting here so calm if I had? Personally, I think we're wasting our time here in the first place. She always tries to go by train.

LUDIE: But she can't go by train, Jessie Mae. How many times do I have to explain that to you? There hasn't been a train to Bountiful in twenty-five years.

JESSIE MAE: She doesn't know that.

LUDIE: She does by now.

JESSIE MAE: But we've always found her there. Remember that. (*A pause.*) Ludie, I know she's there. I know it. I'm never wrong about these things.

LUDIE: All right. Have it your way. Let's go.

JESSIE MAE: Well, now we're here, might as well inquire from someone if they've seen her wandering around.

LUDIE: I thought you said she wouldn't come here.

JESSIE MAE: I said I didn't think she would come here. I don't know what the crazy thing will do. I think we ought to turn it over to the police. That would scare her once and for all.

LUDIE: Well, we're not going to call any police.

JESSIE MAE: It's for her own good. She's crazy.

LUDIE: Why do you talk like that? You know Mama isn't crazy.

JESSIE MAE: Then why does she keep running off from a perfectly good home to try and get to some old swamp? Don't you call that crazy? I mean, she doesn't have to turn her hand. Hardly. We only have a bedroom and a living room and a kitchen. We're all certainly very light eaters, so cooking three meals a day isn't killing her.

LUDIE: Well, let's don't stand here arguing about it. People are looking at us. Do you want to go to the depot or not?

JESSIE MAE: It's your mother. I don't care what you do. Only you better do something. Let me tell you that. She's gonna clonk out some place. She'll get to Bountiful and die from the excitement and then we'll have all kinds of expenses bringing her body back here. Do you know what a thing like that could cost? Do you realize she had a sinking spell this morning?

LUDIE: I know you've told me a hundred times. What can I do about it?

JESSIE MAE: Call the police. It's their job to find missing persons.

LUDIE: I'm not going to call the police.

JESSIE MAE: Then I think I will. That'll settle it once and for all.

LUDIE: You're not calling any police. It would kill her.

JESSIE MAE: Well, this is killing me. I'm going to call the police. I'm tired of it, Ludie. I'm just tired of it.

(She goes marching off. He sits down dejectedly in the seat. THELMA *has been watching all this time . . . She has tried not to be seen, but it should be apparent to the audience that she has heard all that has gone on.* LUDIE *looks helpless and desperate. He mops his face with his handkerchief. He sees the movie magazine in his hand. He turns to* THELMA.*)*

LUDIE: Would you like this? I never read them, and my wife has seen it.

THELMA: Thank you.

(She takes it and puts it in her lap. LUDIE *looks on the floor and sees a handkerchief that has been dropped by* MRS. WATTS. *He picks it up. He looks at* THELMA *and is about to question her.* THELMA *averts her eyes. He runs to the ticket window. There is a new man on duty.)*

LUDIE: Excuse me. Did an old lady come here and buy a ticket to Bountiful?

TICKET MAN: Sorry. I just came here for the night.

LUDIE: Where is the man that was on duty?

TICKET MAN: He's gone home.

LUDIE: Oh. *(LUDIE sees* THELMA *again and goes back to her.)* Excuse me. But I found a handkerchief there that belongs, I think, to my mother. She's run off from home. She has a heart condition and it might be serious for her to be all alone. I don't think she has much money, and I'd like to find her. Do you remember having seen her?

THELMA: Well . . . I . . .

LUDIE: She's in her sixties and she'd be on her way to a town called Bountiful . . .

THELMA: Yes, I did see her. She was here talking to me. She left suddenly.

LUDIE: Did she say that she had a ticket on the bus?

THELMA: I believe so.

LUDIE: Thank you so much. *(JESSIE MAE comes in.)* I was right. She was here. This lady says so. She says she has bought herself a ticket . . .

JESSIE MAE: Well, we're not going to wait. I've turned it over to the police.

LUDIE: Jessie Mae.

JESSIE MAE: Well, I have. It's the best thing, Ludie—I explained the whole thing to them. They said we should just go home. That she will never leave. She's just trying to get our attention. And once we show her we don't care if she goes or not, she'll come home of her own accord. The police say such things are quite common in young people and old people.

LUDIE: Now look, Jessie Mae . . .

JESSIE MAE: And that's just what we're going to do.

LUDIE: Jessie Mae.

JESSIE MAE: Come on, Ludie. *(She starts off.)* Come on, I say.

LUDIE: All right. *(He wearily follows JESSIE MAE.)*

DISSOLVE back to the waiting room.
THELMA *is still there. A man has now taken* MRS. WATTS's *chair. An announcer calls stations . . . "Harrison. Cotton. Old Gulf . . ."* THELMA *gathers her things together.*

DISSOLVE TO: The inside of a bus.
People are getting themselves settled for the ride. THELMA *comes in, gives her ticket to the* BUS DRIVER *and gets into a seat. Everyone is settled down. Then* MRS. WATTS *comes hurrying in . . . She seats herself next to* THELMA.

THELMA: Hello.

(MRS. WATTS jumps up from her seat. Then she recognizes THELMA.)

MRS. WATTS: Oh. It's you. How do you do. Well, I made it. It's a small world. I didn't know you'd be on the same bus. Where do you go, honey?

THELMA: Harrison.

MRS. WATTS: Harrison!

THELMA: Yes. I change buses there.

MRS. WATTS: So do I go there. Isn't that nice?

(She settles herself down in the seat as the BUS DRIVER *says, "All aboard," and is closing the bus door and starting the motor.)*

DISSOLVE TO: The bus station.

LUDIE *comes running in. He goes to an* ATTENDANT.

LUDIE: Has the bus for Harrison left?

ATTENDANT: Just pulled out.

LUDIE: Did you see an old lady get on there?

ATTENDANT: Have on a black hat? In her sixties?

LUDIE: Yes.

ATTENDANT: Yes, I did.

LUDIE: Oh. *(JESSIE MAE comes in.)* Well, she's gone.

JESSIE MAE: I don't understand that. The police said . . .

LUDIE: The police! The police! I knew if she wasn't home when we got there, she wouldn't be coming home.

JESSIE MAE: Let me go phone the police and report it. They'll stop the bus and get her off.

LUDIE: You won't do any such thing. I'll get me a ticket and go after her.

JESSIE MAE: And not be here for work tomorrow and lose this job?

LUDIE: I'll get us back in time for work.

JESSIE MAE: Don't be a fool. I'm calling the police.

LUDIE: You're not.

JESSIE MAE: I am.

LUDIE: You're not.

JESSIE MAE: I am. *(They are screaming at each other.)*

DISSOLVE TO: The inside of the bus.

It is on its way. We dolly in for a close-up of MRS. WATTS's *face. She seems serene and content. She is humming softly . . . "There's not a friend like the lowly Jesus" as there is music for the curtain.*

Act II

The inside of the bus. THELMA *and* MRS. WATTS *are looking out the window. It is later that night.*

MRS. WATTS: The bus is nice to ride, isn't it?

THELMA: Yes. It is.

MRS. WATTS: I'm sorry I couldn't take a train though.

THELMA: I tried to go by train but you couldn't get connections tonight.

MRS. WATTS: I know. When I was a girl I used to take excursions from Bountiful to Houston or Galveston. For the day, you know. Leave at five in the morning and return at ten that night. The whole town would be down to see you get off the train. I have such fond memories of those trips. *(A pause.)* Excuse me for getting personal, but what's a pretty girl like you doing traveling alone?

THELMA: My husband has just been sent overseas. I'm going to stay with my family.

MRS. WATTS: Oh, I'm sorry to hear that. Just say the ninety-first Psalm over and over to yourself. It will be a bower of strength and protection for him. *(She begins to recite.)* "He that dwelleth in the secret place of the most high shall abide under the shadow of the Almighty. I will say of the Lord he is my refuge and my fortress: My God; in Him will I trust. Surely He shall deliver thee from the snare of the fowler and the noisesome pestilence. He shall cover thee with His feathers and under his wing shalt thou trust: His truth shall be thy shield and buckler." *(THELMA begins to cry.)* Oh, I'm sorry, I'm sorry, honey.

THELMA: That's all right. I'm just lonesome for him.

MRS. WATTS: Keep him under the Lord's wing, honey, and he'll be safe.

THELMA: Yes, ma'am. *(She dries her eyes.)* I'm sorry. I don't know what gets into me.

MRS. WATTS: Nobody needs be ashamed of crying. I guess we've all dampened our pillows sometime or other. I have, Lord knows.

THELMA: If I could only learn not to worry.

MRS. WATTS: I know. I guess we all ask that. Jessie Mae, my daughter-in-law, don't worry. What for? she says. Well, like I tell her that's certainly a fine attitude if you can cultivate it. Trouble is I can't any longer.

THELMA: It is hard.

MRS. WATTS: I didn't use to worry. I was so carefree as a girl. Had lots to worry me, too. Everybody was poor in Bountiful. But we got along. I said to Papa once after our third crop failure in a row, whoever gave this place the name of Bountiful. His papa did, he said. He said in those days it was a land of plenty. You just had to drop seeds in the ground and the crops would spring up. Cotton and corn and sugar cane. I still think it's the prettiest place I know of. Jessie Mae, my daughter-in-law, says it's the ugliest. But she just says that I know to get my goat. She only saw it once. And then on a rainy day, at that. She says it's nothing but a swamp. That may be, I said, but it's a mighty pretty swamp, to me. And then Sonny, that's my boy Ludie, I call him Sonny, he said not to answer her back. He said it only caused arguments. And nobody ever won an argument with Jessie Mae, and I guess that's right.

(*A pause. They look out the window.*)

THELMA: Mrs. Watts . . .

MRS. WATTS: Yes?

THELMA: I think I ought to tell you this . . . I . . . I don't want you to think I'm interfering in your business . . . but . . . well . . . you see your son and your daughter-in-law came in just after you left.

MRS. WATTS: I know. I saw them coming. That's why I left so fast.

THELMA: Your son seemed very concerned.

MRS. WATTS: Bless his heart.

THELMA: He found a handkerchief that you had dropped.

MRS. WATTS: Oh, mercy, that's right, I did.

THELMA: He asked me if I had seen you. I felt I had to say yes. I wouldn't have said anything if he hadn't asked me . . .

MRS. WATTS: Oh, that's all right. I would have done exactly the same thing in your place. Did you talk to Jessie Mae?

THELMA: Yes.

MRS. WATTS: Isn't she a sight? I bet she told you I was crazy . . .

THELMA: Well . . .

MRS. WATTS: Oh, don't be afraid of hurting my feelings. Everybody's crazy according to Jessie Mae that don't want to sit in the beauty parlor all day and read movie magazines. She tells me I'm crazy about a million times a day. That's the only time Ludie will talk back to her. He gets real mad when she calls me crazy. I think Ludie knows how I feel about getting back to Bountiful. I bet he'd like to be along right now. Once when I was talking about something we did back there in the old days, he just broke out crying. He was so overcome he had to leave the room.

(A pause. MRS. WATTS *starts to hum and sing "There's not a friend like the lowly Jesus.")*

THELMA: That's a pretty hymn. What's the name of it?

MRS. WATTS: "There's not a friend like the lowly Jesus." Do you like hymns?

THELMA: Yes, I do.

MRS. WATTS: So do I. Jessie Mae says they've gone out of style, but I don't agree. I always sing one walking down the street or riding the streetcar. Keeps my spirits up. What's your favorite hymn?

THELMA: Oh, I don't know.

MRS. WATTS: The one I was singing is mine. I bet I sing it a hundred times a day. When Jessie Mae isn't home. Hymns make Jessie Mae nervous. *(A pause.)* Did Ludie mention my heart condition?

THELMA: Yes, he did.

MRS. WATTS: Poor Ludie. He worries about it so. I hated to leave him. Well, I guess he'll forgive me in time. He's just gotten himself a job. Thank the Lord. He's been out of work for two years. He had a good living as an accountant and then his nerves gave out on him. So many people are nervous today. He wasn't nervous back in Bountiful. Neither was I. The breeze from the Gulf would always quiet your nerves . . . You could sit on our front gallery and smell the ocean blowing in around you. *(A pause.)* I regret the day we left. But, I thought it was the best thing at the time . . . There were only three families there then. Farming was so hard to make a living by, and I had to see to our farm myself; our house was old and there was no money to fix it, nor send Ludie to school. So I sold off the land and gave him an education. Callie said I could always come back and visit her. She meant it, too. That's who I'm going to stay with now. Callie. I got a card from her every Christmas except for the last five. I wrote her last week and told her to expect me. Told her not to answer though on account of Jessie Mae opens all my mail. I didn't want her to know I was going. She'd try to stop it. Jessie Mae hates me. I don't know why, but she hates me. *(A pause.)* Hate me or not, I gotta get back and smell that salt air and work that dirt. I'm gonna spend the whole first month of my visit working in Callie's garden. I haven't had my hands in dirt in twenty years. My hands need the feel of dirt. *(A pause.)* Do you like to work the ground?

THELMA: I never have.

MRS. WATTS: Try it sometimes. It'll do wonders for you. I bet I'll live to be a hundred once I can get outside again. It was being cooped up in those two rooms that was killing me. I used to work the land like a man. Had to when Papa died. I got two little babies buried there. Renee Sue and Douglas. Diphtheria got Renee Sue. I never knew what carried Douglas away. He was just weak from the start. I know Callie's kept their graves weeded. Oh, if my heart just holds out until I get there. *(A pause.)* Where do you go from Harrison?

THELMA: Old Gulf. My family have just moved there from Louisiana. I'll stay with them until my husband comes home again.

MRS. WATTS: That's nice.

THELMA: It'll be funny living at home again.

MRS. WATTS: How long have you been married?

THELMA: Three years. My husband was anxious for me to go. He said he'd worry about my being alone.

MRS. WATTS: What's your husband's name?

THELMA: Robert.

MRS. WATTS: That's a nice name.

THELMA: I think so. But I guess any name he had I would think was nice. I love my husband very much. Lot of girls I know think I'm silly about him. But I can't help it.

MRS. WATTS: I wasn't in love with my husband. *(A pause.)* Do you believe we are punished for what we do wrong? I sometimes think that's why I've had all my trouble. I've talked to many a preacher about it, all but one said they didn't think so. But I can't see any other reason. Of course, I didn't lie to my husband. I told him I didn't love him, that I admired him, which I did, but I didn't love him. That I'd never love anybody but Ray John Murray as long as I lived and I didn't, and I couldn't help it. Even after my husband died and I had to move back with Papa and Mama I used to sit on the front gallery every morning and every evening just to nod hello to Ray John Murray as he went by the house to work at the post office. He went a block out of his way to pass the house. He never loved nobody but me.

THELMA: Why didn't you marry him?

MRS. WATTS: His papa and my papa didn't speak. My papa forced me to write a letter saying I never wanted to see him again and he got drunk and married out of spite. I felt sorry for his wife. She knew he never loved her. *(A pause.)* I don't think about those things much any more. But they're all part of Bountiful and I guess that's why I'm starting to think of them again. You're lucky to be married to the man you love, honey.

THELMA: Yes, I know I am.

MRS. WATTS: Awfully lucky. *(A pause.)* Did you see that star fall over there?

THELMA: No.

MRS. WATTS: It was the prettiest thing I ever saw. You can make a wish on a falling star, honey.

THELMA: I know. It's too bad I didn't see it.

MRS. WATTS: You take my wish.

THELMA: Oh, no.

MRS. WATTS: Go on. I've gotten mine already. I'm on my way to Bountiful.

THELMA: Thank you. *(A pause.)*

MRS. WATTS: Did you make your wish?

THELMA: Yes. I did.

(MRS. WATTS closes her eyes. THELMA puts her coat over MRS. WATTS. She leans her head back against the seat and closes her eyes as we fade out.)

FADE IN: The interior of the bus.
Two hours later. It has stopped. THELMA *is shaking* MRS. WATTS.

THELMA: Mrs. Watts. Mrs. Watts.
  (MRS. WATTS *opens her eyes.*)
MRS. WATTS: Yes?
THELMA: We're here. It's Harrison.
MRS. WATTS: Oh, yes. Thank you, honey.
THELMA: I'll take our suitcases and meet you inside the bus station.
MRS. WATTS: Oh, yes. That's very kind of you.
  (THELMA *takes the suitcases down and goes out the bus.* MRS. WATTS *slowly gets out of her seat and is straightening her hat.*)

DISSOLVE TO: The inside of the bus station.
A man is lying against the inside of the ticket window half asleep. He wakes himself and sees the bus has come in. He comes out of the ticket office and goes halfway to the front door, as THELMA *comes in with the two bags.*

TICKET MAN: Want any help with those bags?
THELMA: No, thank you. (*He goes back inside the office.* THELMA *takes the bags and puts them down beside a bench. She goes over to the ticket window.*) Excuse me.
TICKET MAN: Yes?
THELMA: Is the bus to Old Gulf going to be on time?
TICKET MAN: Always is.
THELMA: Thank you.
  (*She goes back to a seat near her suitcase. The* TICKET MAN *closes his eyes.* MRS. WATTS *come in.*)
MRS. WATTS: What time is it, honey?
THELMA: Two o'clock.
MRS. WATTS: Two o'clock. I bet Callie will be surprised to see me walk in at two o'clock in the morning.
THELMA: Did you tell her you were coming today?
MRS. WATTS: No. I couldn't. Because I didn't know. I had to wait until Jessie Mae went to the beauty parlor which wasn't until this afternoon.
THELMA: My bus is leaving in half an hour.

MRS. WATTS: Oh, I see. I guess I'd better be finding out how I'm going to get on out to Bountiful.

THELMA: You sit down. I'll ask the man.

MRS. WATTS: Thank you.

(She sits on the bench. THELMA *goes over to the* TICKET MAN.*)*

THELMA: Excuse me again.

(The TICKET MAN *opens his eyes.)*

TICKET MAN: Yes?

THELMA: My friend here wants to know how she can get to Bountiful.

TICKET MAN: Bountiful?

THELMA: Yes.

TICKET MAN: What's she going there for?

*(*MRS. WATTS *comes up to the window.)*

MRS. WATTS: I'm going to visit a girlhood friend.

TICKET MAN: I don't know who that's gonna be. The last person in Bountiful was Mrs. Callie Davis. She died day before yesterday. That is they found her day before yesterday. She lived all alone so they don't know exactly when she died.

MRS. WATTS: Callie Davis?

TICKET MAN: Yes, ma'am. They had the funeral this morning. Was she the one you were going to visit?

MRS. WATTS: Yes, sir. She was the one. She was my friend. My girl-hood friend. *(A pause.)* I guess I better sit down and think. *(She goes over to the bench.)*

THELMA: Is there a hotel here?

TICKET MAN: Yes'm. The Riverview. It's a nice hotel. You can get meals there, too.

THELMA: How far is it?

TICKET MAN: About five blocks.

THELMA: Is there a taxi around?

TICKET MAN: No, ma'am. Not this time of night.

THELMA: Thank you. *(She goes over to* MRS. WATTS *at the bench.)* What'll you do now, Mrs. Watts?

MRS. WATTS: I'm thinking, honey. I'm thinking. It's come as quite a blow.

THELMA: I'm sorry. I'm so sorry.

MRS. WATTS: I know. I know. *(A pause.)* It's come to me what to do. I'll go on. That much has come to me. To go on. I feel my strength and my purpose strong within me. I'll go on to Bountiful. I'll walk those twelve miles if I have to.

THELMA: But if there's no one out there what would you do at this time of night?

MRS. WATTS: I guess that's right.

THELMA: I think you should wait until morning.

MRS. WATTS: Yes. I guess I should. Then I can hire someone to drive me out. You know what I'll do. I'll stay at my own house, or what's left of it. Put me in a garden. I'll get along fine with the help of my government checks.

THELMA: Mrs. Watts, the man says there's a hotel not too far away. I think you'd better let me take you there.

MRS. WATTS: Oh, no, thank you. I wouldn't want to waste my money on a hotel. They're high as a cat's back, you know. I'll just sleep right here on this bench. Put my coat under my head, hold my purse under my arm. *(She puts the coat down on the bench like a pillow. She begins to look around for her purse.)* Have you seen my purse, honey?

THELMA: Why, no.

(They begin to look around for it.)

MRS. WATTS: Oh, my Lord. I remember now. I left my purse on the bus. Has it gone?

(THELMA turns to the door and looks out.)

THELMA: Yes, it has. You're sure you left it there?

MRS. WATTS: Yes, I am. I remember now. I didn't have it when I got off that bus. I kept thinking something was missing, but then I decided it was my suitcase that you had brought in for me. What am I gonna do, honey? All I have in the world is in that purse.

THELMA: I'll get the ticket man to call ahead. He can get someone to look on the bus in the next town.

MRS. WATTS: Thank you.

(THELMA goes back to the ticket window. The TICKET MAN is drowsing.)

THELMA: Excuse me again.

TICKET MAN: Yeah?

THELMA: This lady left her purse on the bus.

TICKET MAN: All right. I'll call ahead. How can you identify it?

MRS. WATTS: It's a plain black purse.

TICKET MAN: How much money?

MRS. WATTS: Thirty-five cents and a pension check.

TICKET MAN: Who was the check made out to?

MRS. WATTS: To me, Mrs. Carrie Watts.

TICKET MAN: All right. I'll call up about it.

MRS. WATTS: Oh, thank you. You're most kind.

THELMA: How long will it take to get it back?

TICKET MAN: Depends. If I can get ahead of the bus at Don Tarl, I can get them to send it back on the Victoria bus and it should be here in a couple of hours.

(He goes. THELMA *and* MRS. WATTS *go back to the bench.)*

MRS. WATTS: I don't know what I would have done without you.

THELMA: Try not to worry about the purse.

MRS. WATTS: I won't. I'm too tired to worry. Be time enough to start worrying when I wake up in the morning.

THELMA: Why don't you go on to sleep now if you can.

MRS. WATTS: Oh, I thought I'd stay up and see you off.

THELMA: No. You go on to sleep.

MRS. WATTS: I couldn't go right off to sleep now. I'm too wound up. You know I don't go on a trip every day of my life.

*(*TICKET MAN *comes back to the window.)*

TICKET MAN: You're lucky. Bus hadn't gotten to Don Tarl yet. If they can find the purse it'll be here around five.

MRS. WATTS: Thank you. Thank you so much.

THELMA: Make you feel better?

MRS. WATTS: Yes. It does. Of course, everything has seemed to work out today. Why is it some days everything works out, and some days nothing works out. What I mean is, I've been trying to get on that bus for Bountiful for over five years. Usually Jessie Mae and Ludie find me before I even get inside the station good. Today, I got inside both the railroad station and the bus station. Bought a ticket, seen Ludie and Jessie Mae before they saw me. Hid out until they were gone. Met a nice friend like you. Lost my purse, and now I'm having it found for me. I guess the good Lord is just with me today. *(A pause.)* I wonder why the Lord isn't with us every day? It would be so nice if He was. Well, maybe then we wouldn't appreciate so much the days when He's on our side. Or maybe He's always on our side and we don't know it. Maybe I had to wait twenty years cooped up with Jessie Mae in a city before I could appreciate getting back here. *(A pause.* THELMA *rests her head back on the bench.* MRS. WATTS *rests her head back. She is humming "There's not a friend like the lowly Jesus.")* It's so nice being able to sing a hymn when you want. I'm a happy woman, young lady—a very happy woman.

*(*TICKET MAN *goes to the door and looks out.)*

TICKET MAN: You better get outside, Miss. Bus is coming up the road. It won't wait unless it sees we have a passenger.

THELMA: All right. *(She gets her bag.)* Good-by, Mrs. Watts.

MRS. WATTS: Good-by, honey. Good luck to you. And thank you for everything.

THELMA: That's all right. Good luck to you.

MRS. WATTS: Thank you.

*(*THELMA *goes out. The* TICKET MAN *follows her out. We can hear a bus pulling up.* MRS. WATTS *goes to the door. She stands waving. The bus is heard pulling out. The* TICKET MAN *comes back in.)*

TICKET MAN: Are you gonna stay here all night?

MRS. WATTS: I have to. Everything I have is in that purse and we can't go anyplace without money.

TICKET MAN: I guess that's right. *(He goes back inside the ticket window.)* Well, good night. See you in the morning.

MRS. WATTS: Good night.

(He puts his head on the window ledge and dozes off. MRS. WATTS *sits on the bench. She rests her head back on the ledge. She is singing the hymn softly to herself as we fade out.)*

FADE IN: The ticket office an hour later.

We dolly in to the TICKET MAN. *He is sound asleep and snoring slightly. The door opens. A man comes in. He is the* SHERIFF. *He stands by the door for a moment looking around the bus station. He sees* MRS. WATTS *lying on the bench asleep. He goes over to her and looks down. He stands for a moment watching her sleep. He looks over at the ticket window and sees the man is asleep. The* SHERIFF *goes over to the* TICKET MAN. *He shakes him.*

TICKET MAN: Yeah? *(He opens his eyes. He sees the* SHERIFF.) Oh, hello, Sheriff.

SHERIFF: How long has that old woman been here?

TICKET MAN: About two hours.

SHERIFF: Did she get off the bus from Houston?

TICKET MAN: Yes, sir. I know her name. It's Watts. She left her purse on the bus and I had to call up to Don Tarl about it.

SHERIFF: Have you got her purse?

TICKET MAN: No. It hasn't come yet.

SHERIFF: She's the one, all right. I've had a call from the Houston police to hold her until her son can come for her.

TICKET MAN: She said she used to live in Bountiful.

SHERIFF: Yeah. I believe I remember some Wattses a long time ago over that way. I think that old ramshackly house about to fall into the Brazos River belonged to them.

TICKET MAN: That right? They must have been before my time. She claimed she was going to visit Miss Callie Davis. I told her she was dead. What do the police want her for?

SHERIFF: Police don't. It's her son. He wants to take her back home. Claims she's not responsible. Did she act crazy to you?

TICKET MAN: Not that I noticed. Is she crazy?

SHERIFF: They say so. Harmless, but hipped on running away from Houston to get back here. *(He starts over to her. He stands looking at her for a moment. He comes back to the* TICKET MAN.*)* Poor old thing. She's sleeping so sound, I don't have the heart to wake her up. I tell you what. I'll leave her here. You keep your eye on her. I'll come on back about daylight and take her over. Her son is coming in his car. He should be here around seven-thirty. I'll go let them know in Houston she's here. If she gives you any trouble you just call me. But I don't think she will.

TICKET MAN: All right. I guess she can't go very far without her purse, and I'm gonna have that.

SHERIFF: I'll be back around six. If she isn't up by then, I'll wake her.

TICKET MAN: All right.

(The SHERIFF *goes out.)*

DISSOLVE TO: Bus station.

Daybreak is just beginning. MRS. WATTS *is waking up. She sits up on the bench. She goes over to the door and looks outside. She looks around the waiting room. She sees the* TICKET MAN *asleep. She goes over to him and shakes him by the sleeve.*

MRS. WATTS: Excuse me, sir. *(He doesn't hear her. She shakes his sleeve again.)* I said excuse me, sir. *(He opens his eyes. He lifts his head up.)*

TICKET MAN: Yes?

MRS. WATTS: Did my purse arrive?

TICKET MAN: Yes, ma'am. *(He reaches under the window to a ledge and gets it for her.)*

MRS. WATTS: Thank you so much. I wonder if you would cash a check for me?

TICKET MAN: I'm sorry. I can't.

MRS. WATTS: It's a government check and I have identification.

TICKET MAN: I'm sorry. I can't.

MRS. WATTS: Do you know where I could get a check cashed?

TICKET MAN: Why?

MRS. WATTS: I need money to get me started in Bountiful. I want to hire someone to drive me out there and look at my house and get a few groceries. Try to find a cot to sleep on . . .

TICKET MAN: I'm sorry, lady. You're not going to Bountiful.

MRS. WATTS: Oh, yes I am. You see . . .

TICKET MAN: I'm sorry, lady. You're not going any place right now. I have to hold you here for the Sheriff.

MRS. WATTS: The Sheriff?

TICKET MAN: Yes, ma'am.

(A pause.)

MRS. WATTS: *(Almost afraid he isn't.)* You're joking with me. Don't joke with me. I've come too far . . .

TICKET MAN: I'm sorry. That's how it is.

MRS. WATTS: What has the Sheriff got to do with me?

TICKET MAN: He came in here last night while you were asleep and said I was to keep you here until your son arrived in his car this morning . . .

MRS. WATTS: I don't believe you. I don't believe you . . .

TICKET MAN: It's the truth. He'll be in here in a little while and you can ask him yourself. *(A pause.)*

MRS. WATTS: Then you're not joking?

TICKET MAN: No.

MRS. WATTS: All right. But I'm going, do you understand? You'll see. This is a free country. And I'll tell him that. No sheriff or king or president will keep me from going back to Bountiful.

TICKET MAN: All right. You tell him that. *(A pause. He turns away.)* *(She goes back to the bench. She is suddenly very nervous.)*

MRS. WATTS: What time is my son expected?

TICKET MAN: Sheriff says around seven-thirty.

MRS. WATTS: What time is it now?

TICKET MAN: Around six. *(He looks up at the clock.)* Five of six. To be exact.

MRS. WATTS: Where can I get a driver?

TICKET MAN: Ma'am?

MRS. WATTS: If you can get me a driver, I can make it to Bountiful and back before seven-thirty.

TICKET MAN: Look, lady . . .

MRS. WATTS: That's all I want. That's all I ask. Just to see it. To stand on the porch of my own house, once more. Walk under the trees. I swear, I would come back then meek as a lamb . . .

TICKET MAN: Lady . . .

MRS. WATTS: Last night, I thought I had to stay. I thought I'd die if I couldn't stay. But I'll settle for less now. Much, much less. An hour. A half-hour. Fifteen minutes.

TICKET MAN: Lady, it ain't up to me. I told you the Sheriff . . .

MRS. WATTS: *(Screaming)* Then get me the Sheriff . . .

TICKET MAN: Look, lady . . .

MRS. WATTS: Get me the Sheriff. The time is going. They'll have me locked in those two rooms again soon. The time is going . . . The time is . . .

(She begins to cry. She goes to the bench crying. The SHERIFF comes in. She doesn't hear him. He looks at the TICKET MAN. The TICKET MAN shakes his head as much as to say: "Pitiful." The SHERIFF goes over to her.)

SHERIFF: Mrs. Watts?

MRS. WATTS: Yes sir. *(She looks up.)* Are you the Sheriff?

SHERIFF: Yes, ma'am.

MRS. WATTS: I understand my son will be here at seven-thirty to take me back to Houston . . .

SHERIFF: Yes, ma'am.

MRS. WATTS: Then listen to me, sir. I've waited a long time. Just to get to Bountiful. Twenty years I've been walking the streets of the city, lost and grieving. And as I've grown older and my time approaches to die, I've made one promise to myself, to see my home again . . .

SHERIFF: Lady . . . I . . .

MRS. WATTS: I'm not asking that I not go back. I'm willing to go back. Only let me travel these twelve miles first. I have money. I can pay . . .

SHERIFF: I think that's between you and your son.

MRS. WATTS: Ludie? Why, he has to do whatever Jessie Mae tells him to. I know why she wants me back. It's for my government check. She takes it from me to buy herself Cokes and movie magazines.

SHERIFF: I don't know nothing about that. That's between you and your son.

MRS. WATTS: Won't you let me go?

SHERIFF: Not unless your son takes you.

MRS. WATTS: All right. Then I've lost. I've come all this way only to lose. *(A pause. She sinks wearily down on the bench. After a moment she begins to talk. She speaks half to herself.)* I kept thinking back there day and night in those two rooms. I kept thinking . . . And it may mean nothing at all, but it did occur to me . . . That if I could just set foot there for a minute, even . . . or a second . . . I might get some understanding of why . . . *(She turns to the SHERIFF. She begins to talk directly to him.)* Why my life has grown so petty and so meaningless. Why I've turned into a hateful, quarrelsome, old woman. And before I die I'd like to recover some of the dignity . . . the peace I used to know. For I'm going to die. Do you hear me? I'm going to die. Jessie Mae knows that. She's willful and it's her will I die in those two rooms. Well, she shan't have her way. It's my will to die in Bountiful . . .

(She sobs and starts to run out of the bus station. The SHERIFF starts after her. But she doesn't get far. She stops herself. She seems suddenly very weak and is about to fall. He goes to her and takes her arm.)

MRS. WATTS: I beg you . . . Let me go those twelve miles . . . *(A pause. For a moment her strength seems to come back.)* Understand me. Suffering I don't mind. Suffering I understand. I never protested once. Though my heart was broken when those babies died. I could stand seeing the man I loved go through life with another woman. But this twenty years of bickering. Endless, petty bickering . . . *(She again is overcome with weakness. She stands gasping for breath. They help her back to the bench.)* It's made me just like Jessie Mae sees me. It's ugly. I won't be that way. I want to go home . . . I want to go home. I want to go . . . *(She is unable to speak any more. She is on the verge of collapse. The* SHER-IFF *helps her over to the bench and settles her there.)*

SHERIFF: *(To the* TICKET MAN*)* Roy! Call a doctor.

MRS. WATTS: *(Struggling with her last bit of strength.)* No. No doctor. Bountiful . . . Bountiful . . .

She is whispering the words. They grow indistinct. Music for the curtain.

Act III

The front porch of an old ramshackle two-story house. The house hasn't been painted for years. The roof of the lower porch is sagging, the steps and the flooring are rotting away. There is no glass in the windows, no door in the doorway. The SHERIFF *and* MRS. WATTS *come in walking very slowly. They stop every few minutes while she looks around.*

SHERIFF: Feeling better?

MRS. WATTS: Yes. I am. Much better.

SHERIFF: I hope I've done the right thing bringing you here. Well, I don't see what harm it can do. As long as you mind the doctor and don't get over-excited.

MRS. WATTS: I'm home. I'm home. I'm home . . . Thank you. I thank you. I thank you.

SHERIFF: You better sit down and rest now.

MRS. WATTS: Yes sir.

(He takes her to the steps. She sits.)

SHERIFF: I'll go on back to my car. Call me if you need anything. I'll stay until your son arrives.

MRS. WATTS: Thank you. You have been very kind. You say the store burned fifteen years ago?

SHERIFF: What was left of it. You see with the good roads we have now in the county, these little towns and their country stores are all disappearing. The farmers ride into Cotton or Harrison to trade . . .

MRS. WATTS: But what's happened to the farms? For the last five miles I've seen nothing but woods . . .

SHERIFF: I know. The land around Bountiful just played out. People like you got discouraged and moved away, sold off the land for what they could get. H. T. Mavis bought most of it up . . . He let it go back into timber. He keeps a few head of cattle out here. That's all . . .

MRS. WATTS: Callie Davis kept her farm going.

SHERIFF: Yes. She did. She learned how to treat her land right and it began paying off for her towards the end. I've heard she was out riding her tractor the day before she died. Lonely death she had. All by herself in that big old house.

MRS. WATTS: There are worse things. *(A pause.)*

SHERIFF: Well, I'll go on back to the car now. You call me if you need anything.

MRS. WATTS: Thank you.

(He goes. MRS. WATTS *is sitting on the steps looking out into the yard. There is great peace in her face.)*

DISSOLVE TO: The house and yard an hour later.

The SHERIFF *comes up on the gallery. It is empty. He calls.*

SHERIFF: *(Calling.)* Mrs. Watts. Mrs. Watts . . .

(She comes to the door . . . She stands just outside of it.)

MRS. WATTS: Yes sir?

SHERIFF: Your son and daughter-in-law are out on the road in their car. They said they had to hurry back. I told them I'd bring you.

MRS. WATTS: Won't you ask them to please come in for a minute?

SHERIFF: All right. *(He comes up to the gallery.)* I have to be going on back to town now. Good-by, Mrs. Watts. *(He holds his hand out. She takes it.)*

MRS. WATTS: Good-by and thank you. You'll never know what this has meant to me.

SHERIFF: Glad I could oblige. (LUDIE *comes up.)* I was just coming to tell you your mother wanted you to come in for a few minutes.

LUDIE: Thank you.

SHERIFF: I've got to get on back to town.

LUDIE: All right, Sheriff. Thank you.

SHERIFF: That's all right. Have a nice trip back.

LUDIE: Thank you.

(The SHERIFF *goes.* LUDIE *goes up on the porch.)*

LUDIE: Hello, Mama.

MRS. WATTS: Hello, son.

LUDIE: How do you feel?

MRS. WATTS: I'm feeling better, Ludie.

LUDIE: I'm sorry I had to have the Sheriff stop you that way, Mama, but I was worried.

MRS. WATTS: I know, son. Callie Davis died.

LUDIE: Is that so? When?

MRS. WATTS: They don't know. They found her dead. She'd been seen riding a tractor the day before they found her. Buried her yesterday. *(A pause.)* Sheriff took me by our burial ground. Callie had kept it free of weeds. Even planted a few rose bushes. Least I reckon it was Callie. I don't know of anyone else who would have taken the trouble. That was nice, wasn't it?

LUDIE: Yes. It was.

MRS. WATTS: The old house has gotten run down, hasn't it?

LUDIE: Yes, it has.

MRS. WATTS: I don't think it'll last through the next Gulf storm.

LUDIE: It doesn't look like it could. *(Car horn is heard in the distance, loud and impatient.)* That's Jessie Mae. We have to start back now, Mama. Jessie Mae is nervous that I might lose my job.

MRS. WATTS: Did you ask for the day off?

LUDIE: No. I only asked for the morning off. I said I'd be there by one.

MRS. WATTS: What time is it now?

LUDIE: Eight o'clock. We were a little late getting here.

MRS. WATTS: We can drive it in three hours.

LUDIE: I know, but we might run into some traffic. Besides I borrowed Billy Davidson's car and I promised to get it back to him by twelve.

MRS. WATTS: All right. *(She starts up from the gallery. She cries.)* Ludie. Ludie. What's happened to us? Why have we come to this?

LUDIE: I don't know, Mama.

MRS. WATTS: To have stayed and fought the land would have been better than this.

LUDIE: Yes'm.

MRS. WATTS: It's strange how much I had forgotten, Ludie. Pretty soon it'll all be gone. Five . . . years . . . ten . . . our house . . . You . . . Me . . .

LUDIE: Yes'm.

MRS. WATTS: But the river will be here. The fields. The woods. The smell of the Gulf. That's what I always took my strength from, Ludie. Not from houses, not from people. *(A pause.)* It's so quiet. It's so eternally quiet. I had forgotten the peace. The quiet. And it's given me strength once more, Ludie. To go on and bear what I have to bear. Do you hear me, Ludie? I've found my dignity and my strength.

LUDIE: I'm glad, Mama.

MRS. WATTS: And I'll never fight with Jessie Mae again—or complain. *(She points into the distance.)* Do you remember how my papa always had that field over there planted in cotton?

LUDIE: Yes, ma'am.

MRS. WATTS: See, it's all woods now. But I expect some day people will come again and cut down the trees and plant the cotton and maybe even wear out the land again and then their children will sell it and go to the cities and then the trees will come up again . . .

LUDIE: I guess.

(A pause.)

MRS. WATTS: I'm ready, Ludie.

LUDIE: All right, Mama.

(He reaches his arm up to help her down the steps. JESSIE MAE *comes in.)*

JESSIE MAE: Ludie, are you coming or not?

LUDIE: We were just starting, Jessie Mae.

MRS. WATTS: Hello, Jessie Mae.

JESSIE MAE: I'm not speaking to you. I guess you're proud of the time you gave us. Dragging us all this way this time of morning. If Ludie loses his job over this, I hope you're happy.

LUDIE: I'm not going to lose my job, Jessie Mae.

JESSIE MAE: Well, you could.

LUDIE: All right, Jessie Mae.

JESSIE MAE: And she should realize that. She's selfish. That's her trouble. Always has been. Just puredee selfish . . . Where's your purse?

MRS. WATTS: Are you talking to me, Jessie Mae?

JESSIE MAE: Who else would I be talking to? Since when did Ludie start walking around with a pocketbook under his arm?

*(*MRS. WATTS *is looking around.)*

MRS. WATTS: Oh, I guess I left it inside.

JESSIE MAE: Where?

MRS. WATTS: I'll get it.

JESSIE MAE: No. Let me. You'll take all day. Where did you leave it?

MRS. WATTS: In one of the rooms downstairs.

JESSIE MAE: Wait and I'll get it. *(They start to go on.)* You all wait right there on that porch. I don't want to be left alone in this spooky old house. No telling what's running around in there.

MRS. WATTS: There's nothing in there.

JESSIE MAE: There might be rats or snakes or something.

LUDIE: I'll go.

JESSIE MAE: No. I'll go. Just stay here so if I holler you can come. *(JESSIE MAE goes into the house . . . LUDIE helps his mother down the steps. By the time they have reached the bottom step, JESSIE MAE comes out of the house with the purse.)*

JESSIE MAE: Here's your purse. Where's that money for that government check?

MRS. WATTS: I haven't cashed it.

JESSIE MAE: Where is it?

MRS. WATTS: It's right inside the purse.

(JESSIE MAE begins to search the purse.)

JESSIE MAE: No. It isn't.

MRS. WATTS: Here. Give the purse to me. *(JESSIE MAE hands her the purse. MRS. WATTS rummages around the purse. She suddenly begins to laugh.)*

JESSIE MAE: What's the matter with you?

(MRS. WATTS continues laughing.)

MRS. WATTS: Oh, my Lord. What a good joke on me.

JESSIE MAE: Well, what's so funny?

MRS. WATTS: I just remembered. I left this purse on the bus last night and the ticket man had to phone ahead and get them to take it off the bus and send it back to me. I asked him to do it for that check. I certainly didn't put them to all that trouble for a dollar ninety-eight pocketbook. And do you know the check wasn't in that purse all that time?

JESSIE MAE: Where was it?

MRS. WATTS: Right here. *(She reaches into her bosom.)* Been there since yesterday afternoon. I forgot I never put it in that purse at all.

JESSIE MAE: Give it to me. *(She reaches to grab it out of MRS. WATTS's hands. MRS. WATTS pulls her hand back.)*

MRS. WATTS: Where's your manners?

JESSIE MAE: I'm too aggravated to have manners. Give it to me.

MRS. WATTS: All right. *(She takes the check and she tears it into little pieces. She throws them on the ground.)* Here's your check.

JESSIE MAE: You spiteful old thing.

LUDIE: Jessie Mae . . .

JESSIE MAE: That's what she is. Just spiteful and spoiled . . .

LUDIE: Go on to the car. I want to have a talk with Mama. We're gonna stop this wrangling once and for all else I'm walking out on you both.

JESSIE MAE: Well, you better hurry, or else I won't be here to walk out on. She's not coming into my house again. Not as long as I'm there. Now both of you talk that over. *(She goes out.)*

MRS. WATTS: I'm sorry, Ludie. I shouldn't have fought with her. I know. I know. I swore to myself I wouldn't ever again. I just don't know what got into me. *(A pause.)* I can get the check back for you.

LUDIE: It's not the check, Mama. You know that. It's not the check. *(He starts to cry.)*

MRS. WATTS: Don't, son.

LUDIE: I don't mean to. But you and Jessie Mae make it so hard for me. Always pulling me this way and that. I try to please both of you . . . I . . . And it's killing me, Mama. It's killing me.

MRS. WATTS: I know. I know. Jessie Mae is right. We shouldn't live together. She brings out the worst in me and I reckon I bring out the worst in her.

LUDIE: But we have to live together, Mama.

MRS. WATTS: I know. I know. *(A pause.)* You go tell Jessie Mae I'm sorry. I won't fight any more. I've found my dignity and my strength. I'd lost it there for a minute, but I won't lose it again.

LUDIE: *(Wearily.)* All right, Mama. Come on, let's go.

MRS. WATTS: No. You run ahead first and tell her I apologize. Ask her to let me come. That's the nice way to do it.

LUDIE: All right, Mama.

(He goes. MRS. WATTS *rests her body against the pillars of the porch. She goes down the steps and stoops in the earth by the steps. She scoops up a handful and looks at it, letting it run through her fingers back to the ground.* LUDIE *comes back in.)*

LUDIE: Jessie Mae says all is forgiven.

MRS. WATTS: All right, son.

LUDIE: So come on and let's try and have a pleasant ride home.

MRS. WATTS: All right, son. *(They start away. She breaks out crying.)* Ludie. Ludie.

LUDIE: Now, Mama. Please . . .

MRS. WATTS: All right, son. All right. I'm sorry. I won't cry ever again. *(She wipes her eyes. She starts out.)* I've had my trip. That's more than enough to keep me happy the rest of my life. *(She takes* LUDIE *by the arm. They start out. She turns.)* Good-by, Bountiful. Good-by.

She takes one last look at the house. She waves one last farewell. She and LUDIE *go out. Music for curtain.*

II

The Stageplay

Lillian Gish and Eva Marie Saint (© *Eileen Darby*)

Lillian Gish (© *Eileen Darby*)

The Stageplay

The *Trip to Bountiful* was in the vanguard of television plays to make the transition to the Broadway stage. Almost immediately after the show's airing on NBC, Fred Coe, in conjunction with the Theatre Guild—then one of the leading theatrical production organizations in the United States—arranged to present a stage version of the teleplay. Horton Foote was asked to make the adaptation, and he agreed eagerly.

Lillian Gish and Eva Marie Saint reprised their roles for the Broadway production. John Beal was to keep his role as Ludie, but he and Fred Coe disagreed over whether the actor should wear a toupee, and Beal left the cast. He was replaced by Gene Lyons. Jo Van Fleet took over the role of Jessie Mae from Eileen Heckart and won a Tony Award for best supporting actress.

As the play went through tryouts, Foote made only a few cuts in his playscript. For example, he omitted a scene in which a neighbor played by Jean Stapleton visited Mrs. Watts in the apartment. And some adjustments were made for the performers. According to Foote, Jo Van Fleet was very inventive: "She brought a lot of ideas to the part, which were new. And the other actors had to react differently."[1] Theresa Helburn, a board member and one of the three founders of the Theatre Guild, asked Foote to make additional changes, but he refused: "I won out. I just said I wasn't going to do it. I don't even remember what she asked me to do, but I knew I was upset. She backed down, for good or bad. I think for good myself. But mostly it was a very calm time."[2]

After *Bountiful* was tried out in the Guild's summer theater in Westport (Connecticut), the company went on a road tour to Wilmington (Delaware) and Philadelphia, where the play received good reviews, and in November 1953 *Bountiful* opened on Broadway with Vincent Donehue as director. The 1953–54 season on Broadway saw several new hits, including *Tea and Sympathy, The Teahouse of the August Moon, The Seven Year Itch,* and *The Solid Gold Cadillac;* several musical hits from past seasons such as *Wonderful Town* and *Can-Can* remained strong at the box office.

Expectations for *Bountiful* were high because the road reviews were so favorable. Some had even talked about the play as a new *Glass Menagerie.* Despite some minor reservations, the response from the New York critics was generally positive. John Chapman's comments were typical: "Author Foote is admirably skillful as he sets forth his play. He has a fine sense of humor, a true eye for character and a good ear for talk. In spite of its sentimentality . . . *The Trip to Bountiful* is good theatre."[3] William Hawkins of the *New York World-Telegram and The Sun* wrote, *"The Trip to Bountiful* . . . is that rarest of theater experiences, an evening which will prove an indelible memory. . . . Horton Foote has done and done beautifully, the one thing it is important for a playwright to do. That is, provide the disciplined material for expert actors to completely capture an audience and hold it through the evening."[4] Under ordinary circumstances, the producers could have used the favorable quotes as the basis for a strong publicity campaign with the hope of stimulating a long run on the Broadway stage. But soon after the opening, New York City was hit by a prolonged newspaper strike. In the 1950s, print was the most important source for entertainment news. Coe and the Guild had no outlet to build public support for the play, and it closed after thirty-nine performances.

Bountiful was within the mainstream of one of the two prevailing currents of the time in theater. After World War II, dramatists such as Jean Genet, Eugene Ionesco, Samuel Beckett, Harold Pinter, and Edward Albee emphasized "the event and the conception . . . over the message and the word."[5] Arthur Miller, Tennessee Williams, and William

Inge, among others, prized realism and clarity. Foote and most of the other television writers preferred the latter approach. *Bountiful* also followed in the tradition of Thornton Wilder and William Saroyan in dealing with the common person, although Foote did not offer an unrealistic, sentimental ending guaranteeing happiness to all of his characters.

Although the writers for television's weekly dramatic presentations shared a style and vision similar to those of their theatrical predecessors, one critic has pointed out some subtle differences. Kenneth Hey believes television writers were less fatalistic than playwrights such as Miller and Williams. Conflicts on the television screen "revolved less around illusion versus reality and more around tradition versus modernity."[6] Teleplays contained less social comment. While theater dramatists expressed "anguish at the degradation of modern life, the television dramatists focused on doubt and potential shortcomings, most of which dissolved after troubled consideration."[7]

Stage drama depicted an alienated world with psychologically disturbed people while live television drama was less cynical, more comfortable for mostly a home audience with middle-class values. On the small screen, problems were resolved more easily. While stageplays dealt with broad questions of the human condition, television looked at the problems of individuals. Both media were realistic, in that they examined aspects of ordinary lives in settings with which the audience could easily identify, and both dealt with the characters' search for personal honor and a sense of dignity. Generally, television dramatists, possibly because of the demands of this advertising-supported medium, tended to be more optimistic than their counterparts writing for the stage.[8]

While *Bountiful* was one of the first scripts to make the transition from television to Broadway, other authors and their works soon followed. In 1954, Foote and five other alumni of anthology drama formed a group with Fred Coe to produce the plays of its members. The production company was not a commercial success, but "this gathering of forces and the publicity that grew out of it is an indication of the respect with which the television dramatist . . . was treated at the time."[9]

Bountiful was an example of the way live television inspired innovation in handling spatial mobility on the stage. "The multiple set and the use of lights for transition are the two techniques that owe much to television. For the most part, television plays are made up of brief scenes, often supposed to take place in different rooms of a house or different parts of town. The sets, of course, may actually be no more than a chair or two and a piece of wall, but cribbed and cramped as they are they suggest space and movement impossible in a single-room set."[10]

In the second act of *Bountiful,* Mrs. Watts walks from the Houston bus terminal to the bus and then arrives at the Harrison bus station. Instead of lowering the curtain and setting up the stage separately for each scene, the set designer for the stageplay put all three sets in a simplified form on the stage, just as they had all shared the television playing area. The Broadway audience, suspending disbelief, watched Mrs. Watts as she walked from the Houston bus station on one side of the stage to the bus seats in the middle, and then to the Harrison bus station on the other side of the stage. Each area was lit only when action took place there; therefore, the audience knew where to look and when. No longer did the curtain have to come down to signal a change in scene; transitions could be made quickly and easily—before the audience's eyes.[11]

Bountiful led the way for other television dramas to make the transition to the stage. Television writers such as Gore Vidal and Paddy Chayefsky would follow Horton Foote's lead. The brief Broadway run of *Bountiful* was significant not only for breaking innovative ground, but also for the strong performances of Lillian Gish and Jo Van Fleet. Foote has commented that the original Broadway performance inspired a special kind of loyalty and remained a "remembered event" for those who saw it. He noted that through the years many people have remarked that they were deeply moved by the production.[12] Professional and amateur groups both in this country and abroad are still entertaining and moving audiences with the story of Mrs. Watts's journey home.

The second version of the *Bountiful* drama gave Horton Foote the opportunity to shape and deepen his story. The more detailed characterization of Mrs. Watts, Ludie, and Jessie Mae through dialogue and action in the first act is the major benefit the film version inherited from the stageplay.

Notes

1. Horton Foote, personal interview with Barbara Moore, New York City, July 1987.

2. Foote interview.

3. John Chapman, *New York Daily News,* Nov. 4, 1953.

4. William Hawkins, *New York World-Telegram and The Sun,* Nov. 4, 1953. For other critics' responses, see Brooks Atkinson, *New York Times,* Nov. 4, 1953, 30; Richard Watts, Jr., *New York Post,* Nov. 4, 1953; Robert Coleman, *New York Daily Mirror,* Nov. 4, 1953.

5. George Terry Barr, "The Ordinary World of Horton Foote" (Ph.D. diss., University of Tennessee, 1986), 20.

6. Kenneth Hey, "*Marty:* Aesthetics vs. Medium in Early Television Drama," in *American History/American Television: Interpreting the Video Past,* ed. John E. O'Connor (New York: Frederick Ungar, 1983), 99.

7. Hey, 101.

8. Hey, 103.

9. Gerald Weales, *American Drama since World War II* (New York: Harcourt, Brace & World, Inc., 1962), 57.

10. Weales, 68.

11. Weales, 68.

12. Foote interview.

The Trip to Bountiful

First produced at
Henry Miller's Theatre, New York City
November 3, 1953

Director: Vincent Donehue
Producers: The Theatre Guild and Fred Coe
Set Designer: Otis Riggs

Cast

MRS. CARRIE WATTS: Lillian Gish
LUDIE WATTS: Gene Lyons
JESSIE MAE WATTS: Jo Van Fleet
THELMA: Eva Marie Saint
HOUSTON TICKET MAN: Will Hare
A TRAVELER: Salem Ludwig
SECOND HOUSTON TICKET MAN: David Clive
HARRISON TICKET MAN: Frederick Downs
SHERIFF: Frank Overton
TRAVELERS: Patricia MacDonald, Neil Laurence,
Helen Cordes

Scenes

ACT I: A Houston Apartment
ACT II: The Trip
ACT III: A Country Place

Production Notes

ACT I: *The bedroom and living room of a Houston apartment. The walls of these two rooms can be defined by the placement of furniture and by the use of certain necessary fragments of flats needed to contain a door or a window frame.*

ACT II: *The Houston bus station, a seat on a bus, the Harrison bus station. The Houston and Harrison bus stations require no more than a bench each and cutouts to represent ticket windows. Two chairs are all that are required for the bus seats.*

ACT III: *The house at Bountiful. Since this house is seen through the eyes and heart of Mrs. Watts, the actual house can be as symbolic or as realistic as the individual designer chooses. An atmospheric description of this set is included in the text for groups wanting to make use of it.*

Act I

SCENE I

The curtain rises. The stage is dark. The lights are slowly brought up and we see the living room and bedroom of a small three-room apartment. The two rooms have been furnished on very little money. The living room is downstage right. In the living room is a sofa that at night has to serve as a bed. It has been made up for the night. Upstage left of the room is a door leading out to the hallway, kitchen, and bathroom. At the opposite end of this hallway is a door leading to the bedroom. To get back and forth, then, between these two rooms it is necessary to go out into the hallway. Center right, in the living room, is a window looking out on the street. Above the window is a wardrobe in which MRS. WATTS'*s clothes and other belongings are kept. On top of the wardrobe are a suitcase and* MRS. WATTS'*s purse. A rocking chair is beside the window, and about the room are an easy chair and another straight chair. Center, in the living room, is a drop-leaf table with two straight chairs at either end. On the table are a small radio and a book. Upstage center is a door leading to the outside stairs. Against the rear wall, stage right, is a desk and on the desk are a phone, a newspaper, and a movie magazine.*

A full moon shines in the window. The two rooms are kept immaculately.

The bedroom is smaller than the living room. There is a bed with its headboard against the upstage center wall. A small table with a bed light stands by the bed. Right center is a vanity with its back against the imaginary wall separating the living room from the bedroom. There are two straight chairs in the room, one in front of the vanity. Upstage left is a closet with dresses hanging in it.

In the living room a woman of sixty is sitting in the rocking chair, rocking back and forth. She is small and thin and fragile. The woman is MRS. WATTS. *She lives in the apartment with her son,* LUDIE, *and her daughter-in-law,* JESSIE MAE.

The lights are out in the bedroom and we can't see much. LUDIE *and* JESSIE MAE *are both in bed.* JESSIE MAE *is asleep and* LUDIE *isn't.*

LUDIE *slips out of his bed, in the bedroom. He starts tiptoeing out the door that leads to the hallway.*

MRS. WATTS *continues to rock back and forth in the chair. She doesn't hear* LUDIE. *She hums a hymn to herself, "There's Not a Friend Like the Lowly Jesus."*

Then she hears LUDIE.

LUDIE *is in his early forties. He has on pajamas and a robe.* LUDIE *has had a difficult life. He had been employed as an accountant until his health broke down. He was unable to work for two years. His mother and his wife are both dependent on him, and their small savings were depleted during his illness. Now he has started working again, but at a very small salary.*

MRS. WATTS: Don't be afraid of makin' noise, Sonny. I'm awake.

LUDIE: Yes, Ma'am.

> *(He comes into the living room. He comes over to the window.* MRS. WATTS *is looking back out the window, rocking and singing her hymn. He stands behind his mother's chair looking out the window at moonlight. We can clearly see his face now. It is a sensitive face. After a moment* MRS. WATTS *looks up at* LUDIE. *The rocking ceases for a second.)*

MRS. WATTS: Pretty night.

LUDIE: Sure is.

MRS. WATTS: Couldn't you sleep?

LUDIE: No, Ma'am.

MRS. WATTS: Why couldn't you sleep?

LUDIE: I just couldn't. (MRS. WATTS *turns away from* LUDIE *to look out the window again. She starts her rocking once more, and hums her hymn to herself. She is opening and closing her hands nervously.)* Couldn't you sleep?

MRS. WATTS: No. I haven't been to bed at all. *(Outside the window in the street we hear a car's brakes grind to a sudden stop.)*

LUDIE: There's going to be a bad accident at that corner one of these days.

MRS. WATTS: I wouldn't be surprised. I think the whole state of Texas is going to meet its death on the highways. *(Pause.)* I don't see what pleasure they get drivin' these cars as fast as they do. Do you?

LUDIE: No, Ma'am. *(A pause.* MRS. WATTS *goes back to her humming and her rocking.)* But there's a lot of things I don't understand. Never did and never will, I guess. *(A pause.)*

MRS. WATTS: Is Jessie Mae asleep?

LUDIE: Yes, Ma'am. That's why I thought I'd better come out here. I got to tossin' an' turnin' so I was afraid I was gonna wake up Jessie Mae. *(A pause.)*

MRS. WATTS: You're not worryin' about your job, are you, Sonny?

LUDIE: No, Ma'am. I don't think so. Everybody seems to like me there. I'm thinking about askin' for a raise.

MRS. WATTS: You should, hard as you work.

LUDIE: Why couldn't you sleep, Mama?

MRS. WATTS: Because there's a full moon. *(She rocks back and forth opening and closing her hands.)* I never could sleep when there was a full moon. Even back in Bountiful when I'd been working out in the fields all day, and I'd be so tired I'd think my legs would give out on me, let there be a full moon and I'd just toss the night through. I've given up trying to sleep on nights like this. I just sit and watch out the window and think my thoughts. *(She looks out the window smiling to herself.)* I used to love to look out the window back at Bountiful. Once when you were little and there was a full moon, I woke you up and dressed you and took you for a walk with me. Do you remember?

LUDIE: No, Ma'am.

MRS. WATTS: You don't?

LUDIE: No, Ma'am.

MRS. WATTS: I do. I remember just like it was yesterday. I dressed you and took you outside and there was an old dog howlin' away off somewhere and you got scared an' started cryin' an' I said, "Son, why are you cryin'?" You said someone had told you that when a dog howled a person was dyin' some place. I held you close to me, because you were tremblin' with fear. An' then you asked me to explain to you about dyin', an' I said you were too young to worry about things like that for a long time to come. *(A pause.)* I was just sittin' here thinkin', Sonny. *(She looks up at* LUDIE. *She sees he is lost in his own thoughts.)* A penny for your thoughts.

LUDIE: Ma'am?

MRS. WATTS: A penny for your thoughts.

LUDIE: I didn't have any, Mama. *(She goes back to her rocking).* I wish we had a yard here. Part of my trouble is that I get no exercise. *(A pause.)* Funny the things you think about when you can't sleep. I was trying to think of the song I used to like to hear you sing back home. I'd always laugh when you'd sing it.

MRS. WATTS: Which song was that, Son?

LUDIE: I don't remember the name. I just remember I'd always laugh when you'd sing it. *(A pause.* MRS. WATTS *thinks a moment.)*

MRS. WATTS: Oh, yes. That old song. *(She thinks for another moment.)* What was the name of it?

LUDIE: I don't know. *(A pause.)*

MRS. WATTS: Let's see. Oh, I hate not to be able to think of something. It's on the tip of my tongue. *(A pause. She thinks. She recites the words.)*

Hush little baby, don't say a word.
Mama's gonna buy you a mockin' bird.
And if that mockin' bird don't sing,
Mama's gonna buy you a diamond ring.

I used to think I was gonna buy you the world back in those days. I remember remarking that to my Papa. He said the world can't be bought. I didn't rightly understand what he meant then. *(She suddenly turns to him, taking his hand.)* Ludie. *(He looks down at her, almost afraid of the question she intends to ask. She sees his fear and decides not to ask it. She lets go of his hand.)* Nothin'. Nothin'. *(A pause.)* Would you like me to get you some hot milk?

LUDIE: Yes, Ma'am. If you don't mind.

MRS. WATTS: I don't mind at all. *(She gets up out of her chair and exits to the kitchen.* LUDIE *repeats the lines of the song to himself quietly.)*

LUDIE:

Hush little baby, don't say a word.
Mama's gonna buy you a mockin' bird.
And if that mockin' bird don't sing,
Mama's gonna buy you a diamond ring.

(Another car comes to a sudden stop out in the street, screeching its brakes. He peers out the window, his face close against the screen, trying to see the car. JESSIE MAE *is awakened by the screech. She gets out of bed and puts on a dressing gown.)*

JESSIE MAE: *(From the bedroom.)* Ludie! Ludie!

MRS. WATTS: *(Reenters from hallway.)* You want butter and pepper and salt in it?

LUDIE: Yes, Ma'am, if it's not too much trouble.

MRS. WATTS: No trouble at all. *(Exits to hallway.)*

JESSIE MAE: *(From the bedroom.)* Ludie.

LUDIE: Come in, Jessie Mae. Mama isn't asleep.

(JESSIE MAE *goes out the bedroom into the living room. She immediately turns on the lights, flooding the room with an ugly glare.* JESSIE MAE *was probably called very cute when she was young. Now she is hard, driven, nervous, and hysterical.)*

JESSIE MAE: Why don't you turn on the lights? What's the sense of sitting around in the dark? I don't know what woke me up. I was sleeping as sound as a log. All of a sudden I woke up and looked over in bed and you weren't there. Where is your mama?

LUDIE: In the kitchen.

JESSIE MAE: What's she doing out there?

LUDIE: Fixing some hot milk for me.

JESSIE MAE: *(She glances out the hallway.)* Putter, putter, putter. Honestly! Do you want a cigarette?

LUDIE: No, thanks. (JESSIE MAE *takes cigarettes and a lighter from her dressing gown pocket. She struggles with the cigarette lighter.)*

JESSIE MAE: Do you have a match? My lighter is out of fluid. I have to remember to get some tomorrow. (LUDIE *lights her cigarette. A pause. She takes a drag off her cigarette.* LUDIE *gives her a package of matches.)* Thanks. Couldn't you sleep?

LUDIE: Uh-uh.

JESSIE MAE: How do you expect to work tomorrow if you don't get your sleep, Ludie?

LUDIE: I'm hopin' the hot milk will make me sleepy. I slept last night. I don't know what got into me tonight.

JESSIE MAE: You didn't sleep the night before last.

LUDIE: I know. But I slept the night before that.

JESSIE MAE: I don't think your mama has even been to bed. *(MRS. WATTS comes in from the hallway with the milk.)* What's the matter with you that you can't sleep, Mother Watts?

MRS. WATTS: It's a full moon, Jessie Mae.

JESSIE MAE: What's that got to do with it?

MRS. WATTS: I never could sleep when there's a full moon.

JESSIE MAE: That's just your imagination. *(MRS. WATTS doesn't answer. She hands* LUDIE *the hot milk. He takes it and blows it to cool it off before drinking.* JESSIE MAE *goes over to a small radio on the drop-leaf table and turns it on.)* I don't know what's the matter with you all. I never had trouble sleepin' in my life. I guess I have a clear conscience. The only time that I remember having had any trouble sleeping was the night I spent out at Bountiful. The mosquitoes like to have chewed me up. I never saw such mosquitoes. Regular gallow nippers. *(The radio plays a blues.* JESSIE MAE *picks up a movie magazine from the desk and sits in the chair by the radio.)* Mother Watts, where did you put that recipe that Rosella gave me on the phone today?

MRS. WATTS: What recipe was that, Jessie Mae?

JESSIE MAE: What recipe was that? She only gave me one. The one I wrote down while I was talkin' to Rosella this mornin'. You remember, I asked you to find me a pencil.

MRS. WATTS: Yes, I remember something about it.

JESSIE MAE: Then I handed it to you and asked you to put it away on the top of my dresser.

MRS. WATTS: Jessie Mae, I don't remember you havin' given me any recipe.

JESSIE MAE: Well, I did.

MRS. WATTS: I certainly have no recollection of it.

JESSIE MAE: You don't?

MRS. WATTS: No, Ma'am.

JESSIE MAE: I swear, Mother Watts, you just don't have any memory at all anymore.

MRS. WATTS: Jessie Mae, I think I . . .

JESSIE MAE: I gave it to you this mornin' in this very room and I said to please put it on my dresser and you said I will and went out holding it in your hand.

MRS. WATTS: I did?

JESSIE MAE: Yes, you did.

MRS. WATTS: Did you look on your dresser?

JESSIE MAE: Yes, Ma'am.

MRS. WATTS: And it wasn't there?

JESSIE MAE: No, Ma'am. I looked just before I went to bed.

MRS. WATTS: Oh. Well, let me look around. *(She gets up and goes out the door into the hallway.* JESSIE MAE *paces around the room.)*

JESSIE MAE: I swear. Have you noticed how forgetful she's getting? I think her memory is definitely going. Honestly, it just gets on my nerves. We're just gonna have to get out a little more, Ludie.

No wonder you can't sleep. You get up in the morning, you go to work, you come home, you have your supper, read the paper, and then go right off to bed. Every couple I know goes out three or four times a week. I know we couldn't afford it before, so I kept quiet about it. But now you're working again I don't think a picture show once or twice a week would break us. We don't have a car. We don't go to nightclubs. We have to do something.

LUDIE: OK. Why don't we go out one night this week?

JESSIE MAE: I mean, I think we have to. I was talkin' to Rosella about it this morning on the phone and she said she just didn't see how we stood it. Well, I said, Rosella, we have Mother Watts and it's hard for us to leave her alone.

LUDIE: When did you and Rosella get friendly again?

JESSIE MAE: This morning. She just all of a sudden called me up on the telephone. She said she would quit being mad if I would. I said shucks, I wasn't mad in the first place. She was the one that was mad. I told her I was plain-spoken and said exactly what I felt and people will just have to take me as I am or leave me alone. I said furthermore, I had told her the truth when I remarked that the beauty parlor must have seen her coming a long way down the road when they charged her good money for that last permanent they gave her. She said she agreed with me now entirely and had stopped patronizing that beauty shop. *(A pause. She goes back to her movie magazine.)* Rosella found out definitely that she can't have any children . . . *(MRS. WATTS comes into the living room. To MRS. WATTS.)* Walk, don't run. *(MRS. WATTS looks around the room for the recipe. A pause.)* You know your mother's pension check didn't come today. It's the eighteenth. I swear it was due. I just can't understand the government. Always late. *(Looking up from her reading—then to MRS. WATTS.)* Did you find it?

MRS. WATTS: Not yet.

JESSIE MAE: Well, then forget about it. Look for it in the morning.

MRS. WATTS: No, I'm going to look for it until I find it. *(MRS. WATTS goes out of the room.)*

JESSIE MAE: Honestly, Ludie, she's so stubborn. *(She goes back to her movie magazine. Turns the radio dial—the radio plays a popular tune.)* I just love this song and this singer: I could just listen to him all day. *(JESSIE MAE begins to sing with the singer. There is an immediate knocking upstairs. She continues singing louder than ever. The knocking continues. Finally she jumps up out of her chair. She is very angry.)* Now what are they knocking about? Do you consider this on too loud?

LUDIE: No sense in arguing with them, Jessie Mae.

JESSIE MAE: They'd like it if we didn't breathe.

LUDIE: Well, it is kinda late. (LUDIE *turns the radio down.* JESSIE MAE *yawns. She goes over to the sofa with the movie magazine.)*

JESSIE MAE: Who played the captain in *Mutiny on the Bounty?*

LUDIE: Search me.

JESSIE MAE: They're running a contest in here but I never saw such hard questions. *(A pause. She looks up at* LUDIE.*)* Rosella said Jim used to have trouble sleepin'. She said a man told him to lie in bed and count backwards and that would cure him. He tried it and she said it did. She said you start with a hundred and instead of going forward you go backwards. One hundred, ninety-nine, ninety-eight, ninety-seven, ninety-six, ninety-five . . . She said it would just knock him out.

LUDIE: Jessie Mae, maybe we can take in a baseball game one night this week. The series is getting exciting. I think Houston has the best team they've had in a long time. I'd sure like to be there when they play Shreveport. *(Pause.)* I used to play baseball back at Bountiful. I used to rather play baseball than eat, when I was a kid.

JESSIE MAE: Come on, let's go to bed. *(She gets up. There is another screech of brakes.)* There goes another car smashed up. *(She runs to the window and stands looking out.)* Nope, they missed each other. Six cars smashed up on the freeway to Galveston I read yesterday in the Chronicle. One right on top of another. One car was trying to pass another car and ran right smack into a third car. Then the ones behind both cars started pilin' up. A lot of them were killed. I bet they were all drunk. Been down to Galveston, gamblin', likely. I think the whole of Houston goes into Galveston gambling and drinking. Everybody but us. I don't see how some people hold down a job the way they drink and gamble. Do you?

LUDIE: No . . . I don't.

JESSIE MAE: That's why I told Rosella I could hardly keep from callin' up your boss and givin' him a piece of my mind for payin' you the salary he pays you. Like I said to Rosella, you're so steady and so conscientious and they just take advantage of your good nature. Maybe you're too steady, Ludie. (LUDIE *has taken a book off the drop-leaf table. He goes to the chair, reading it. A pause.* MRS. WATTS *goes into the bedroom. She turns on the lights in the bedroom and begins a systematic search for the recipe. To* LUDIE.) Rosella was glad to hear you're workin' again. She said she was cleanin' out some drawers night before last and had come across some pictures of you and me she'd taken when we started goin' together. I said I don't care to see them. No, thank you. (MRS. WATTS *is looking, now, in* JESSIE MAE's *vanity drawer. She finds the recipe.*) The passin's of time makes me sad. That's why I never want a house with the room to keep a lot of junk in to remind you of things you're better off forgetting. If we ever get any money you wouldn't catch me buying a house. I'd move into a hotel and have me room service. (MRS. WATTS *comes into the living room, holding the recipe.*)

MRS. WATTS: Here's your recipe, Jessie Mae.

JESSIE MAE: Thank you but I told you not to bother. Where did you find it? (*She takes the recipe.*)

MRS. WATTS: In your room.

JESSIE MAE: In my room?

MRS. WATTS: Yes, Ma'am.

JESSIE MAE: Where in my room?

MRS. WATTS: In your dresser drawer. Right-hand side.

JESSIE MAE: In my dresser drawer?

MRS. WATTS: Yes, Ma'am. I looked on top of the dresser and it wasn't there an' something said to me . . . (JESSIE MAE *rises and angrily throws her package of matches down on the table.*)

JESSIE MAE: Mother Watts.

MRS. WATTS: Ma'am.

JESSIE MAE: Ludie, how many times have I asked her never to go into my dresser drawer?

MRS. WATTS: I thought you wanted me to find your recipe?

JESSIE MAE: Well, I don't want you to go into my dresser drawers. I'd like a little privacy if you don't mind.

MRS. WATTS: Yes, Ma'am. (*She turns away. She is trying to avoid a fight.*)

JESSIE MAE: (*She is very angry now. She takes* MRS. WATTS *by the shoulder and shakes her.*) And just let me never catch you looking in them again. For anything. I can't stand people snoopin' in my dresser drawers. (MRS. WATTS *grabs the paper from* JESSIE MAE *and throws it on the floor. She is hurt and angry.*)

MRS. WATTS: All right. Then the next time you find it yourself.

JESSIE MAE: Pick that recipe up, if you please.

MRS. WATTS: Pick it up yourself. I have no intention of picking it up.

JESSIE MAE: *(Shouting.)* You pick that up!

MRS. WATTS: *(Shouting back.)* I won't.

LUDIE: Mama.

JESSIE MAE: *(Shouting even louder.)* You will!

LUDIE: Jessie Mae. For God sakes! You're both acting like children. It's one-thirty in the morning.

JESSIE MAE: You tell her to pick that up.

MRS. WATTS: I won't. (MRS. WATTS *stubbornly goes to her rocking chair and sits.)*

JESSIE MAE: *(Screaming.)* You will! This is my house and you'll do as you're told. (LUDIE *walks out of the room. He goes into his bedroom.* JESSIE MAE *crosses to* MRS. WATTS.) Now. I hope you're satisfied. You've got Ludie good and upset. He won't sleep for the rest of the night. What do you want to do? Get him sick again? *(There is a knocking upstairs.* JESSIE MAE *screams up at them.)* Shut up. *(To* MRS. WATTS.) You're going too far with me one of these days, old lady.

(JESSIE MAE *walks out of the room.* MRS. WATTS *is ready to scream back at her, but she controls the impulse. She takes her anger out in rocking violently back and forth.* JESSIE MAE *throws open the door to the bedroom and comes in.* LUDIE *is sitting on the edge of the bed. She marches over to the vanity and sits. She starts to throw things around on top of the vanity. After a moment,* LUDIE *gets up and starts toward her.)*

LUDIE: Jessie Mae.

JESSIE MAE: I just can't stand this, Ludie. I'm at the end of my rope. I won't take being insulted by your mother or anyone else. You hear that?

(LUDIE *rises and stands uncomfortably for a moment. He turns and goes out the bedroom door and into the living room. He stands by the living room door looking at his mother. She stops her rocking. She goes and picks up the recipe.* LUDIE *sees what she is doing and tries to get there first. He is not able to. She hands the recipe to him. He stands there for a moment looking at it. He turns to his mother and speaks with great gentleness.)*

LUDIE: Mama. Will you give this recipe to Jessie Mae?

MRS. WATTS: All right, Ludie. *(She takes the recipe. She starts out of the living room and* LUDIE *stops her. He obviously hates asking the next question.)*

LUDIE: Mama, will you please tell Jessie Mae you're sorry?

MRS. WATTS: Ludie . . .

LUDIE: Please, Mama.

MRS. WATTS: All right, Ludie.

LUDIE: Jessie Mae.

*(*MRS. WATTS *goes out of the room to the bedroom.)*

JESSIE MAE: What do you want, Ludie?

LUDIE: Mama has something to say to you.

JESSIE MAE: What is it? *(*MRS. WATTS *hands her the recipe.)*

MRS. WATTS: I'm sorry, Jessie Mae, for throwing the recipe on the floor.

JESSIE MAE: I accept your apology.

*(*MRS. WATTS *goes out, reappears in living room.)*

JESSIE MAE: *(Calling.)* Come on, Ludie. Let's all go to bed.

LUDIE: All right. *(He starts for the living room door.)*

JESSIE MAE: *(Calling.)* And you'd better go to bed too, Mother Watts. A woman your age ought to have better sense than to sit up half the night.

MRS. WATTS: Yes, Ma'am. Good night, Ludie.

LUDIE: Good night, Mama.

(He waits until his mother sits in the rocking chair and then he turns the lights off in the living room and goes into the bedroom, taking his book with him. MRS. WATTS *buries her face in her hands. She is crying.)*

LUDIE: *(Now in bedroom.)* Jessie Mae. I know it's hard and all, but for your own sake, I just think sometimes if you'd try to ignore certain things.

JESSIE MAE: Ignore? How can you ignore something when it's done right under your very nose?

LUDIE: Look, Jessie Mae.

JESSIE MAE: I know her, Ludie. She does things just to aggravate me. Well, I hope she's happy now. She aggravated me. Now you take her hymn singin'. She never starts until I come into a room. And her poutin'! Why sometimes she goes a whole day just sittin' and starin' out that window. How would you like to spend twenty-four hours a day shut up with a woman that either sang hymns or looked out the window and pouted? You couldn't ignore it and don't tell me you could. No. There's only one thing to do and that's to say quit it, every time she does something like that until she stops for good and all.

LUDIE: I'm not sayin' it's easy, Jessie Mae. I'm only sayin' . . .

JESSIE MAE: Well, let's change the subject. I don't want to get mad all over again. She keeps me so nervous never knowing when I leave whether she is going to try to run off to that old town or not.

LUDIE: Well, she's not going to run off again, Jessie Mae. She promised me she wouldn't.

JESSIE MAE: What she promised and . . .

LUDIE: Now, she can't run off. Her pension check hasn't come. You said yourself . . .

(MRS. WATTS hears them. She goes to the edge of the rug, lifts it up, and takes the pension check. She stands there for a moment, looking at it, trying to decide whether to take this in to JESSIE MAE.)

JESSIE MAE: Well, I am not too sure that that check hasn't come. Sometimes I think she hides that check and I tell you right now if it is not here tomorrow I am going to search this house from top to bottom.

LUDIE: Well, I know the check will come tomorrow.

JESSIE MAE: I hope so. Rosella says she thinks it's terrible how close I have to stay here. Well, I told Rosella ever since your mother started that running-off business I don't feel easy going. I used to love it when I could get up from the breakfast table with an easy mind and go downtown and shop all morning, then get a sandwich and a Coke, or a salad at the cafeteria, see a picture show in the afternoon and then come home. That was fun. Shhh. I think I hear your mother still up.

(MRS. WATTS has decided not to give them the check. She is now sitting in her rocking chair, rocking and looking out the window. LUDIE comes into the living room. She puts the check inside her nightgown.)

LUDIE: Mama. Are you still up?

MRS. WATTS: Yes. I don't feel like sleeping, Ludie. You go on back to bed and don't worry about me.

LUDIE: All right, Mama.

(He goes back to bedroom.)

JESSIE MAE: Was she still up?

LUDIE: Yes.

JESSIE MAE: I knew it. I never get to go out of the house except for the beauty parlor. I'm not giving that up for anyone. I told Rosella that. I said no one was more faithful to a husband than

I was to Ludie, when he was sick, but even then I went out to the beauty parlor once a week. I mean, I had to.

LUDIE: I wanted you to.

JESSIE MAE: I know you did. (JESSIE MAE *sings absentmindedly. She is sitting at the vanity, brushing her hair, putting on face lotion, etc. A pause.*) Next time I see one of those little portable radios on sale, I'm going to get one. It would be nice to have by our bed. It would be so much company for us. (*A pause.*) That was a good supper we had tonight, wasn't it?

LUDIE: Uh-huh. Mama is a good cook.

JESSIE MAE: Yes. She is. I'll have to hand that to her. And an economical one. Well, she enjoys cooking. I guess you're born to enjoy it. I could never see how anyone could get any pleasure standing over a hot stove, but she seems to. (*A pause.*) Rosella asked me if I realized that it would be fifteen years this August since we were married. I hadn't realized it. Had you? (LUDIE *thinks for a moment. He counts back over the years.*)

LUDIE: That's right, Jessie Mae. It'll be fifteen years this August.

JESSIE MAE: I hate to think of time going that fast. (*A pause.*) I never will forget the night I came home and told Rosella you had proposed. I thought you were the handsomest man alive.

LUDIE: And I thought you were the prettiest girl.

JESSIE MAE: Did you, Ludie? I guess I did have my good features. People used to tell me I looked like a cross between Joan Crawford and Clara Bow. And I thought you were the smartest man in the world. I still do. The thing that burns me up is that you don't let other people know it. Do you remember Sue Carol in the movies?

LUDIE: Sure.

JESSIE MAE: I loved her. She was my ideal when I was growing up. She was always so cute in whatever she did. I always tried to act like her, be good company and a sport. (*A pause.*) Sue Carol's married to Alan Ladd now. They've got a bunch of kids. Well, she can afford them. They've got servants and I don't know what all. (LUDIE *has his book in his hand. He is walking around the room.*)

LUDIE: Jessie Mae, I've just got to start makin' some more money. I'm thinkin' about askin' for a raise. I'm entitled to it. I've been there six months now. I haven't been late or sick once. I've got to do it. I've got to ask for a raise tomorrow. (*He continues to walk around the room.*) I'm gonna walk into Mr. Douglas' office the first thing in the mornin' and I'm just gonna take the bull by the horns and I'm gonna say, Mr. Douglas, I've got to have a raise starting as of now. We can't live on what you pay us. We have my mother's pension check to help us out and if we didn't have that I don't know what we'd do.

JESSIE MAE: Well, I would.

LUDIE: I don't understand it, Jessie Mae. I try not to be bitter. I try not to . . . Oh, I don't know. All I know is that a man works eight years with a company. He saves a little money. He gets sick and has to spend two years in bed watching his savings all go. Then start all over again with a new company. *(A pause. He sits on the bed, placing his book on it.)* Of course, the doctor says I shouldn't worry about it. He says I've got to take things like they come. Every day, and that's what I try to do. But how can you help worryin' when you end up every month holding your breath to see if you're gonna make ends meet. (JESSIE MAE *gets up from the vanity. She crosses to the bed.)*

JESSIE MAE: You can't help being nervous. A lot of people get nervous. *(She sits on the bed and picks up the book.)* What's this book?

LUDIE: It's mine. I bought it at the drugstore coming home from the office.

JESSIE MAE: *How to Become an Executive.* What's that about?

LUDIE: It tells you how to prepare yourself for an executive position. It looks like there might be some helpful things in it. (LUDIE *takes the book and leans back against the headboard of the bed, reading.* JESSIE MAE *restlessly looks around the room.)*

JESSIE MAE: You sleepy, Ludie?

LUDIE: No, not yet.

JESSIE MAE: I'm not either. I wish I had something good to eat. I wish the drugstore was open. We could get us some ice cream. I wish I had my movie magazine.

LUDIE: Where is it?

JESSIE MAE: In the living room. (LUDIE *starts off the bed.)*

LUDIE: I'll get it.

JESSIE MAE: No, honey. I don't want to get your mother awake. (JESSIE MAE *lies across the foot of the bed. She hums and gets off the bed.)* I think I'll get me a cigarette. Want me to get you one?

LUDIE: Thanks. I think I will have one. I can get them.

JESSIE MAE: No. You rest. *(She goes to the vanity and gets a package of cigarettes.)* Rosella cried like her heart would break when she told me she couldn't have children. *(She lights a cigarette and gives one to* LUDIE.*)*

LUDIE: Thanks.

JESSIE MAE: She wanted to know how I stood it not havin' children. I said I don't know about Ludie 'cause you can't always tell what he feels, but I stand it by never thinking about it. *(She walks back to the foot of the bed and sits.)* I have my own philosophy about those things, anyway. I feel things like that are in the hands of the Lord. Don't you, Ludie?

LUDIE: I guess so.

JESSIE MAE: I've been as good a wife to you as I know how. But if the Lord doesn't want to give us children, all the worryin' in the world won't help. Do you think?

LUDIE: No. It won't.

JESSIE MAE: Anyway, like I told Rosella, I don't have the money to be runnin' around the doctors about it, even if I wanted to. *(A pause.)* Do you have an ashtray?

LUDIE: Right here. *(*LUDIE *gets an ashtray from the vanity and brings it to her.)* Jessie Mae, if I get a raise the first thing I want you to do is buy yourself a new dress.

JESSIE MAE: Well, thank you, Ludie. *(She goes back to the vanity and puts pin curlers in her hair. She puts a hairnet on and is finished by the end of speech.)* Besides, when you were sick what would I have done if I'd had a bunch of kids to worry me? Your mother said to me the other day, Jessie Mae, I don't know how you and Ludie stand livin' in the city. What are you talkin' about, I said. I didn't start livin' until I moved to the city. Who but a fool would want to live in the country? She wouldn't even listen to my arguments. Honestly, she's so stubborn. I declare, I believe your mother's about the stubbornest woman in forty-eight states. *(She looks at herself in the vanity mirror and then gets up laughing.)* Well, I don't look like Joan Crawford now. But who cares? I don't. What are you thinking about?

LUDIE: Oh, I was just thinking about this book. *(A pause.* LUDIE *gets into bed.)*

JESSIE MAE: Ludie, do you ever think back over the past?

LUDIE: No.

JESSIE MAE: I don't either. I started today a little when Rosella brought up that fifteen year business. But I think it's morbid. Your mother does that all the time.

LUDIE: I know.

JESSIE MAE: Turn your head the other way. *(He does so. She takes her dressing gown off and slips into bed.)*

LUDIE: My boss likes me. Billie Davison told me today he was positive he did. Billie has been there ten years now, you know. He said he thought he liked my work a lot. *(A pause.)* Feelin' sleepy now?

JESSIE MAE: Uh-huh. Are you?

LUDIE: Yes, I am. Good night.

JESSIE MAE: Good night.

(LUDIE turns off the bed light by the side of the bed. MRS. WATTS is rocking back and forth in her rocker now, working her hands nervously, humming quietly to herself. LUDIE hears her and sits up in bed. He gets out of bed and goes into the living room.)

LUDIE: Mama.

MRS. WATTS: I'm all right, Ludie. I'm just still not sleepy.

LUDIE: You're sure you're feelin' all right?

MRS. WATTS: Yes, I am.

LUDIE: Good night. *(He starts out of the room. She turns to him.)*

MRS. WATTS: Ludie, please, I want to go home.

LUDIE: Mama, you know I can't make a living there. We have to live in Houston.

MRS. WATTS: Ludie, son, I can't stay here any longer. I want to go home.

LUDIE: I beg you not to ask me that again. There's nothing I can do about it.

(LUDIE goes back to the bedroom. He gets into bed.)

JESSIE MAE: Was she still up?

LUDIE: Uh-huh. Good night.

JESSIE MAE: Good night.

(MRS. WATTS is standing at the back of the rocking chair. She paces around the room thinking what to do. She listens for a moment to see if they are asleep. She decides they are and quietly takes a suitcase down from the top of the wardrobe. She waits a moment then takes some clothing from the drawer of the cupboard and puts them in the suitcase, then she quietly closes it and hides the suitcase under the sofa. She then goes back to her chair, sits, and is rocking back and forth violently as the lights fade.)

Curtain

Act I

SCENE II

At rise of curtain, MRS. WATTS *is discovered sleeping in the rocker.* JESSIE MAE *is in bed.* LUDIE *is offstage in the bathroom, washing.* MRS. WATTS *awakens, looks for the check, finds it inside her nightgown, and hides it under the mattress. She looks out the window to see the time, runs over to* LUDIE'*s bedroom to see if he's awake, and runs into the kitchen to put some water on for coffee, calling as she goes.*

MRS. WATTS: Ludie, it's eight-fifteen by the drugstore clock . . .

LUDIE: *(Calling back, offstage.)* Yes'm. *(*MRS. WATTS *is back in the living room with a breakfast tray and dishes.* JESSIE MAE *has gotten out of bed and is at the vanity.* LUDIE *sticks his head in the living room door.)* Good morning, Mama.

MRS. WATTS: Good morning, son.

LUDIE: Did you get any sleep at all last night?

MRS. WATTS: Yes. Don't worry about me. *(*MRS. WATTS *goes back into the kitchen, takes the tray out with her.* MRS. WATTS *comes back with the tray and finishes setting the table, humming to herself, absentmindedly.* JESSIE MAE *hollers from the next room.)*

JESSIE MAE: It's too early for hymn singing. *(*JESSIE MAE *comes into the living room.)*

MRS. WATTS: Good morning, Jessie Mae.

JESSIE MAE: Good morning, Mother Watts.

*(*MRS. WATTS *goes out to the kitchen.* JESSIE MAE *turns on the radio and we hear a popular song. She goes out to the bathroom.* LUDIE *enters the living room from the hallway, puts his jacket on the chair.)*

JESSIE MAE: *(Calling.)* Ludie, turn that radio down, please, before they start knocking again. *(*MRS. WATTS *enters from the kitchen with coffee, which she sets on the table.)*

LUDIE: *(At the radio.)* Would you like me to turn if off?

JESSIE MAE: *(Calling.)* Oh, you might as well.

MRS. WATTS: I'll have your toast ready for you in a minute. *(Crosses into the kitchen.* JESSIE MAE *enters the living room from the hallway as* MRS. WATTS *is rushing out.)*

JESSIE MAE: Walk, don't run. I've just got to get me out of this house today, if no more than to ride downtown and back on the bus.

LUDIE: *(Sits at table, drinking coffee.)* Why don't you?

JESSIE MAE: If Mother Watts's pension check comes I'll go to the beauty parlor. I'm just as tense. I think I've got a trip to the beauty parlor comin' to me.

LUDIE: You ought to go if the check comes or not. It doesn't cost that much. *(*MRS. WATTS *comes in with toast.)*

JESSIE MAE: Mother Watts, will you skip down and see if the mail has come yet? Your pension check ought to be here and I want to get me to that beauty parlor.

MRS. WATTS: Yes, Ma'am. *(*MRS. WATTS *goes out for the mail at outside door.* JESSIE MAE *looks after her suspiciously.)*

JESSIE MAE: Ludie, she's actin' silent again. Don't you think she's actin' silent again?

LUDIE: I hadn't noticed. *(He takes a last swig out of his coffee.)*

JESSIE MAE: Well, she definitely is. You can say what you please, but to me it's always a sure sign she's gonna try and run off when she starts actin' silent.

LUDIE: She's not going to run off again, Jessie Mae. She promised me last time she wouldn't. *(He starts up from the table.)*

JESSIE MAE: She just better not. What do you want, Ludie?

LUDIE: I want more coffee.

JESSIE MAE: Well, keep your seat. I'll get it.

LUDIE: No, I'll get it.

JESSIE MAE: No. I want to get it. You'll have a tiring day ahead of you. Now rest while you can. *(She goes out to the hallway for coffee.* MRS. WATTS *enters.)*

MRS. WATTS: Where's Jessie Mae?

LUDIE: In the kitchen.

MRS. WATTS: There was no mail, Jessie Mae. *(*JESSIE MAE *comes in with coffee.)*

JESSIE MAE: Had it been delivered yet?

MRS. WATTS: I don't know.

JESSIE MAE: Did you look in the other boxes to see if there was mail?

MRS. WATTS: No, Ma'am. I didn't think to. *(MRS. WATTS goes to the bedroom.)*

LUDIE: I'll look on my way out. Why don't we have an early supper tonight? Six-thirty if that's all right with you and Mama. After supper I'll take you both to the picture show.

JESSIE MAE: That's fine. What would you like to see, Ludie?

LUDIE: Whatever you want to see, Jessie Mae. You know best about picture shows.

JESSIE MAE: Do you want to go downtown or to one of the neighborhood movies? *(She picks up a paper from the desk.)*

LUDIE: Whatever you want to do, Jessie Mae.

JESSIE MAE: Maybe it would do us good to go downtown. There's something about walkin' into the Majestic or the Metropolitan, or the Loew's State that just picks me up. People dress so much nicer when they're going to see a movie downtown. Of course, on the other hand, I could stand a good double bill myself.

LUDIE: *(Half to himself.)* I want to get to the office a little early this morning. Mr. Douglas is usually in by nine. I'd like a chance to talk to him before the others get there. I think I'm doin' the right thing, askin' for a raise. Don't you?

JESSIE MAE: Sure. I think I'll phone the beauty parlor for an appointment. I hope I can still get one. *(She goes to the phone on the desk. MRS. WATTS has been making up the bed. She stops when she hears JESSIE MAE dial the phone and goes to the bedroom door to listen.)* Hello, Rita. This is Jessie Mae Watts. Can I have an appointment for my hair? The usual. Uh-huh. *(She laughs.)* Four o'clock. Nothin' earlier. All right. See you then. *(She hangs up the phone.)* Well, I can't get an appointment until four o'clock.

LUDIE: I'm ready to go. Wish me luck on my raise.

JESSIE MAE: Good luck, Ludie. *(He kisses her on the cheek. He calls into the bedroom.)*

LUDIE: Goodbye, Mama.

MRS. WATTS: Goodbye, son. *(MRS. WATTS goes back to making up the bed.)*

LUDIE: Goodbye, Jessie Mae.

JESSIE MAE: So long. Holler if there's any mail down there so we won't be runnin' up and down lookin' for mail that won't be there.

LUDIE: *(Calling back.)* All right. *(Exits outside door.)*

JESSIE MAE: *(Calling into the bedroom.)* That pension check should have been here yesterday, shouldn't it, Mother Watts?

MRS. WATTS: *(Calling back and trying to seem unconcerned.)* I reckon so.

LUDIE: *(Calling from offstage downstairs.)* No mail for us.

JESSIE MAE: All right! I can't understand about that pension check, can you?

MRS. WATTS: No, Ma'am. *(JESSIE MAE casually takes MRS. WATTS's purse off the wardrobe and looks inside. Finding nothing, she closes it and puts it back.)*

JESSIE MAE: I sure hope it isn't lost. You know you're so absent-minded, you don't think you put it around the room someplace by mistake and forgot all about it. *(MRS. WATTS comes into the living room.)*

MRS. WATTS: I don't believe so. *(JESSIE MAE looks around the room. MRS. WATTS watches anxiously everything she does.)*

JESSIE MAE: You know you said you lost that check once before and it took us five days to find it. I came across it under this radio.

MRS. WATTS: I don't think I did that again, Jessie Mae.

(JESSIE MAE begins a halfhearted search of the room, looking under a vase, a pillow on the sofa, and when she gets to the corner of the rug where the check is hidden, she stoops as if to look under it, but it is only a strand of thread that has caught her attention. She picks it up and goes over to the radio, looking under that. JESSIE MAE gives up the search and MRS. WATTS goes back to the bedroom. JESSIE MAE calls after her.)

JESSIE MAE: What could I do 'til four o'clock? What are you gonna do today? *(JESSIE MAE goes into the bedroom.)*

MRS. WATTS: Well, I'm going to give the kitchen a good cleaning and put fresh paper on the shelves and clean the icebox.

JESSIE MAE: Well, I have a lot of things I have to do. I got some drawers I can straighten up. Or maybe I'll put some flowers on that red dress of mine. If I wear the red dress tonight. I really don't know yet which dress I'm going to wear. Well, if I wear my red dress tonight, I'll wear this print one to the beauty parlor. *(She has taken a dress out of her closet and goes out the hallway to the bathroom to try it on. MRS. WATTS decides to use this opportunity to run into the living room to get the check. JESSIE MAE hears her running and calls to her from the bathroom before she can reach the rug.)* Mother Watts! *(MRS. WATTS quickly finds something to do in the living room.)*

MRS. WATTS: Yes, Ma'am.

(JESSIE MAE *comes into the living room.*)

JESSIE MAE: There you go again. You never walk when you can run. (JESSIE MAE *goes back into the bathroom.* MRS. WATTS *quickly reaches under the rug and gets the check. She puts it inside her dress. Then she takes the dishes out to the kitchen.* JESSIE MAE *continues to lecture her from the bathroom.*) You know it's none of my business, and I know you don't like me to suggest anything, but I don't think a woman your age should go running around a three-room apartment like a cyclone. It's really not necessary, Mother Watts. You never walk when you can run. (JESSIE MAE *comes out to the living room with the dress on. She watches* MRS. WATTS.) I wish for once you'd listen to me.

MRS. WATTS: I'm listening, Jessie Mae.

JESSIE MAE: You're not listening to a word. Mother Watts, are you feeling all right? You look a little pale.

MRS. WATTS: I'm feeling fine, Jessie Mae. (JESSIE MAE *zips up her dress, straightens out the skirt etc. during following speech.*)

JESSIE MAE: That movie magazine Ludie brought me last night is running a contest. First prize is a free trip to Hollywood. I'd like to enter it if I thought I could win. I wouldn't win. I don't have that kind of luck. I want you to look at the hem of this dress for me, to see if it's straight.

MRS. WATTS: Yes, Ma'am. (MRS. WATTS *gets a tape measure from her wardrobe and measures the dress.*)

JESSIE MAE: I'm gonna make Ludie take me to Hollywood one of these days. I want to visit Hollywood as bad as you want to visit Bountiful.

MRS. WATTS: It measures straight, Jessie Mae. (*She returns the tape measure to the wardrobe and starts to make her own bed.* JESSIE MAE *walks restlessly around the living room.*)

JESSIE MAE: Do you need anything from the drugstore?

MRS. WATTS: Just let me think a moment, Jessie Mae.

JESSIE MAE: Because if you do, I'd walk over to the drugstore and have me a fountain Coke with lots of chipped ice. We don't need toothpaste. We don't need toothbrushes. I got a bottle of Listerine yesterday. Can you think of anything we need from the drugstore?

MRS. WATTS: Did you get that nail polish you mentioned?

JESSIE MAE: Oh, yes I have that. I hate to wait around here until four o'clock. I think I'm gonna call Rosella and tell her to meet me at the drugstore for a Coke. *(She goes to the phone and dials.* MRS. WATTS *is humming to herself as she finishes making up her bed.)* Will you stop that hymn singing? Do you want me to jump right out of my skin? You know what hymns do to my nerves. *(MRS. WATTS *stops her humming.)* And don't pout. You know I can't stand pouting.

MRS. WATTS: I didn't mean to pout, Jessie Mae. I only meant to be silent.

JESSIE MAE: *(Hangs up the phone.)* Wouldn't you know it. She's not home. I bet she's at the drugstore right now. I think I'll go on over to the drugstore and just take a chance on Rosella's being there. *(*JESSIE MAE *begins to put her hat on.* MRS. WATTS *has gotten a hand sweeper from the kitchen and is sweeping around the room.)* I can't make up my mind what movie I want to see tonight. Well, I'll ask Rosella. Will you stop that noise for a minute. I'm nervous. *(*MRS. WATTS *stops sweeping and gets a dustrag from the kitchen. She begins to dust the room.* JESSIE MAE *continues putting on her hat and arranging her dress in front of the mirror.)* You know when I first came to Houston, I went to see three picture shows in one day. I went to the Kirby in the morning, and the Metropolitan in the afternoon, and the Majestic that night. People don't go to see picture shows the way they used to. Well, I'm ready. *(She turns to* MRS. WATTS.*)* I just want you to promise me one thing. That you won't put a foot out of this house and start that Bountiful business again. You'll kill Ludie if he has to chase all over Houston looking for you. And I'm warning you. The next time you run off I'm calling the police. I don't care what Ludie says. *(*JESSIE MAE *starts out of the room.)* If Rosella calls just tell her I'm at the drugstore. *(*MRS. WATTS *has done her best to continue dusting the furniture during the latter speech, but she has been getting physically weaker and weaker. Finally in a last desperate attempt to keep* JESSIE MAE *from noticing her weakness she grabs hold again of the sweeper, trying to support herself. She sways, drops the sweeper, and reaches for the sofa to keep from falling, just as* JESSIE MAE *is ready to leave the room.)* Mother Watts . . . *(*JESSIE MAE *runs to her. She is very frightened.)*

MRS. WATTS: *(Trying desperately to control herself.)* I'm all right, Jessie Mae.

JESSIE MAE: Is it your heart?

MRS. WATTS: No. Just a sinkin' spell. Just let me lie down on the sofa for a minute and I'll be all right.

JESSIE MAE: Can I get you some water?

MRS. WATTS: Thank you. (JESSIE MAE *runs into the kitchen for water.*)

JESSIE MAE: (*Offstage, from the kitchen.*) Do you want me to call a doctor?

MRS. WATTS: No, Ma'am.

JESSIE MAE: Do you want me to call Ludie?

MRS. WATTS: No, Ma'am. (JESSIE MAE *reenters the living room with a glass of water.* MRS. WATTS *drinks it.*)

JESSIE MAE: Are you feelin' better?

MRS. WATTS: Yes, I am, Jessie Mae. (MRS. WATTS *gets up off the sofa.*)

JESSIE MAE: Do you think you ought to get up so soon?

MRS. WATTS: Yes, Ma'am. I'm feeling much better already. I'll just sit here in the chair.

JESSIE MAE: All right. I'll sit here for a while and keep you company. (MRS. WATTS *sits in her rocking chair.* JESSIE MAE *sits in her chair, restless as a cat.*) How do you feel now?

MRS. WATTS: Better.

JESSIE MAE: That's good. It always scares the daylights out of me when you get one of those sinkin' spells. Of course, like I told you this morning, you wouldn't be having these sinkin' spells if you'd stop this running around. Well, it's your heart. If you don't want to take care of it no one can make you. But I tell you right now all I need is to have an invalid on my hands. I wish you'd think of Ludie. He's got enough to worry him without your gettin' down flat on your back. (*Phone rings. She goes to it.*) Oh, hello, Rosella. I tried to call you earlier. Oh. You're at the drugstore. That's what I just figured. Well, I'd like to, Rosella, but Mother Watts has had a sinking spell again and . . .

MRS. WATTS: You go on, Jessie Mae. I'm gonna be all right. I'll just rest here. There's nothing you can do for me.

JESSIE MAE: Are you sure?

MRS. WATTS: Yes, Jessie Mae. I'm sure.

JESSIE MAE: Well, all right then. Rosella, Mother Watts says she won't need me here. So I think I will come over for a little while. All right. I'll see you in a few minutes. Goodbye. (*She hangs up the phone.*) Now you're sure you'll be all right?

MRS. WATTS: Yes, Jessie Mae.

JESSIE MAE: Well, then I'll go on over. Now you call me at the drugstore if you need me. You hear?

MRS. WATTS: Yes, Ma'am.

(JESSIE MAE *goes out the entrance to stairs.* MRS. WATTS *sits for a moment, rocking and using all her will to get her strength back. After a moment she slowly and weakly gets up and goes to the door, listening. She is sure* JESSIE MAE *has gone. She gets her suitcase from under the bed. Then she remembers the check, which she takes out, and goes to the desk to endorse it. She takes writing paper and an envelope from the desk at the same time. While* MRS. WATTS *is endorsing the check,* JESSIE MAE *comes running back in.* MRS. WATTS *doesn't see her until she has opened the door.)*

JESSIE MAE: I forgot to take any money along with me. (JESSIE MAE *is in such a hurry she doesn't see* MRS. WATTS. *She goes into the bedroom to get her money, which she takes from the vanity.* MRS. WATTS *has just time to get the suitcase and get it back in the wardrobe, stuff the check inside her dress, and get back to the writing desk when* JESSIE MAE *comes in again.)* Who are you writing to?

MRS. WATTS: I thought I'd drop a line to Callie Davis, Jessie Mae. Let her know I'm still alive.

JESSIE MAE: Why did you decide to do that all of a sudden?

MRS. WATTS: No reason. The notion just struck me.

JESSIE MAE: All right. *(She starts out.)* But just in case you're trying to put something over on me with that pension check, I've told Mr. Reynolds at the grocery store never to cash anything for you.

(She goes out the door. MRS. WATTS *again stands quietly waiting. Then she goes to the door, listening. She decides* JESSIE MAE *has really gone. She gets her hat and coat from the wardrobe. She gets her suitcase and goes quietly out the door.)*

Curtain

Act II

The lights are brought up on part of a bus terminal in Houston, Texas. It is placed stage right. Upstage center right of this area is a door to the street. Downstage right is an exit to washrooms, etc.

There is a man sitting on one of the benches eating a sandwich. A pretty blond girl, carrying a suitcase and a magazine, is standing at the ticket window right center waiting to buy a ticket. A man is standing behind her. The girl's name is THELMA.

The TICKET MAN *is busy on the telephone. He puts the phone down and comes to the front of the window.*

TICKET MAN: Yes?

THELMA: I want a ticket to Old Gulf, please.

TICKET MAN: Yes, Ma'am. *(He reaches for a ticket.)* Here you are. You change buses at Harrison.

THELMA: I know. How much, please?

TICKET MAN: Four eighty.

THELMA: Yessir. *(She gives him the money and steps out of line. Goes to bench and sits, reading a magazine. The man steps up to the window.)*

MAN: Ticket to Leighton.

TICKET MAN: Leighton. Yes, indeed. (MRS. WATTS, *carrying a suitcase and purse, comes into the terminal from the street entrance. She is looking all around her to see if* JESSIE MAE *or* LUDIE *has put in an appearance. Satisfied that they haven't, she hurries to the ticket window. She gets in line behind the man. She is humming the hymn to herself and keeps an eye on the doors all the time.* TICKET MAN *hands the man his ticket.)* Be seven sixty, please.

MAN: Yessir. *(He gets the money for the* TICKET MAN. *Two people have come up behind* MRS. WATTS. *The man gives the* TICKET MAN *the money for the tickets, the* TICKET MAN *reaches for change.)*

TICKET MAN: Seven sixty out of ten dollars.

MAN: Thank you. *(He takes his change and exits.* MRS. WATTS *is so busy watching the doors that she doesn't notice it's her turn.)*

TICKET MAN: *(Calling.)* Lady. *(She is still so absorbed in watching, she doesn't hear him.)* Lady. It's your turn. *(MRS. WATTS turns and sees she is next in line. She moves up to the counter.)*

MRS. WATTS: Oh, yes. Excuse me. I'd like a ticket to Bountiful, please.

TICKET MAN: Where?

MRS. WATTS: Bountiful.

TICKET MAN: What's it near?

MRS. WATTS: It's between Harrison and Cotton.

TICKET MAN: Just a minute. *(He takes a book from behind the window on a shelf. He looks inside it. MRS. WATTS is again watching the doors. He looks up.)* Lady.

MRS. WATTS: Oh. Yessir.

TICKET MAN: I can sell you a ticket to Harrison or to Cotton. But there's no Bountiful.

MRS. WATTS: Oh, yes there is, it's between . . .

TICKET MAN: I'm sorry, lady. You say there is, but the book says there isn't. And the book don't lie.

MRS. WATTS: But . . . I . . .

TICKET MAN: *(Impatiently.)* Make up your mind, lady. Cotton or Harrison. There are other people waiting.

MRS. WATTS: Well . . . let me see . . . How much is a ticket to Harrison?

TICKET MAN: Three fifty . . .

MRS. WATTS: Cotton?

TICKET MAN: Four twenty.

MRS. WATTS: Oh, yes. Well, I'll have the one to Harrison, please.

TICKET MAN: All right. That'll be three fifty, please.

MRS. WATTS: Yessir. *(She reaches for her pocketbook and is about to open it. She turns to the TICKET MAN.)* Can you cash a pension check? You see I decided to come at the last minute and I didn't have time to stop by the grocery store.

TICKET MAN: I'm sorry, lady. I can't cash any checks.

MRS. WATTS: It's perfectly good. It's a government check.

TICKET MAN: I'm sorry. It's against the rules to cash checks.

MRS. WATTS: Oh, is that so? I understand. A rule's a rule. How much was that again?

TICKET MAN: Three fifty.

MRS. WATTS: Oh, yes. Three fifty. Just a minute, sir. I've got it all here in nickels and dimes and quarters. *(She opens her purse and takes a handkerchief out. The money is tied in the handkerchief. She unties it, places it on the counter, and begins to count out the amount for the ticket. She counts half aloud as she does it. She shoves a pile of silver toward the* TICKET MAN.) Here. I think this is three fifty.

TICKET MAN: Thank you. *(He rakes the money into his hand. She ties her handkerchief back up.)*

MRS. WATTS: That's quite all right. I'm sorry to have taken up so much of your time. *(She picks up her suitcase and starts off.)*

TICKET MAN: Here, lady. Don't forget your ticket. *(She comes running back.)*

MRS. WATTS: Oh, my heavens. Yes. I'd forget my head if it wasn't on my neck. *(She takes the ticket and goes away. The man next in line steps up to the window.* MRS. WATTS *goes back to the entrance. She peers out and then comes back into the bus station. She comes down to the bench.* THELMA *is seated there, reading. Looks up from her magazine. There is an empty space next to her.* MRS. WATTS *comes up to it.)* Good evening.

THELMA: Good evening.

MRS. WATTS: Is this seat taken?

THELMA: No, Ma'am.

MRS. WATTS: Are you expectin' anyone?

THELMA: No, Ma'am.

MRS. WATTS: May I sit here then?

THELMA: Yes, Ma'am. *(MRS. WATTS puts the suitcase down along the side of the bench. She looks nervously around the station. All of a sudden she jumps up.)*

MRS. WATTS: Would you watch my suitcase, honey?

THELMA: Yes, Ma'am.

MRS. WATTS: I'll be right back.

THELMA: Yes'm.

(MRS. WATTS goes running back toward the door to the street. THELMA *watches her go for a minute and then goes back to reading her magazine. The* TICKET MAN *is joined by the man who is to relieve him for the night. They greet each other and the first* TICKET MAN *leaves the bus station.* MRS. WATTS *comes back to the bench. She sits down and takes a handkerchief out of her purse. She wipes her forehead.)*

MRS. WATTS: Thank you so much.

THELMA: That's all right. *(MRS. WATTS wipes her brow again.)*

MRS. WATTS: Little warm isn't it when you're rushing around?

THELMA: Yes'm.

MRS. WATTS: I had to get myself ready in the biggest kind of hurry.

THELMA: Are you going on a trip?

MRS. WATTS: Yes, I am. I'm trying to get to a town nobody ever heard of around here.

THELMA: What town is that?

MRS. WATTS: Bountiful.

THELMA: Oh.

MRS. WATTS: Did you ever hear of it?

THELMA: No.

MRS. WATTS: You see. Nobody has. Well, it's not much of a town now, I guess. I haven't seen it myself in thirty years. But it used to be quite prosperous. All they have left is a post office and a filling station and a general store. At least they did when I left.

THELMA: Do your people live there?

MRS. WATTS: No. My people are all dead except my son and his wife, Jessie Mae. They live here in the city. I'm hurrying to see Bountiful before I die. I had a sinking spell this morning. I had to climb up on the bed and rest. It was my heart.

THELMA: Do you have a bad heart?

MRS. WATTS: Well, it's not what you call a good one. Doctor says it would last as long as I needed it if I could just cut out worrying. But seems I can't do that lately. *(She looks around the bus station again. She gets up out of her seat.)* Excuse me. Would you keep your eye on that suitcase again?

THELMA: Yes, Ma'am. (MRS. WATTS *hurries back to the entrance of the bus station.* THELMA *picks up her magazine and goes back to reading.* MRS. WATTS *comes hurrying back to the seat. She doesn't sit down, but stands over by the side.)* Lady. Is there anything wrong?

MRS. WATTS: No, honey. I'm just a little nervous. That's all. *(She hurries back toward the door. This time she opens it and goes outside.* THELMA *goes back to her reading.* MRS. WATTS *comes running back in. She hurries over to the seat and picks up the suitcase. In her confusion, she drops her handkerchief on the floor. Neither she nor* THELMA *sees it fall.)* Say a prayer for me, honey. Good luck.

THELMA: Good luck to you.

(MRS. WATTS goes running out toward the rest room. LUDIE *comes in the outside door to the bus station. He stands a moment at the entrance, looking all around. He wanders slowly down until he gets to the bench*

where THELMA *is sitting. He pauses here, looking out in front of him and to each side.* JESSIE MAE *comes in. She is in a rage. She walks over to* LUDIE.*)*

LUDIE: You want to sit down, Jessie Mae?

JESSIE MAE: Yes, I do. If you want to look around, go ahead. I'll wait here.

LUDIE: You looked carefully in the coffee shop?

JESSIE MAE: Yes.

LUDIE: Want me to bring you a Coke?

JESSIE MAE: No.

LUDIE: Want me to buy you a movie magazine?

JESSIE MAE: Yes.

LUDIE: All right. I'll be right back. *(He goes back out the outside door he came in, looking around as he goes.* JESSIE MAE *sits down next to* THELMA. *She takes out a package of cigarettes. She gets her lighter. It doesn't work. She opens her purse and starts looking for a match. She can't find one. She turns to* THELMA.*)*

JESSIE MAE: Excuse me. Do you have a match? My lighter's out of fluid. *(*THELMA *reaches in the pocket of her jacket. She finds matches and gives them to her.)* Thank you. *(She lights her cigarette and hands the matches back to* THELMA. JESSIE MAE *takes a deep drag off her cigarette.)* I hope you're lucky enough not to have to fool with any in-laws. I've got a mother-in-law about to drive me crazy. At least twice a year we have to try and keep her from getting on a train to go back to her hometown. *(She takes another drag off her cigarette.)* I swear, she always has to spoil everything. My husband was goin' to take us to a double bill tonight at the picture show for the first time in I don't know when. I had called the beauty parlor for an appointment and I couldn't get one till four o'clock, see, and I was nervous sitting around the house, and so I went to the drugstore for a fountain Coke and I come home and what did I find . . . no Mother Watts. So I had to call my husband at the office and say the picture show was off. We've got to go looking for Mother Watts. Oh, she's so stubborn. I could just wring her neck. Her son spoils her that's the whole trouble. She's just rotten spoiled. Do you live with your in-laws?

THELMA: No.

JESSIE MAE: Well, you're lucky. They're all stubborn. My husband is as stubborn as she is. We should be over at the depot right now instead of sitting here. She always tries to go by train, but no.

We wait at one railroad station five minutes and the other railroad station for five minutes and because she isn't there, right then, he drags me over here. And don't ask me why she always tries to go by train. That's just how she is. *(She takes another drag off her cigarette. It has gone out.)* Could I trouble you for another match, please? My cigarette has gone out. (THELMA *gets the match for her.* JESSIE MAE *takes it and lights her cigarette.)* Of course, there hasn't been a train to that town in I don't know when. But if you try to tell her that she just looks at you like you're making it up. Always before we've been there waitin' for her when she walks into the railroad station, but today I was too trustin'. I gave her all the time in the world to get away. Well, we're payin' for it now. I told Ludie at breakfast she had that silent look, and I bet she tries to run away. But no, he said she wouldn't, because she had promised she wouldn't, and Ludie believes anything she says. I'm just worn out. I've had my fourth Coca-Cola today, just to keep my spirits up. People ask me why I don't have any children. Why? I say I've got Ludie and Mother Watts. That's all the children I need. (LUDIE *comes in with a movie magazine. He comes up to* JESSIE MAE.*)* What did you bring me? *(He shows her the magazine.)* Oh, I've seen that one.

LUDIE: *(He puts it absentmindedly under his arm. He looks around the station.)* Have you seen Mama?

JESSIE MAE: No, you goose. Do you think I'd be sittin' here so calm if I had! Personally, I think we're wastin' our time sittin' here. She always tries to go by train.

LUDIE: But she can't go by train, Jessie Mae.

JESSIE MAE: She doesn't know that.

LUDIE: She's bound to by now. What time did she leave again?

JESSIE MAE: I don't know what time she left. I told you I called from the drugstore at 11:30 and she was gone, the sneaky thing.

LUDIE: Well, you see she's had the time to find out a lot of things she hasn't known before. (JESSIE MAE *gets up and goes to him.)*

JESSIE MAE: I don't care what you say, Ludie. My hunch is that she's at one of those train stations. We've always found her there. You know how she is. Stubborn. Why, she won't believe them at the depot if they tell her there's not a train to Bountiful. She says there is and you watch, as far as she's concerned that's how it'll have to be. Ludie, I know she's there. I'm never wrong about these things.

LUDIE: All right. Have it your way. Let's go.

JESSIE MAE: Well, now we're here we might as well inquire from someone if they've seen her wanderin' around.

LUDIE: I thought you said she wouldn't come here.

JESSIE MAE: I said I didn't think she would come here. I don't know what the crazy thing will do. I could wring her neck. I can tell you that. I ought to be sitting at the beauty parlor right this very minute.

LUDIE: All right, Jessie Mae. Let's go on back to the depot.

JESSIE MAE: Will you stop rushing me around. I'm so mad I could chew nails. I tell you again I think we ought to just turn this whole thing over to the police. That would scare her once and for all.

LUDIE: Well, we're not going to call any police. We've been through that once and we're . . .

JESSIE MAE: It's for her own good. She's crazy.

LUDIE: *(He is very angry with her.)* Now why do you talk like that? You know Mama isn't crazy. *(A pause.)* I just wish you wouldn't say things like that.

JESSIE MAE: *(JESSIE MAE has taken off her hat, and hands it to LUDIE. She is combing her hair and freshening her makeup during the following speech.)* Then why does she keep runnin' off from a perfectly good home like this? To try and get to some old swamp. Don't you call that crazy? I mean, she doesn't have to turn her hand. Hardly. We only have a bedroom and a living room and a kitchen. We're all certainly very light eaters, so cooking three meals a day isn't killing her. And like I told her this morning. She wouldn't be havin' her sinkin' spells if she'd start walkin' like a normal human bein' and not go trottin' all over the place. I said, Mother Watts, please tell my why with a bad heart you insist on running . . . *(LUDIE is getting more and more embarrassed. He sees people looking at them.)*

LUDIE: Well, let's don't stand here arguing. People are looking at us. Do you want to go to the depot or not? *(JESSIE MAE turns and sees they're being watched. She lowers her voice but not her intensity.)*

JESSIE MAE: It's your mother. I don't care what you do. Only you better do something. Let me tell you that, or she's gonna clonk out some place. She'll get to Bountiful and die from the excitement and then we'll have all kinds of expenses bringing her body back here. Do you know what a thing like that could cost? Do you realize she had a sinkin' spell this mornin'?

LUDIE: I know. You've told me a hundred times. What can I do about it, Jessie Mae?

JESSIE MAE: I'm trying to tell you what you can do about it. Call the police.

LUDIE: I'm not going to call the police.

JESSIE MAE: Oh, you won't.

LUDIE: No.

JESSIE MAE: Then I think I will. That'll settle it once and for all. *(She goes outside.* LUDIE *looks around for a minute, then sits down dejectedly in the seat next to* THELMA. THELMA *has been watching the preceding scene. She has tried not to be seen by them, but the audience should know that she has taken in every single word.* LUDIE *reaches in his back pocket and takes out a handkerchief. He mops his forehead. He notices the magazine under his arm. He takes it in his hand and turns to* THELMA.*)*

LUDIE: Would you like this? I never read them, and my wife has seen it.

THELMA: Thank you. *(She takes the magazine and puts it in her lap. She goes back to her reading.* LUDIE *looks on the floor and sees the handkerchief that was dropped by* MRS. WATTS. *He reaches down and picks it up. He recognizes it. He gets up and goes running over to the ticket window.)*

LUDIE: Excuse me. Did an old lady come here and buy a ticket to a town named Bountiful?

TICKET MAN: Where?

LUDIE: Bountiful!

TICKET MAN: Not since I've been on duty.

LUDIE: How long have you been on duty?

TICKET MAN: About fifteen minutes.

LUDIE: Where is the man that was on before?

TICKET MAN: He's gone home.

LUDIE: Oh. *(He walks away thinking what to do next. He sees* THELMA *and goes to her.)* Excuse me, Miss.

THELMA: Yes?

LUDIE: I found this handkerchief here that belongs, I think, to my mother. She's run off from home. She has a heart condition and it might be serious for her to be all alone. I don't think she has much money, and I'd like to find her. Do you remember having seen her?

THELMA: Well . . . I . . .

LUDIE: She'd be on her way to a town called Bountiful.

THELMA: Yes, I did see her. She was here talkin' to me. She left all of a sudden.

LUDIE: Thank you so much. (JESSIE MAE *has come back in.* LUDIE *goes up to her.*)

JESSIE MAE: Ludie.

LUDIE: I was right. She was here. The lady there said so.

JESSIE MAE: Well, it's too late now.

LUDIE: But this lady was talking to her.

JESSIE MAE: We're not going to wait. The police and I talked it over. (THELMA *takes advantage of their argument to slip out of the station.*)

LUDIE: *(Turning on* JESSIE MAE.*)* You didn't really call them!

JESSIE MAE: I did, and they said in their opinion she was just trying to get our attention this way and we should just go home and pay her no mind at all.

LUDIE: How can I go home with Mama . . .

JESSIE MAE: The police tell me they have hundreds of cases like this every day. They say such things are very common among young people and old people, and they're positive that if we just go home and show her that we don't care if she goes or stays, she'll come home of her own free will.

LUDIE: Jessie Mae . . .

JESSIE MAE: Now, we're going to do what the police tell us to. They say she will come home when she's tired and hungry enough and that makes a lot of sense to me. Now, Ludie, I wish you'd think of me for a change . . . I'm not going to spend the rest of my life running after your mother.

LUDIE: All right, Jessie Mae. *(He stands there, thinking.)*

JESSIE MAE: Now, come on, let's go. Come on. *(She starts out.* LUDIE *pauses for a moment, thinking. He goes after her.)*

LUDIE: All right. But if Mama is not home in an hour I'm going after her . . .

JESSIE MAE: Honestly, Ludie, you're so stubborn.

(They go out as the lights are brought down. Over the loudspeaker we hear the stations being called: Bus leaving for Newton, Sugarland, Gerard, Harrison, Cotton, Old Gulf, Don Tarle . . . In the darkness

we hear the sound of a bus starting, then the noise of the traffic of a downtown city. Brakes grinding, horns honking. This is brought down to almost a whisper. The lights are brought up on the center section and we see a seat in the bus. MRS. WATTS *and* THELMA *are sitting there.* MRS. WATTS *is gazing out into the night.* THELMA *is casually glancing at the movie magazine. After a moment* MRS. WATTS *turns to her.)*

MRS. WATTS: Isn't it a small world? I didn't know we'd be on the same bus. Where do you go, honey?

THELMA: Harrison.

MRS. WATTS: Harrison!

THELMA: Yes. I change buses there.

MRS. WATTS: So do I go there. Isn't that nice? Is that a moving picture magazine?

THELMA: Yes, Ma'am. Would you like to look at it?

MRS. WATTS: No, thank you. *(She leans her head back on the seat and turns her head away.)* The bus is nice to ride, isn't it?

THELMA: Yes. It is.

MRS. WATTS: I'm sorry I couldn't take a train, though.

THELMA: I tried to go by train, but you couldn't get connections tonight.

MRS. WATTS: I know. When I was a girl I used to take excursions from Bountiful to Houston to Galveston. For the day, you know. Leave at five in the morning and return at ten that night. The whole town would be down to see you get off the train. I have such fond memories of those trips. *(A pause. She looks over at* THELMA.*)* Excuse me for getting personal, but what's a pretty girl like you doing traveling alone?

THELMA: My husband has just been sent overseas. I'm going to stay with my family.

MRS. WATTS: Oh, I'm sorry to hear that. Just say the Ninety-first Psalm over and over to yourself. It will be a bower of strength and protection for him. *(She begins to recite with closed eyes.)* "He that dwelleth in the secret place of the most high, shall abide under the shadow of the Almighty. I will say of the Lord, He is my refuge and my fortress: My God; in Him will I trust. Surely He shall deliver thee from the fowler and the noisome pestilence. He shall cover thee with His feathers and under his wing shalt thou trust: His truth shall be thy shield and buckler."

(THELMA *covers her face with her hands—she is crying.* MRS. WATTS *looks up and sees her.*) Oh, I'm sorry. I'm sorry, honey.

THELMA: That's all right. I'm just lonesome for him.

MRS. WATTS: Keep him under the Lord's wing, honey, and he'll be safe.

THELMA: Yes, Ma'am. *(She dries her eyes.)* I'm sorry. I don't know what gets into me.

MRS. WATTS: Nobody needs be ashamed of crying. I guess we've all dampened our pillows sometime or other. I have, goodness knows.

THELMA: If I could only learn not to worry.

MRS. WATTS: I know. I guess we all ask that. Jessie Mae, my daughter-in-law, don't worry. What for? she says. Well, like I tell her, that's a fine attitude if you can cultivate it. Trouble is I can't any longer.

THELMA: It is hard.

MRS. WATTS: I didn't use to worry. I was so carefree as a girl. Had lots to worry me, too. Everybody was so poor back in Bountiful. But we got along. I said to Papa once after our third crop failure in a row, whoever gave this place the name of Bountiful? His Papa did, he said, because in those days it was a land of plenty. You just had to drop seeds in the ground and the crops would spring up. Cotton and corn and sugar cane. I still think it's the prettiest place I know of. Jessie Mae says it's the ugliest. But she just says that I know to make me mad. She only saw it once, and then on a rainy day, at that. She says it's nothing but a swamp. That may be, I said, but it's a might pretty swamp to me. And then Sonny, that's my boy, Ludie, I call him Sonny, he said not to answer her back. He said it only caused arguments. And nobody ever won an argument with Jessie Mae, and I guess that's right. *(A pause. She looks out into space.)*

THELMA: Mrs. Watts . . .

MRS. WATTS: Yes?

THELMA: I think I ought to tell you this . . . I . . . I don't want you to think I'm interfering in your business . . . but . . . well . . . you see your son and your daughter-in-law came in just after you left . . .

MRS. WATTS: I know. I saw them coming. That's why I left so fast.

THELMA: Your son seemed very concerned.

MRS. WATTS: Bless his heart.

THELMA: He found a handkerchief that you had dropped.

MRS. WATTS: Oh, mercy. That's right, I did.

THELMA: He asked me if I had seen you. I felt I had to say yes. I wouldn't have said anything if he hadn't asked me.

MRS. WATTS: Oh, that's all right. I would have done the same thing in your place. Did you talk to Jessie Mae?

THELMA: Yes.

MRS. WATTS: Isn't she a sight? I bet she told you I was crazy . . .

THELMA: Well . . .

MRS. WATTS: Oh, don't be afraid of hurting my feelings. Poor Jessie Mae, she thinks everybody's crazy that don't want to sit in the beauty parlor all day and drink Coca-Colas. She tells me a million times a day I'm crazy. That's the only time Ludie will talk back to her. He gets real mad when she calls me crazy. I think Ludie knows how I feel about getting back to Bountiful. Once when I was talkin' about somethin' we did back there in the old days, he just broke out cryin'. He was so overcome he had to leave the room. (*A pause.* MRS. WATTS *starts to hum "There's Not a Friend Like the Lowly Jesus."*)

THELMA: That's a pretty hymn. What's the name of it?

MRS. WATTS: "There's Not a Friend Like the Lowly Jesus." Do you like hymns?

THELMA: Yes, I do.

MRS. WATTS: So do I. Jessie Mae says they've gone out of style . . . but I don't agree. I always sing one walking down the street or riding in the streetcar. Keeps my spirits up. What's your favorite hymn?

THELMA: Oh, I don't know.

MRS. WATTS: The one I was singin' is mine. I bet I sing it a hundred times a day. When Jessie Mae isn't home. Hymns make Jessie Mae nervous. (*A pause.*) Did Ludie mention my heart condition?

THELMA: Yes, he did.

MRS. WATTS: Poor Ludie. He worries about it so. I hated to leave him. Well, I hope he'll forgive me in time. So many people are nervous today. He wasn't nervous back in Bountiful. Neither was I. The breeze from the Gulf would always quiet your nerves. You could sit on your front gallery and smell the ocean blowing in around you. (*A pause.*) I regret the day I left. But I thought it was the best thing at the time. There were only three families left there then. Farming was so hard to make a living by, and I had to see to our farm myself; our house was old and there was no money to fix it with, nor send Ludie to school. So I sold off the land and gave him an education. Callie said I could always come back and visit her. She meant it, too. That's who I'm going to stay with now. Callie Davis. I get a card from her every Christmas. I wrote her last week and told her to expect me. Told her not to answer though on account of Jessie Mae opens all my mail. I didn't want her to know I was going. She'd try to stop me. Jessie Mae hates me. I don't know why, but she hates me. *(A pause.)* Hate me or not. I gotta get back and smell that salt air and work that dirt. I'm gonna spend the whole first month of my visit workin' in Callie's garden. I haven't had my hands in dirt in twenty years. My hands feel the need of dirt. *(A pause.)* Do you like to work the ground?

THELMA: I never have.

MRS. WATTS: Try it sometimes. It'll do wonders for you. I bet I'll live to be a hundred once I can get outside again. It was being cooped up in those two rooms that was killing me. I used to work the land like a man. Had to when Papa died . . . I got two little babies buried there. Renee Sue and Douglas. Diphtheria got Renee Sue. I never knew what carried Douglas away. He was just weak from the start. I know Callie's kept their graves weeded. Oh, if my heart just holds out until I get there. *(A pause.)* Where do you go from Harrison?

THELMA: Old Gulf. My family have just moved there from Louisiana. I'll stay there with them until my husband comes home again.

MRS. WATTS: That's nice.

THELMA: It'll be funny living at home again.

MRS. WATTS: How long have you been married?

THELMA: A year. My husband was anxious for me to go. He said he'd worry about my being alone. I'm the only child and my parents and I are very close.

MRS. WATTS: That's nice.

THELMA: My father being in the oil business we've always moved around a lot. I guess I went to school in fifteen different towns along the Coast. I guess moving around like that made me and my mother and father even closer. I hoped so my mother and daddy would like my husband and he'd like them. I needn't have worried. They hit it off from the very first. Mother and Daddy say they feel like they have two children now. A son and a daughter.

MRS. WATTS: Isn't that nice? I've heard people say that when your son marries you lose a son, but when your daughter marries you get a son. *(A pause.)* What's you husband's name?

THELMA: Robert.

MRS. WATTS: That's a nice name.

THELMA: I think so. But I guess any name he had I would think was nice. I love my husband very much. Lots of girls I know think I'm silly about him, but I can't help it. *(A pause.)*

MRS. WATTS: I wasn't in love with my husband. *(A pause.)* Do you believe we are punished for what we do wrong? I sometimes think that's why I've had all my trouble. I've talked to many a preacher about it, all but one said they didn't think so. But I can't see any other reason. Of course, I didn't lie to my husband. I told him I didn't love him, that I admired him, which I did, but I didn't love him. That I'd never love anybody but Ray John Murray as long as I lived and I didn't, and I couldn't help it. Even after my husband died and I had to move back with Mama and Papa I used to sit on the front gallery every morning and every evening just to nod hello to Ray John Murray as he went by the house to work at the store. He went a block out of his way to pass the house. He never loved nobody but me.

THELMA: Why didn't you marry him?

MRS. WATTS: His papa and my papa didn't speak. My papa forced me to write a letter saying I never wanted to see him again and he got drunk and married out of spite. I felt sorry for his wife. She knew he never loved her. *(A pause.)* I don't think about those things anymore. But they're all part of Bountiful and I guess that's why I'm starting to think of them again. You're lucky to be married to the man you love, honey.

THELMA: I know I am.

MRS. WATTS: Awfully lucky. *(A pause. She looks out the window.)* Did you see that star fall over there?

THELMA: No.

MRS. WATTS: It was the prettiest thing I ever saw. You can make a wish on a falling star, honey.

THELMA: I know. It's too bad I didn't see it.

MRS. WATTS: You take my wish.

THELMA: Oh, no.

MRS. WATTS: Go on. I've gotten mine already. I'm on my way to Bountiful.

THELMA: Thank you. *(A pause.* THELMA *closes her eyes.* MRS. WATTS *watches her for a moment.)*

MRS. WATTS: Did you make your wish?

THELMA: Yes, I did.

(MRS. WATTS *leans her head back on the seat. She hums to herself.* THELMA *leans her head back, too. They close their eyes. The lights fade. The lights on the area stage left are brought up. It is the Harrison bus station. An old man is inside the ticket window, with his head on the ledge, asleep. He wakes up. He comes out of the cage into the room, yawning and stretching. We hear a bus pull up in the distance and stop. He starts for the entrance of the bus station, as* THELMA *comes in carrying her suitcase and* MRS. WATTS'*s suitcase.)*

TICKET MAN: Want any help with those bags?

THELMA: No, thank you. *(The* TICKET MAN *turns a light on in the station.* THELMA *takes the bags and puts them down beside a bench. She goes over to the* TICKET MAN.*)* Excuse me.

TICKET MAN: Yes?

THELMA: Is the bus to Old Gulf going to be on time?

TICKET MAN: Always is.

THELMA: Thank you. *(*THELMA *goes back to her seat near the suitcases.* MRS. WATTS *comes in. She sees the* TICKET MAN. *She speaks to him.)*

MRS. WATTS: Good evening. *(To* THELMA.*)* What time is it, honey?

THELMA: Twelve o'clock.

MRS. WATTS: Twelve o'clock. I bet Callie will be surprised to see me walk in at twelve o'clock.

THELMA: Did you tell her you were coming today?

MRS. WATTS: No. I couldn't. Because I didn't know. I had to wait until Jessie Mae went to the drugstore.

THELMA: My bus is leaving in half an hour.

MRS. WATTS: Oh, I see. I guess I'd better be finding out how I'm going to get on out to Bountiful.

THELMA: You sit down. I'll find the man.

MRS. WATTS: Thank you. *(She sits on the bench.* THELMA *goes over to the* TICKET MAN *at the door. He is busy bringing in morning papers left by the bus.)*

THELMA: Excuse me again.

TICKET MAN: Yes?

THELMA: My friend here wants to know how she can get to Bountiful.

TICKET MAN: Bountiful?

THELMA: Yes.

TICKET MAN: What's she going there for? (MRS. WATTS *comes up to the* TICKET MAN.)

MRS. WATTS: I'm going to visit my girlhood friend.

TICKET MAN: I don't know who that's gonna be. The last person in Bountiful was Mrs. Callie Davis. She died day before yesterday. That is they found her day before yesterday. She lived all alone so they don't know exactly when she died.

MRS. WATTS: Callie Davis!

TICKET MAN: Yes, Ma'am. They had the funeral this morning. Was she the one you were going to visit?

MRS. WATTS: Yessir. She was the one. She was my friend. My girlhood friend. (MRS. WATTS *stands for a moment. Then she goes to the bench. She seems very old and tired and defeated.* THELMA *crosses to the* TICKET MAN.)

THELMA: Is there a hotel here?

TICKET MAN: Yes'm. The Riverview.

THELMA: How far is it?

TICKET MAN: About five blocks.

THELMA: Is there a taxi around?

TICKET MAN: No, Ma'am. Not this time of night.

THELMA: Thank you. (*The* TICKET MAN *goes back into the ticket window.* THELMA *goes over to* MRS. WATTS *at the bench. She speaks to her with great sympathy.*) What'll you do now, Mrs. Watts?

MRS. WATTS: I'm thinking, honey. I'm thinking. It's come as quite a blow.

THELMA: I'm sorry. I'm so sorry.

MRS. WATTS: I know. I know. (*A pause. Her strength and her will reviving.*) It's come to me what to do. I'll go on. That much has come to me. To go on. I feel my strength and my purpose strong within me. I'll go on to Bountiful. I'll walk those twelve miles if I have to. (*She is standing now.*)

THELMA: But if there's no one out there what'll you do this time of night? (THELMA *gets her to sit back down.*)

MRS. WATTS: Oh, yes. I guess that's right.

THELMA: I think you should wait until morning.

MRS. WATTS: Yes. I guess I should. Then I can hire someone to drive me out. You know what I'll do. I'll stay at my own house, or what's left of it. Put me in a garden. I'll get along fine with the help of my government checks.

THELMA: Mrs. Watts, the man says there's a hotel not too far away. I think you'd better let me take you there.

MRS. WATTS: Oh, no thank you. I wouldn't want to waste my money on a hotel. They're high as cats' backs you know. I'll just sleep right here on this bench. Put my coat under my head, hold my purse under my arm. *(She puts the coat down on the bench like a pillow. She begins to look around for her purse. She has lost it.)* My purse! *(She begins to search frantically.)* Have you seen my purse, honey?

THELMA: Why, no. *(They begin to look around for it.)*

MRS. WATTS: Oh, good heavens. I remember now. I left my purse on the bus. *(THELMA runs to the entrance and looks out.)*

THELMA: You're sure you left it there?

MRS. WATTS: *(Joining her.)* Yes. I am. I remember now. I didn't have it when I got off that bus. I kept thinking something was missing, but then I decided it was my suitcase that you had brought in for me. What am I gonna do, honey? All I have in the world is in that purse. *(THELMA and MRS. WATTS go back to the ticket window. The TICKET MAN is drowsing.)*

THELMA: Excuse me again.

TICKET MAN: Yeah?

THELMA: This lady left her purse on the bus.

TICKET MAN: All right. I'll call ahead. How can you identify it?

MRS. WATTS: It's a plain brown purse.

TICKET MAN: How much money?

MRS. WATTS: Thirty-five cents and a pension check.

TICKET MAN: Who was the check made out to?

MRS. WATTS: To me. Mrs. Carrie Watts.

TICKET MAN: All right. I'll call up about it.

MRS. WATTS: Oh, thank you. You're most kind.

THELMA: How long will it take to get it back?

TICKET MAN: Depends. If I can get ahead of the bus at Don Tarle, I can get them to send it back on the Victoria bus and it should be here in a couple of hours.

MRS. WATTS: That's awful kind of you. *(He goes.* THELMA *and* MRS. WATTS *go back to the bench.)* I don't know what I would have done without you.

THELMA: Try not to worry about the purse.

MRS. WATTS: I won't. *(They sit on the bench.)* I'm too tired to worry. Be time enough to start worrying when I wake up in the morning.

THELMA: Why don't you go on to sleep now if you can?

MRS. WATTS: Oh, I thought I'd stay up and see you off.

THELMA: No. You go on to sleep.

MRS. WATTS: I couldn't go right off to sleep now. I'm too wound up. You know I don't go on a trip every day of my life. *(The* TICKET MAN *comes over to them on the bench.)*

TICKET MAN: You're lucky. Bus hadn't gotten to Don Tarle yet. If they can find the purse it'll be here around five.

MRS. WATTS: Thank you. Thank you so much.

THELMA: Make you feel better?

MRS. WATTS: Yes. It does. Of course, everything has seemed to work out today. Why is it some days everything works out, and some days nothing works out. What I mean is, I've been trying to get on that bus for Bountiful for over five years. Usually Jessie Mae and Ludie find me before I ever get inside the railroad station good. Today, I got inside both the railroad station and the bus station. Bought a ticket, seen Ludie and Jessie Mae before they saw me. Hid out. Met a pretty friend like you. Lost my purse, and now I'm having it found for me. I guess the good Lord is just with me today. *(A pause.)* I wonder why the Lord isn't with us every day? It would be so nice if He was. Well, maybe then we wouldn't appreciate so much the days when He's on our side. Or maybe He's always on our side and we don't know it. Maybe I had to wait twenty years cooped up in a city before I could appreciate getting back here. *(A pause.* THELMA *rests her head back on the bench.* MRS. WATTS *rests her head. She hums her hymn.)* It's so nice being able to sing a hymn when you want to. I'm a happy woman, young lady. A very happy woman.

THELMA: I still have a sandwich left. Will you have one?

MRS. WATTS: Sure you don't want it?

THELMA: No. I'm full.

MRS. WATTS: Then I'll have a half, thank you. *(THELMA gets the sandwich from her suitcase and unwraps it.)*

THELMA: Take the whole sandwich. I'm not hungry.

MRS. WATTS: No, thank you. Just half. You know I don't eat much. Particularly if I'm excited. *(She rises and stands nibbling on the sandwich and walking around the room.)* You know, I came to my first dance in this town.

THELMA: Did you?

MRS. WATTS: Yes, Ma'am. It was the summertime. My father couldn't decide if he thought dancin' was right or not. But my mother said she had danced when she was a girl and I was gonna dance. And so I went. The girls from all over the county came for this dance. It was at the Opera House. I forget what the occasion was. Somethin' special though. *(A pause. She looks at THELMA. She goes over to her.)* Do you know something, young lady? If my daughter had lived I would have wanted her to be just like you.

THELMA: Oh, thank you.

MRS. WATTS: *(With great tenderness.)* Just like you. Sweet and considerate and thoughtful.

THELMA: Oh, no . . . I'm . . .

MRS. WATTS: Oh, yes. Sweet and considerate and thoughtful. And pretty.

THELMA: Well, thank you. *(A pause.)* Mrs. Watts . . . I hope you don't mind my askin' this, but I worry about your son. Are you going to let him know where you are?

MRS. WATTS: Oh, yes, Ma'am. As soon as I get that check cashed I'm going to send him a telegram. *(The TICKET MAN comes by checking his watch as he passes. MRS. WATTS follows after him.)* I was tellin' my little friend here that I came to my first dance in this town.

TICKET MAN: Is that so?

MRS. WATTS: Yes. And I've been to Harrison quite a few times in my life, shopping.

TICKET MAN: *(To THELMA.)* You'd better get outside, Miss. Bus will be up the road. It won't wait this time of night unless it sees we have a passenger.

THELMA: All right. *(She gets her suitcase.)* Goodbye, Mrs. Watts.

MRS. WATTS: *(Following her to the door.)* Goodbye, honey. Good luck to you. And thank you for everything.

THELMA: That's all right. Good luck to you.

MRS. WATTS: Thank you.

(THELMA kisses her. THELMA goes out into the night, followed by the TICKET MAN. MRS. WATTS stands at the door watching THELMA. We

hear a bus pulling up. MRS. WATTS *waves. We hear the bus leave. The* TICKET MAN *comes back inside the bus station.)*

TICKET MAN: Are you gonna stay here all night?

MRS. WATTS: I have to. Everything I have is in that purse and we can't go anyplace without money.

TICKET MAN: I guess that's right. *(He starts away.)*

MRS. WATTS: Do they still have dances in Borden's Opera House?

TICKET MAN: No, Ma'am. It's torn down. They condemned it, you know. *(He starts on. He pauses.)* Did you ever know anybody in Harrison?

MRS. WATTS: I knew a few people when I was a girl. Priscilla Nytelle. Did you know her?

TICKET MAN: No, Ma'am.

MRS. WATTS: Nancy Lee Goodhue?

TICKET MAN: No, Ma'am.

MRS. WATTS: The Fay girls?

TICKET MAN: No, Ma'am.

MRS. WATTS: I used to trade in Mr. Ewing's store. I knew him to speak to.

TICKET MAN: Which Ewing was that?

MRS. WATTS: George White Ewing.

TICKET MAN: He's dead.

MRS. WATTS: Is that so?

TICKET MAN: Been dead for twelve years.

MRS. WATTS: Is that so?

TICKET MAN: He left quite a bit of money, but his son took over his store and lost it all. Drank.

MRS. WATTS: Is that so? One thing I can say about my boy is that he never gave me any worry that way.

TICKET MAN: Well, that's good. I've got one boy that drinks and one boy that doesn't. I can't understand it. I raised them the same way.

MRS. WATTS: I know. I've known of other cases like that. One drinks. The other doesn't.

TICKET MAN: A friend of mine has a girl that drinks. I think that's the saddest thing in the world.

MRS. WATTS: Isn't it? *(A pause.)*

TICKET MAN: Well. Good night.

MRS. WATTS: Good night. *(The* TICKET MAN *stands waiting to switch off the light while* MRS. WATTS *takes her suitcase and coat and makes a bed for herself on the bench. She lies down. He goes inside the ticket booth. He sticks his head out the cage.)*

TICKET MAN: Good night.

MRS. WATTS: Good night.

(He turns the light inside the ticket window out. MRS. WATTS is humming quietly to herself. Her humming fades away as the lights are faded out. The lights are brought up. The TICKET MAN is in his office sound asleep and snoring slightly. The door opens and a man comes in. He is the SHERIFF. He stands by the door for a moment looking around the bus station. He sees MRS. WATTS lying on the bench asleep. He goes over to her and looks down. He stands for a moment watching her sleep. He looks over at the ticket window and sees the man is asleep. The SHERIFF goes over to the TICKET MAN. He shakes him.)

SHERIFF: Come on, Roy, wake up.

TICKET MAN: Yeah? *(He opens his eyes. He sees the SHERIFF. He comes out to the SHERIFF.)* Oh, hello, Sheriff.

SHERIFF: How long has that old woman been here?

TICKET MAN: About four hours.

SHERIFF: Did she get off the bus from Houston?

TICKET MAN: Yessir. I know her name. It's Watts. She left her purse on the bus and I had to call up to Don Tarle about it.

SHERIFF: Have you got her purse?

TICKET MAN: Yes. It just came.

SHERIFF: She's the one, all right. I've had a call from the Houston police to hold her until her son can come for her.

TICKET MAN: She said she used to live in Bountiful.

SHERIFF: Yeah. I believe I remember some Wattses a long time ago over that way. I think that old ramshackly house about to fall into the Brazos River belonged to them.

TICKET MAN: That right? They must have been before my time. She asked me about a lot of people I never heard of. She claimed she was going to visit Miss Callie Davis. I told her she was dead. What do the police want her for?

SHERIFF: Police don't. It's her son. He wants to take her back home. Claims she's not responsible. Did she act crazy to you?

TICKET MAN: Not that I noticed. Is she crazy?

SHERIFF: They say so. Harmless, but hipped on running away from Houston to get back here. *(He starts over to her to wake her up. He stands looking at her for a moment. He comes back to the TICKET*

MAN.) Poor old thing. She's sleeping so sound. I don't have the heart to wake her up. I'll tell you what, I'll go down and call Houston . . . tell them she's here. Her son is coming in his car. He should be here around seven-thirty. I'll be back in ten minutes. If she gives you any trouble just call me. Keep your eye on her.

TICKET MAN: All right. *(The* SHERIFF *goes out and the* TICKET MAN *follows him. He comes back in carrying a crate and bumps it accidentally against the door. This wakes* MRS. WATTS *up. She opens her eyes. She looks around trying to remember where she is. Then she sees the* TICKET MAN.)

MRS. WATTS: Good morning.

TICKET MAN: Good morning.

MRS. WATTS: Could you tell me the time?

TICKET MAN: It's around four-thirty.

MRS. WATTS: Thank you. Did my purse arrive?

TICKET MAN: Yes, Ma'am. *(He reaches under the ticket window to a ledge and gets the purse for her. He hands the purse to her.)*

MRS. WATTS: Thank you so much. I wonder if you could cash a check for me?

TICKET MAN: I'm sorry. I can't.

MRS. WATTS: It's a government check and I have identification.

TICKET MAN: I'm sorry. I can't.

MRS. WATTS: Do you know where I could get a check cashed?

TICKET MAN: Why? *(She starts to gather up her coat and suitcase.)*

MRS. WATTS: I need money to get me started in Bountiful. I want to hire someone to drive me out there and look at my house and get a few groceries. Try to find a cot to sleep on. *(She has the coat and suitcase.)*

TICKET MAN: I'm sorry, lady. You're not going to Bountiful.

MRS. WATTS: Oh, yes, I am. You see . . .

TICKET MAN: I'm sorry, lady. You're not going anyplace right now. I have to hold you here for the sheriff.

MRS. WATTS: The sheriff?

TICKET MAN: Yes, Ma'am. *(A pause.)*

MRS. WATTS: You're joking with me!? Don't joke with me. I've come too far.

TICKET MAN: I'm sorry. That's how it is.

MRS. WATTS: What has the sheriff got to do with me?

TICKET MAN: He came a few minutes ago while you were asleep and said I was to keep you here until your son arrived in his car this morning.

MRS. WATTS: My son hasn't got a car, so I don't believe you. I don't believe you.

TICKET MAN: It's the truth. He'll be here in a little while, and you can ask him yourself. *(A pause.)*

MRS. WATTS: Then you're not joking?

TICKET MAN: No. *(She takes her coat and suitcase and runs for the entrance. He senses what she is going to do and gets there first—blocking her way.)*

MRS. WATTS: All right. But I'm going, do you understand? You'll see. This is a free country. And I'll tell him that. No sheriff or king or president will keep me from going back to Bountiful.

TICKET MAN: All right. You tell him that. *(She comes back into the room. She is desperate.)*

MRS. WATTS: What time is my son expected?

TICKET MAN: Sheriff says around seven-thirty.

MRS. WATTS: What time is it now?

TICKET MAN: I told you around four-thirty.

MRS. WATTS: Where can I get me a driver?

TICKET MAN: Ma'am?

MRS. WATTS: If you can get me a driver, I can make it to Bountiful and back way before seven-thirty . . .

TICKET MAN: Look, lady . . .

MRS. WATTS: That's all I want. That's all I ask. Just to see it. To stand on the porch of my own house, once more. Walk under the trees. I swear, I would come back then meek as a lamb . . .

TICKET MAN: Lady . . .

MRS. WATTS: Last night, I thought I had to stay. I thought I'd die if I couldn't stay. But I'll settle for less now. Much, much less. An hour. A half hour. Fifteen minutes.

TICKET MAN: Lady, it ain't up to me. I told you the sheriff.

MRS. WATTS: *(Screaming.)* Then get me the sheriff.

TICKET MAN: Look, lady . . .

MRS. WATTS: Get me the sheriff. The time is going. They'll have me locked in those two rooms again soon. The time is going . . . the time is . . .

(The SHERIFF comes in. The SHERIFF goes over to MRS. WATTS.)

SHERIFF: Mrs. Watts?

MRS. WATTS: Yessir. *(She looks up at him. She puts the coat and suitcase down.)* Are you the sheriff?

SHERIFF: Yes, Ma'am.

MRS. WATTS: I understand my son will be here at seven-thirty to take me back to Houston.

SHERIFF: Yes, Ma'am.

MRS. WATTS: Then listen to me, sir. I've waited a long time. Just to get to Bountiful. Twenty years I've been walkin' the streets of the city, lost and grieving. And as I've grown older and my time approaches, I've made one promise to myself, to see my home again . . . before I die . . .

SHERIFF: Lady . . . I . . .

MRS. WATTS: I'm not asking that I not go back. I'm willing to go back. Only let me travel these twelve miles first. I have money. I can pay . . .

SHERIFF: I think that's between you and your son.

MRS. WATTS: Ludie? Why, he's got to do whatever Jessie Mae tells him to. I know why she wants me back. It's for my government check.

SHERIFF: I don't know anything about that. That's between you and your son.

MRS. WATTS: Won't you let me go?

SHERIFF: No. Not unless your son takes you.

MRS. WATTS: All right. Then I've lost. I've come all this way only to lose. *(A pause. She stands behind the bench supporting herself. She seems very tired and defeated. She speaks very quietly and almost to herself.)* I've kept thinking back there day and night in those two rooms, I kept thinkin' . . . and it may mean nothin' at all to you, but I kept thinkin' . . . that if I could just set foot there for a minute . . . even . . . a second . . . I might get some understanding of why . . . Why my life has grown so empty and meaningless. Why I've turned into a hateful, quarrelsome old woman. And before I leave this earth, I'd like to recover some of the dignity . . . the peace I used to know. For I'm going to die . . . and Jessie Mae knows that . . . and she's willful and it's her will I die in those two rooms. Well, she won't have her way. It's my will to die in Bountiful. *(She sobs and starts to run out of the bus station. The SHERIFF stops her. She suddenly seems very weak, and is about to fall. He has her arm, supporting her.)*

SHERIFF: Mrs. Watts.

MRS. WATTS: Let me go those twelve miles . . . before it's too late. *(A pause. For a moment her strength seems to come back.)* Understand me. Suffering I don't mind. Suffering I understand. I never protested once. Though my heart was broken when those babies died. I could stand seeing the man I love walk through life with another woman. But this fifteen years of bickering. Endless, petty bickering . . . It's made me like Jessie Mae sees me. It's ugly. I won't be that way. *(An anguished cry.)* I want to go home. I want to go home. I want to go . . . *(She is unable to speak any more. She is on the verge of collapse. The* SHERIFF *helps her over to the bench and settles her there. The* SHERIFF *calls to the* TICKET MAN.*)*

SHERIFF: Roy, hurry. Call a doctor. *(She summons up her last bit of strength to get free.)*

MRS. WATTS: No. No doctor. Bountiful . . . Bountiful . . . Bountiful. *(The* SHERIFF *holds her. There is a very fast* CURTAIN.*)*

Act III

It is early morning. The lights are slowly brought up and we can see the house and the yard of MRS. WATTS's *old house in Bountiful. The house, with a sagging porch before it, is stage right. The entrance to the yard is upstage center.*

The house is an old, ramshackle two-story country place that hasn't been painted for years. Vines are growing wild over it, coralvine and Virginia creeper and fig vine. The roof of the front porch is sagging and one of the supporting posts is completely gone. The floorboards of the front porch are rotting away and the steps leading to the porch are loose. The yard has gone to weeds, and wildflowers are everywhere: buttercups, dandelions, and wild iris. In the early morning light there is a peace and tranquility and a wild kind of beauty about the place that is moving and heartwarming and in its own way lovely.

The SHERIFF *and* MRS. WATTS *come in upstage center walking very slowly. They stop every few minutes while she looks at the house and the yard.* MRS. WATTS *is carrying her purse.*

MRS. WATTS: I'm home. I'm home. I'm home. Thank you. I thank you. I thank you. I thank you. *(They pause for a moment in the yard.* MRS. WATTS *is obviously still quite weak.)*

SHERIFF: You'd better sit down and rest for a while. You don't want to overdo it.

MRS. WATTS: Yessir. *(She sits on a tree stump in the yard.)*

SHERIFF: Feeling all right?

MRS. WATTS: Yes, I am. I feel ever so much better.

SHERIFF: You look better. I hope I've done the right thing in bringing you here. Well, I don't see what harm it can do. As long as you mind the doctor and don't get overexcited.

MRS. WATTS: Yessir. *(A pause. She looks around the yard again.)*

SHERIFF: Soon as you've rested for a little I'll go on back to my car and leave you alone. You can call me if you need anything. I'll stay out here until your son arrives.

MRS. WATTS: Thank you. You've been very kind. *(A bird calls. She and the* SHERIFF *sit listening to it. It whistles once again.)* What kind of a bird was that?

SHERIFF: Redbird.

MRS. WATTS: I thought that was a redbird, but I hadn't heard one in so long, I couldn't be sure. *(A pause.)* Do they still have scissortails around here?

SHERIFF: Yes, Ma'am. I still see one every once in a while when I'm driving around the country.

MRS. WATTS: I don't know of anything prettier than a scissortail flying around in the sky. *(A pause.)* My father was a good man in many ways, a peculiar man, but a good one. One of the things he couldn't stand was to see a bird shot on his land. If men came here hunting, he'd take a gun and chase them away. I think the birds knew they couldn't be touched here. Our land was always a home to them. Ducks and geese and finches and blue jays. Bluebirds and redbirds. Wild canaries and blackbirds and mockers and doves and ricebirds . . . *(During the latter speech she gets up and begins to pick weeds out of the yard. At the end of the speech the* SHERIFF *gently stops her and leads her to the porch of the house. She sits on a step.)*

SHERIFF: Ricebirds are gettin' thicker every year. They seem to thrive out here on the coast.

MRS. WATTS: I guess a mockin'bird is my favorite of them all.

SHERIFF: I guess it's mine, too.

MRS. WATTS: I don't know, though. I'm mighty partial to a scissortail. I hope I get to see one soon.

SHERIFF: I hope you can.

MRS. WATTS: My father was born on this land and in this house. Did you know my father?

SHERIFF: No, Ma'am. Not that I can remember.

MRS. WATTS: I guess there are not many around here that remember my father. I do, of course, and my son. Maybe some old-timers around Harrison. *(A pause.)* It's funny, ever since I've been here I've been half expectin' my father and my mother to walk out of the house and greet me and welcome me home. *(A pause.)* When you've lived longer than your house or your family, maybe you've lived too long. *(A pause.)* Or maybe it's just me. Maybe the need to belong to a house and a family and a town has gone from the rest of the world.

SHERIFF: How big was your farm, Mrs. Watts?

MRS. WATTS: Three hundred and seventy-five acres were left when my papa died and I sold off all but the house and the yard. *(A pause.)* You say the store burned fifteen years ago?

SHERIFF: Yes, Ma'am. What was left of it. You see with the good roads we have now in the county, the little towns and their country stores are all disappearing. The farmers ride into Cotton or Harrison to trade . . .

MRS. WATTS: But what's happened to the farms? For the last five miles I've seen nothing but woods . . .

SHERIFF: I know. The land around Bountiful just played out. People like you got discouraged and moved away, sold off the land for what they could get. H. T. Mavis bought most of it up. He let it go back into timber. He keeps a few head of cattle out here. That's about all . . .

MRS. WATTS: Callie Davis kept her farm going.

SHERIFF: Yes. She did. She learned how to treat her land right and it began paying off for her toward the end. I've heard she was out riding her tractor the day before she died. Lonely death she had. All by herself in that big house.

MRS. WATTS: There are worse things. *(The sun is up full now, filling the stage with light.)*

SHERIFF: Looks to me like you're going to have a pretty day.

MRS. WATTS: I hope so. My daughter-in-law has never seen our place in the sunshine. I expect my son will bring her along with him. I'd hate for her to have to see it again in the rain. *(A pause. The* SHERIFF *looks at her.)*

SHERIFF: Feeling more rested now?

MRS. WATTS: Oh, yes, I am.

SHERIFF: Good. Then I'll be getting on back to my car. You just call me if you need anything.

MRS. WATTS: Thank you.

(He gets up and walks to the corner of the yard. Just before he goes out he turns and waves. MRS. WATTS *waves back to him. She sits on the steps for a moment watching him go out. When he is out of sight, she rises slowly from the steps and goes along the porch. When she comes to the front door she stops and stands for a moment. She slowly opens the door and goes inside the house as the lights fade. The lights are slowly brought up. The* SHERIFF *comes into the yard. He goes up to the steps of the porch.)*

SHERIFF: *(Calling.)* Mrs. Watts. Mrs. Watts. Mrs. Watts. *(He runs up on the porch as he calls her.* MRS. WATTS *comes out of the house. She has left her purse inside the house.)*

MRS. WATTS: Yessir.

SHERIFF: It's seven-thirty. Your son and his wife are here.

MRS. WATTS: Yessir.

SHERIFF: They're out on the road in their car. They said they had to hurry on back. I told them I'd come get you.

MRS. WATTS: Yessir. Won't you ask them to please come in for a minute?

SHERIFF: Well, all right. I'll have to be gettin' on back to town now myself, Mrs. Watts. *(He holds his hand out. She takes it.)* Good-bye, and good luck to you.

MRS. WATTS: Thank you. You'll never know what this has meant to me.

SHERIFF: Glad I could oblige. *(He starts away as* LUDIE *comes into the yard.)* Oh, Mr. Watts. I was just coming to tell you your mother wanted you to come in for a few minutes.

LUDIE: Thank you. *(The* SHERIFF *goes up to him.)*

SHERIFF: I've got to be getting back on into town.

LUDIE: All right, Sheriff. Thank you for everything you've done.

SHERIFF: Don't mention it. I was glad I could oblige. You folks have a nice trip home.

LUDIE: Thank you.

SHERIFF: Good-bye, Mrs. Watts.

MRS. WATTS: Good-bye, Sheriff.

SHERIFF: So long, Mr. Watts.

LUDIE: Good-bye, Sheriff. *(He goes out.* MRS. WATTS *and* LUDIE *watch him go.* LUDIE *walks up on the porch to his mother. They both seem embarrassed and ill at ease.)* Hello, Mama.

MRS. WATTS: Hello, son.

LUDIE: How do you feel?

MRS. WATTS: I'm feelin' better, Ludie.

LUDIE: That's good. They told me at the bus station you had another attack.

MRS. WATTS: Yes, I did. All the excitement, I guess. But I feel fine now.

LUDIE: Yes'm.

MRS. WATTS: I got my wish.

LUDIE: Yes'm. (LUDIE *walks away from the porch down to the corner of the yard.* MRS. WATTS *follows him.*)

MRS. WATTS: I hope I didn't worry you too much, Ludie. But I just felt I had to . . .

LUDIE: I know, Mama.

MRS. WATTS: You see, son, I know it's hard for you to understand and Jessie Mae . . . understand—But . . .

LUDIE: Yes, Ma'am. I understand, Mama. It's done now. So let's forget about it.

MRS. WATTS: All right, Sonny. (*A pause.*) You did bring Jessie Mae, didn't you?

LUDIE: Yes, Ma'am.

MRS. WATTS: Well, now she's here isn't she going to get out of the car and look around a little?

LUDIE: She didn't seem to want to, Mama.

MRS. WATTS: You asked her?

LUDIE: Yes, Ma'am. (*A pause.*)

MRS. WATTS: Did you ask about your raise, son?

LUDIE: Yes, Ma'am, and Mr. Douglas told me he liked my work and he'd be glad to recommend a raise for me.

MRS. WATTS: Oh. (*A pause.*) The sky's so blue, Ludie. Did you ever see the sky so blue?

LUDIE: No, Ma'am. (*A pause.*)

MRS. WATTS: Callie Davis died.

LUDIE: Is that so? When did that happen?

MRS. WATTS: They don't rightly know. They found her dead. She'd been ridin' a tractor the day before they found her. Buried her yesterday. (*A pause.*)

LUDIE: Mama, I should have made myself bring you here before. I'm sorry but I thought it would be easier for both of us not to see the house again.

MRS. WATTS: I know, Ludie. (*A pause.*) Now you're here, wouldn't you like to come inside, son, and look around?

LUDIE: I don't think I'd better, Mama. I don't see any use in it. It would just make me feel bad. I'd rather remember it like it was. (*A pause.* MRS. WATTS *looks at the house. She smiles.*)

MRS. WATTS: The old house has gotten kind of run down, hasn't it?

LUDIE: Yes, it has. (*She starts back toward the house slowly.*)

MRS. WATTS: I don't think it'll last out the next Gulf storm.

LUDIE: It doesn't look like it would. *(She turns and looks at him standing in the yard.)*

MRS. WATTS: You know who you look like standing there, Ludie?

LUDIE: Who?

MRS. WATTS: My papa.

LUDIE: Do I?

MRS. WATTS: Just like him. Of course, I've been noticing as you grow older you look more and more like him. My papa was a good-looking man.

LUDIE: Was he?

MRS. WATTS: You've seen his pictures. Didn't you think so?

LUDIE: I don't remember. It's been so long since I looked at his picture.

MRS. WATTS: Well, he was always considered a very nice-looking man. *(A pause.)* Do you remember my papa at all, son? *(MRS. WATTS sits on the steps of the porch.)*

LUDIE: No, Ma'am. Not too well. I was only ten when he died, Mama. I remember the day he died. I heard about it as I was coming home from school. Lee Weems told me. I thought he was joking and I called him a liar. I remember you takin' me into the front room there the day of the funeral to say good-bye to him. I remember the coffin and the people sitting in the room. Old man Joe Weems took me up on his knee and told me that Grandpapa was his best friend and that his life was a real example for me to follow. I remember Grandmama sitting by the coffin crying and she made me promise that when I had a son of my own I'd name it after Grandpapa. I would have, too. I've never forgotten that promise. *(A pause.)* Well, I didn't have a son. Or a daughter. *(A pause.)* Billy Davidson told me his wife is expecting her fourth child. They have two girls and a boy, now. Billy Davidson doesn't make much more than I do and they certainly seem to get along. Own their own home and have a car. It does your heart good to hear them tell about how they all get along. Everybody has their job, even the youngest child. She's only three. She puts the napkins around the table at mealtimes. That's her job. Billy said to me, Ludie, I don't know how I'd keep going without my kids. He said, I don't understand what keeps you going, Ludie. What you work for. I said, Well, Billy . . . Oh, Mama, I haven't made any kind of life for you, either one of you and I try so hard. I try so hard. *(He crosses to her.)* Oh, Mama. I lied to you. I do remember. I remember so much. This house. The life here. The night you woke me up and dressed me and took me for a walk when there was a full moon and I cried because I was afraid and you comforted me. *(He turns abruptly away from his mother and walks to the downstage corner of the porch.)* Mama, I want to stop remembering . . . It doesn't do any good to remember. *(A car horn is heard in the distance—loud and impatient. He looks in the direction of the horn.)* That's Jessie Mae.

MRS. WATTS: Whose car did you come in? *(He crosses to her.)*

LUDIE: I borrowed Billy Davidson's car. He didn't want me to have it at first. You know people are funny about lending their car, but then I explained what happened and he was nice about it. *(The car horn is heard again.)* We have to start back now, Mama. Jessie Mae is nervous that I might lose my job.

MRS. WATTS: *(Frantically trying to find an excuse not to leave.)* Didn't you ask for the day off?

LUDIE: No, Ma'am. I only asked for the morning off.

MRS. WATTS: What time is it now?

LUDIE: Must be after eight. We were a little late getting here.

MRS. WATTS: We can drive it in three hours, can't we, Ludie?

LUDIE: Yes, Ma'am, but we might have a flat or run into traffic or something. Besides, I promised Billy I'd get his car back to him by twelve.

MRS. WATTS: Son, why am I going back at all? Why can't I stay?

LUDIE: Mama, you can't stay. You know that. Now come on. *(He takes her by the arm. She starts to get up from the steps. When she is about halfway up she collapses, crying. She cries passionately, openly, bitterly.)*

MRS. WATTS: Ludie. Ludie. What's happened to us? Why have we come to this?

LUDIE: I don't know, Mama.

MRS. WATTS: To have stayed and fought the land would have been better than this.

LUDIE: Yes'm. *(She gets up.)*

MRS. WATTS: Pretty soon it'll all be gone. Ten years . . . twenty . . . this house . . . me . . . you . . .

LUDIE: I know, Mama. *(A pause. She looks into his suffering face. She looks around. She speaks with great tenderness.)*

MRS. WATTS: But the river will be here. The fields. The woods. The smell of the Gulf. That's what I always took my strength from, Ludie. Not from houses, not from people. *(A pause.)* It's so quiet. It's so eternally quiet. I had forgotten the peace. The quiet. And it's given me strength once more, Ludie. To go on and do what I have to do. I've found my dignity and my strength.

LUDIE: I'm glad, Mama.

MRS. WATTS: And I'll never fight with Jessie Mae again or complain. *(She points out into the distance.)* Do you remember how my papa always had that field over there planted in cotton?

LUDIE: Yes, Ma'am.

MRS. WATTS: See, it's all woods now. But I expect someday people will come again and cut down the trees and plant the cotton and maybe even wear out the land again and then their children will sell it and go to the cities and then the trees will come up again.

LUDIE: I expect so, Mama.

MRS. WATTS: We're part of all this. We left it, but we can never lose what it has given us.

LUDIE: I expect so, Mama.

(He takes her by the arm and they start walking out. JESSIE MAE comes into the yard.)

JESSIE MAE: Ludie. Are you coming or not?

LUDIE: We were just startin', Jessie Mae.

MRS. WATTS: Hello, Jessie Mae.

JESSIE MAE: I'm not speakin' to you. I guess you're proud of the time you gave us. Dragging us all the way out here this time of the mornin'. If Ludie loses his job over this, I hope you're satisfied.

LUDIE: I'm not goin' to lose my job, Jessie Mae.

JESSIE MAE: Well, you could.

LUDIE: All right, Jessie Mae.

JESSIE MAE: And she should realize that. She's selfish. That's her trouble. Always has been. Just puredee selfish. Did you tell your Mama what we were discussing in the car?

LUDIE: No. We can talk it all over driving back to Houston.

JESSIE MAE: I think we should have it out right there. I'd like everything understood right now. *(JESSIE MAE opens her purse and takes out a piece of paper.)* I've gotten everything written down. Do you want to read it or do you want me to read it to you, Mother Watts?

MRS. WATTS: What is it, Jessie Mae?

JESSIE MAE: It's a few rules and regulations that are necessary to my peace of mind. And I think to Ludie's. Ludie says you may have a few of your own to add and that may be and I'm perfectly willin' to listen if you do . . . First of all, I'd like to ask you a question.

MRS. WATTS: Yes, Ma'am. (MRS. WATTS *sits on the steps.*)

JESSIE MAE: Just what possessed you to run away? Didn't you know you'd be caught and have to come back?

MRS. WATTS: I had to come, Jessie Mae. Twenty years is a long time.

JESSIE MAE: But what if you had died from the excitement! Didn't you know you could have died?

MRS. WATTS: I knew.

JESSIE MAE: And you didn't care?

MRS. WATTS: *(With great dignity.)* I had to come, Jessie Mae.

JESSIE MAE: Well, I hope it's out of your system now.

MRS. WATTS: It is. I've had my trip. That's more than enough to keep me happy the rest of my life.

JESSIE MAE: Well, I'm glad to hear it. That's the first thing on my list. *(She reads from list.)* Number one. There'll be no more running away.

MRS. WATTS: There'll be no more running away.

JESSIE MAE: Good. *(She takes the list up again.)* Number two. No more hymn singing, when I'm in the apartment. When I'm gone you can sing your lungs out. Agreed?

MRS. WATTS: Agreed.

JESSIE MAE: Number three.

LUDIE: *(Interrupting.)* Jessie Mae, can't this wait till we get home?

JESSIE MAE: Now, honey, we agreed that I'm going to handle this! *(She goes back to the list.)* No more pouting. When I ask a question, I'd like an answer. Otherwise I'll consider it's pouting.

MRS. WATTS: All right.

JESSIE MAE: Fourth. With the condition that your heart is in I feel you should not run around the apartment when you can walk.

MRS. WATTS: All right, Jessie Mae.

JESSIE MAE: That's all. Is there anything you want to say to me?

MRS. WATTS: No, Jessie Mae.

JESSIE MAE: I might as well tell you now I'm not staying in the house and watching over you anymore. I am joinin' a bridge club and going to town at least twice a week. If you go now, it'll just be your funeral. You understand?

MRS. WATTS: I understand.

JESSIE MAE: All right. *(She puts the list away.)*

LUDIE: And, Mama, we also agreed that we're all gonna try our best to get along together. Jessie Mae also realizes that she gets upset sometimes when she shouldn't. Don't you, Jessie Mae?

JESSIE MAE: Uh-huh.

LUDIE: So let's start by trying to have a pleasant ride home.

JESSIE MAE: Allrightie. *(She takes a cigarette and the lighter from her purse. The lighter works and she lights her cigarette. She crosses down to the far edge of the house.)* Is there any water around here? I'm thirsty.

LUDIE: I don't think so, Jessie Mae. Mama, is there any water around here?

MRS. WATTS: No. The cistern is gone. *(JESSIE MAE notices a scratch on her shoes. She is furious.)*

JESSIE MAE: Look at my shoes! I've got scratches on them. They're my good pair. I ought to have my head examined for wearing my only good pair of shoes out here in this old swamp.

LUDIE: *(Looking out in the distance.)* When I was a boy I used to drink in the creek over there, Jessie Mae. We had a cistern, but I always preferred to drink out of the creek. It seemed to me the water always tasted so much better. *(JESSIE MAE crosses over to the far end of the stage looking out at the creek in the distance.)*

JESSIE MAE: Well, you wouldn't catch me drinking out of any creek. I knew a man once that went on a huntin' trip and drank out of a creek and caught something and died.

MRS. WATTS: There's nothin' like cistern water for washin' your hair with. It is the softest water in the world. *(A bird calls in the distance.)* That's a redbird.

JESSIE MAE: A what?

MRS. WATTS: A redbird.

JESSIE MAE: Oh. I thought you said that. They all sound alike to me. Well, come on. Let's get going. Do we go back by the way of Harrison?

LUDIE: Yes.

JESSIE MAE: Good. Then we can stop at the drugstore. I'm so thirsty I could drink ten Coca-Colas. Are you all ready?

MRS. WATTS: Yes'm. *(They start out. JESSIE MAE looks at her.)*

JESSIE MAE: Where's your purse?

MRS. WATTS: Are you talkin' to me, Jessie Mae?

JESSIE MAE: Who else would I be talkin' to? Since when did Ludie start walkin' around with a pocketbook under his arm? *(MRS. WATTS looks around.)*

MRS. WATTS: Oh, I guess I left it inside.

JESSIE MAE: Where? *(She starts toward the door of the house.)*

MRS. WATTS: I'll get it. *(She turns to go into the house.)*

JESSIE MAE: No. I want to go. You'll take all day. Where did you leave it?

MRS. WATTS: In the parlor. Right off the front hall.

JESSIE MAE: All right. I'll get it. You wait here. *(She starts into the house. She turns and sees them walking off.)* I said wait here now. I don't want to be left alone in this ramshackly old house. No telling what's running around in there.

MRS. WATTS: There's nothing in there.

JESSIE MAE: There might be rats or snakes or something.

LUDIE: I'll go.

JESSIE MAE: No. I'll go. Just stay here so if I holler you can come. *(She goes inside the house. LUDIE turns to his mother.)*

LUDIE: Mama.

MRS. WATTS: It's all right, Ludie, son. *(JESSIE MAE comes back out with the purse.)*

JESSIE MAE: Here's your purse. Now where's the money for that government check?

MRS. WATTS: I haven't cashed it.

JESSIE MAE: Where is it?

MRS. WATTS: It's right inside the purse. *(JESSIE MAE opens the purse and begins to search again.)*

JESSIE MAE: No. It isn't.

MRS. WATTS: Here. Let me look. *(JESSIE MAE hands her the purse and MRS. WATTS, too, begins to rummage around. All of a sudden she bursts out laughing.)*

JESSIE MAE: What's the matter with you?

MRS. WATTS: That's a good joke on me.

JESSIE MAE: Well, what's so funny?

MRS. WATTS: I just remembered. I left this purse on the bus last night and caused a man a lot of trouble because I thought the check was in there. *(She is overcome by laughter again.)* And do you know that check wasn't in that purse all that time?

JESSIE MAE: Where was it?

MRS. WATTS: Right here. *(She reaches inside her dress and takes it out.)* Been here since yesterday afternoon. (JESSIE MAE *reaches for the check.)*

JESSIE MAE: Give it to me before you go and lose it again.

MRS. WATTS: I won't lose it.

JESSIE MAE: Now don't start that business again. Just give it to me.

LUDIE: *(Interrupting angrily.)* Jessie Mae.

JESSIE MAE: Well, I'm not going to—

LUDIE: *(With great positiveness).* We're going to stop this wrangling once and for all. You've given me your word and I expect you to keep your word. We have to live together and we're going to live together in peace.

MRS. WATTS: It's all right, Ludie. *(She gives the check to* JESSIE MAE.) Let Jessie Mae take care of the check. (JESSIE MAE *accepts the check. She looks at it for a moment and then grabs* MRS. WATTS's *purse. She opens it and puts the check inside.)*

JESSIE MAE: Oh, here. You keep the check. But don't go and lose it before you get home. *(She puts the purse back in* MRS. WATTS's *hand. She starts offstage.)* Well, come on. Let's go. *(She leaves.* LUDIE *goes to his mother.)*

LUDIE: Mama, if I get the raise you won't—

MRS. WATTS: It's all right, Ludie. I've had my trip. You go ahead. I'll be right there. (LUDIE *starts out.* MRS. WATTS *points up in the sky.)* Look, isn't that a scissortail?

LUDIE: I don't know. I didn't get to see it if it was. They fly so fast. (LUDIE *takes one last look at the house.)* The house used to look so big.

(He goes out. MRS. WATTS *stands for a moment looking into the sky. Then she drops gently onto her knees, puts her hands in the dirt. She kneels for a moment holding the dirt, then slowly lets it drift through her fingers back to the ground. She begins to walk slowly out until she gets to the corner of the yard. She pauses for a moment, taking one last look at the house, speaks quietly.)*

MRS. WATTS: Good-bye, Bountiful, good-bye. *(Then she turns and walks off the stage.)*

Curtain

III

The Screenplay

Geraldine Page (*Courtesy of Sterling VanWagenen*)

John Heard (*Courtesy of Sterling VanWagenen*)

Rebecca DeMornay and Geraldine Page (*Courtesy of Sterling VanWagenen*)

Geraldine Page (*Courtesy of Sterling VanWagenen*)

Geraldine Page (*Courtesy of Sterling VanWagenen*)

The Screenplay

AFTER *Bountiful* finished its Broadway run, Horton Foote had many offers from producers who wanted to film the story, but he was unwilling to relinquish control of the project. In particular, it was important to him that Lillian Gish reprise the role of Carrie Watts.

It was not until thirty years later in 1984 when his cousin, Peter Masterson, approached him asking to direct a movie based on *Bountiful* that Foote agreed to make a film of the story—if they could find the right person to play Mrs. Watts. Masterson and Foote decided the role was so strenuous that an actress younger than Gish (who was by then nearly ninety) might be needed. Foote suggested Geraldine Page, with whom he had worked earlier in a "Playhouse 90" television production. Foote knew her talent and considered her a close friend: "I just thought she was marvelous. I thought she'd be extraordinary in it, which she was. And Pete knew her and admired her."[1] Masterson suggested that Sterling VanWagenen coproduce the project with Foote, and the three were ready to begin.

The next step was to secure the financing for the production, which took a year. Fearing loss of control over his conception of the film version of *Bountiful,* Foote wanted to avoid the traditional Hollywood studio system. The alternative was independent production, making a small-budget film geared toward a smaller, more sophisticated audience. An average Hollywood production costs $18.1 million; *Bountiful* was made for less than $2 million.

Of his decision to participate in an independent film project, Foote says, "In Hollywood, you're a writer for hire, which means that you write it and turn it over to them. And that's not so in the films I do. But that's been a long, hard battle, and that's not an easy thing for a writer to achieve. You really just have to dig in your heels and say this is what I'm going to do and be willing not to have anything done—because they don't give in to you gladly."[2]

His experience with the film *Tomorrow* inspired Foote's working style. "I learned that film should really be like theater in the sense that the writer is . . . very dominant. . . . I mean we are sought after. We are at the rehearsals. If we don't like something we can speak up our minds. We help with the casting. It is always a collaborative effort."[3]

Once some of the financing had been obtained, Foote began adapting the play into a filmscript: "The task I gave myself in writing the screenplay [was] . . . how to make the trip as interesting and meaningful as its start and conclusion."[4] He accomplished his goal by trimming some of the dialogue from the theatrical script and adding visual elements. By April 1985, the screenplay was finished.

With *Bountiful*, Foote was involved in casting, editing, and rehearsals. He tried to be on the set as much as possible, although he was working on the film *Valentine's Day* at the same time. In casting, for example, in addition to suggesting Geraldine Page for Mrs. Watts, Foote also suggested Carlin Glynn, Masterson's wife, for the role of Jessie Mae. According to Foote, he and Masterson were able to agree on casting because they have a similar theatrical background:

Pete's been trained as an actor and was a wonderful actor and likes the kind of acting I like, and we both know people we admire. . . . We were asked to think about Rebecca [DeMornay]. Neither of us knew her work and she flew in and met with Pete. . . . And Pete seemed to like her and so it was fine with me. And the sheriff [Richard Bradford], we both had known, and Pete suggested him and I was delighted. We had some search for Ludie, and I forget who suggested John [Heard], but whoever it was, we are very grateful because he worked out just wonderfully for us.[5]

Masterson and Foote also worked together on selecting the film sites. Location shooting took place in Texas. Of the *Bountiful* house, situated just outside the small north Texas town of Waxahachie, Foote has said, "The house was just there. There wasn't much we had to do to it. We didn't have to distress it at all. It was pretty well run-down."[6]

Masterson chose the set designer, film editor, and costume designer. After consulting with Foote, who was an admirer of Fred Murphy's work, Masterson chose Murphy as director of photography.

When the film was being shaped into its final form, Foote visited weekly with Masterson and viewed the rough cuts in the editing room:

We'd talk about it. I'd give my ideas. It was a very sharing time. [Pete] is very thorough and thinks out quite logically what he wants to do. Usually people I work with are people I've worked with before, I know about, or we share an aesthetic in common. . . . This was a very constructive time on the whole for everybody. We had disagreements, minor ones. They cropped up from time to time, but they were quickly resolved.[7]

After production was finished in 1985, the next step was distribution by Island Pictures, a leader in specialized films that open in a limited number of cities, appear on fewer than twelve hundred screens simultaneously, and depend on good critical reviews for survival.[8]

The film was released to nearly universal accolades. Rex Reed of the *New York Post* raved, "One of those rarefied, indelible films about the human heart we never seem to get on the screen these days, *The Trip to Bountiful* is a moving, unforgettable experience."[9] In the *New York Times*, Vincent Canby praised both the film and its star: "As Mrs. Watts, Geraldine Page has never been in better form, nor in more firm control of the complex, delicate mechanism that makes her one of our finest actresses. . . . *The Trip to Bountiful* works perfectly as a small, richly detailed film."[10] A handful of critics, like David Denby of *New York* magazine, echoed the concern of some theater critics three decades earlier about its sentimentality and treatment of relatively trivial events in the lives of ordinary people.[11] They were a small minority, however, and *Bountiful* went on to earn an Academy Award for best actress for Geraldine Page and a nomination for best screenplay for Foote.

For a small independent film, *Bountiful* had "an unusually successful theatrical distribution," coproducer Sterling Van-Wagenen noted. "By the time the film finished its theatrical run, there were 250 prints out in theaters across the country. Major, big budget films, those in the thirty to forty million dollar range, will maybe play in two thousand theaters." According to VanWagenen *The Trip to Bountiful* was one of two independent films (the other was *The Kiss of the Spiderwoman*) to make money within the first year of its release. "*Bountiful* is still making money," he said.[12] When *Bountiful* appeared on videocassette, a new audience joined Mrs. Watts on her journey homeward.

Notes

1. Horton Foote, personal interview with Barbara Moore, New York City, July 1987.
2. Gary Edgerton, "A Visit to the Imaginary Landscape of Harrison, Texas: Sketching the Film Career of Horton Foote," *Literature/Film Quarterly* 17 (Winter 1989): 7.
3. Horton Foote, "Writing for Film," in *Film and Literature: A Comparative Approach to Adaptation,* ed. Wendell Aycock and Michael Schoenecke (Lubbock: Texas Tech University Press, 1988), 9.
4. Foote interview.
5. Foote interview.
6. Foote interview.
7. Foote interview.

8. Beverly Walker and Leonard Klady, "Cinema Sanctuaries," *Film Comment* 22 (1986): 61–64.

9. Rex Reed, *New York Post,* Dec. 20, 1985.

10. Vincent Canby, *New York Times,* Dec. 20, 1985.

11. David Denby, *New York,* Apr. 7, 1985, 65.

12. Sterling VanWagenen, telephone interview with Barbara Moore, October 1987.

The Trip to Bountiful

A Filmdallas I and Bountiful Film Partners Production
Distributed by Island Pictures

Producer: Sterling VanWagenen
Director: Peter Masterson
Director of Photography: Fred Murphy
Music: J. A. C. Redford
Art Director: Philip Lamb
Film Editor: Jay Freund
Costumes: Gary Jones

Cast

MRS. CARRIE WATTS: Geraldine Page
LUDIE WATTS: John Heard
JESSIE MAE WATTS: Carlin Glynn
SHERIFF: Richard Bradford
THELMA: Rebecca DeMornay
ROY (*Harrison Ticket Man*): Kevin Cooney
ROSELLA: Mary Kay Mars
TICKET MAN #1: Norman Bennett
TICKET MAN #2: Harvey Lewis
TICKET AGENT (*Houston Train Station*): Kirk Sisco
BILLY DAVIS: Dave Tanner
BUS ATTENDANT, GERARD: Gil Glasgow
BUS OPERATOR: Jerry Nelson
BLACK WOMAN ON BUS: Wezz Tildon
DOWNSTAIRS NEIGHBOR: Peggy Ann Byers
MEXICAN MAN: David Romo

The script printed here is a scene-by-scene
transcription of the feature film.

EXTERIOR: Field of bluebonnets.
As credits roll, a little boy runs through the bluebonnets in slow motion, followed by a young woman. In the background we hear a woman's voice singing the hymn "Softly and Tenderly."

> Softly and tenderly Jesus is calling,
> Calling for you and for me;
> See, on the portals he's waiting and watching,
> Watching for you and for me.
> Come home, come home,
> Ye who are weary, come home;
> Earnestly, tenderly, Jesus is calling,
> Calling, O sinner, come home.

INTERIOR: Living room of the Watts's small Houston apartment.
MRS. CARRIE WATTS *is seated in a rocking chair looking out the window, rocking back and forth, and humming quietly to herself the hymn that has just been heard.*

INTERIOR: Apartment bedroom.
LUDIE WATTS *and his wife,* JESSIE MAE, *are in single beds.* JESSIE MAE *is sound asleep, but* LUDIE *is awake and after a moment gets quietly out of bed.*

INTERIOR: Living room.
MRS. WATTS *continues rocking and humming the hymn.* LUDIE *comes into the room.*

MRS. WATTS: Don't try to be quiet, Sonny. I'm awake.
LUDIE: Yes, Ma'am.
MRS. WATTS: Couldn't you sleep?
LUDIE: No, Ma'am.
MRS. WATTS: Why couldn't you sleep?
LUDIE: I just couldn't. Couldn't you sleep?
MRS. WATTS: No. I haven't been to bed at all. You're not worrying about your job, are you, Sonny?

LUDIE: No, Ma'am. Everybody seems to like me there. I'm thinking about asking for a raise.

MRS. WATTS: Oh, you should, hard as you work.

(LUDIE *sits down.*)

LUDIE: Why couldn't you sleep, Mama?

MRS. WATTS: Because there's a full moon. I never could sleep when there was a full moon. Even back in Bountiful when I worked out in the fields all day, and I got so tired I thought my legs would just give out on me, you let there be a full moon and I'd just toss the night away. *(She gets up and looks out the window.)* I remember once when you were little and there was a full moon, I woke you up and dressed you and took you for a walk with me. Do you remember that?

LUDIE: No, Ma'am.

MRS. WATTS: You don't?

LUDIE: No, Ma'am.

MRS. WATTS: Well, I remember that just like it was yesterday. I dressed you and took you outside and there was an old dog howling away someplace and that scared you, and I held you and you just tremblin' with fear, and you said someone told you that when a dog howled a person was dying somewhere. I held you close to me. And then you asked me to explain to you about dying, and I said, you too young to worry about things like that for a long time to come.

LUDIE: Funny the things you think of when you can't sleep. I was trying to think of that song I used to like to hear you sing.

MRS. WATTS: Oh, what was that, Sonny?

LUDIE: I don't remember the name. I just remember I . . . I'd always laugh when you'd sing it.

MRS. WATTS: *(Laughs.)* That old song.

INTERIOR: Bedroom.

JESSIE MAE *stirs in her sleep.*

MRS. WATTS: *(Off camera.)* How'd that go?

INTERIOR: Living room.

MRS. WATTS: I hate it when I can't think of things. *(A pause. She thinks. She begins to half-sing it.)*

Hush, little baby, don't say a word,
Mama's gonna buy you a mockingbird.
And if that mockingbird don't sing,
Mama's gonna buy you a diamond ring.

(She sits on the sofa beside LUDIE.*)* I used to think I was gonna buy you the world back in those days. I remember remarking that to my papa. He said the world can't be bought. I didn't rightly understand what he meant by that then. *(*LUDIE *looks at her. She suddenly turns to him.)* Oh, Ludie . . . Nothing. Would you like me to get you some hot milk?

LUDIE: Yes, Ma'am. If you don't mind.

*(*MRS. WATTS *kisses* LUDIE *on the cheek and goes to the kitchen.* JESSIE MAE *enters the living room, walks over behind the sofa where* LUDIE *is sitting, and turns on the lights.)*

JESSIE MAE: How do you expect to work tomorrow if you don't get your sleep, Ludie?

INTERIOR: Kitchen.

MRS. WATTS *prepares milk.*

INTERIOR: Living room.

JESSIE MAE *goes over to a small radio on a drop-leaf table and turns it on. She picks up a movie magazine from the desk and sits in a chair by the radio.* MRS. WATTS *comes in with the milk and hands it to* LUDIE.

JESSIE MAE: Mother Watts, what did you do with that recipe that Rosella gave me on the phone today?

MRS. WATTS: Jessie Mae, I don't remember you having given me any recipe.

JESSIE MAE: Well, I did. This morning right here in this very room, and I asked you to please put it on my dresser, and you said "I will" and went out holding it in your hand.

MRS. WATTS: Did you look on your dresser?

JESSIE MAE: Yes, Ma'am.

MRS. WATTS: And it wasn't there?

JESSIE MAE: No, Ma'am. I looked just before I went to bed.

*(*MRS. WATTS *turns back toward the kitchen.)*

INTERIOR: Kitchen.
MRS. WATTS *searches noisily.*

INTERIOR: Living room.

JESSIE MAE: I know we couldn't afford it before, so I kept quiet about it. But now that you're working again, I don't think that a picture show once or twice a week would break us.

LUDIE: Okay. Why don't we go out one night this week?

JESSIE MAE: Well, I mean, I think we have to. I was talking to Rosella about it this morning on the phone.

LUDIE: When did you and Rosella get friendly again?

JESSIE MAE: This morning. She just all of a sudden called me up on the telephone. She said she would quit being mad if I would. I said shucks, I wasn't mad. She was the one that was mad. I told her I was plainspoken and said exactly what I felt and people have to take me as I am or just leave me alone. *(A pause.)* Rosella found out definitely she can't have any children . . .

(MRS. WATTS comes back into the living room.)

JESSIE MAE: Walk, don't run.

(MRS. WATTS moves around the living room looking for the recipe.)

JESSIE MAE: Your mother's pension check didn't come today. It's the eighteenth. I swear it's due. I just don't understand the government. Always late.

(MRS. WATTS goes out of the room. JESSIE MAE gets up and goes over to LUDIE.)

JESSIE MAE: Rosella was glad to hear you're working again.

INTERIOR: Bedroom.
MRS. WATTS *searches for the recipe in the drawers of the dressing table.*

JESSIE MAE: *(Off camera.)* She said she was cleaning some drawers night before last and had come across some pictures of you and me she'd taken when we started going together. I said I don't care to see them.

INTERIOR: Living room.

JESSIE MAE: No, thank you. The passing of time makes me sad.

(MRS. WATTS *comes into the living room holding the recipe.*)

MRS. WATTS: Jessie Mae, here's your recipe.

JESSIE MAE: Oh, thank you. Where did you find it?

MRS. WATTS: In your room.

JESSIE MAE: In my room?

MRS. WATTS: Yes, Ma'am. *(She hands* JESSIE MAE *the recipe.)*

JESSIE MAE: Where in my room?

MRS. WATTS: In your dresser drawer. Right-hand side.

JESSIE MAE: In my dresser drawer?

MRS. WATTS: Yes, Ma'am. I looked on top of the dresser and it wasn't there, and then something just told me . . .

JESSIE MAE: Mother Watts!

MRS. WATTS: Ma'am?

JESSIE MAE: Ludie, how many times have I asked her never to look into my dresser drawers?

MRS. WATTS: I thought you wanted me to find your recipe?

JESSIE MAE: I do not want you to go into my dresser drawers. I'd like a little privacy, if you don't mind.

MRS. WATTS: Yes, Ma'am.

JESSIE MAE: And don't you ever let me catch you looking in them again. For anything. I can't stand people snooping in my dresser drawers.

MRS. WATTS: All right. Next time you just find it yourself.

(MRS. WATTS *grabs the paper from* JESSIE MAE *and throws it on the floor.*)

JESSIE MAE: You pick that recipe up, if you please.

MRS. WATTS: Pick it up yourself. I have no intention of picking that up.

JESSIE MAE: *(Shouting.)* You pick that up!

MRS. WATTS: *(Shouting back.)* I won't!

LUDIE: Mama.

JESSIE MAE: *(Shouting even louder.)* You will!

LUDIE: Jessie Mae. For God sakes! You're both acting like children. It's one-thirty in the morning.

JESSIE MAE: You make her pick that up.

MRS. WATTS: I won't, I won't!

JESSIE MAE: *(Screaming.)* You will! This is my house and you'll do exactly as you're told.

(LUDIE *walks out of the room.*)

JESSIE MAE: Now. I hope you're satisfied. You have got Ludie good and upset. He won't sleep for the rest of the night. *(While she is talking,* MALE VOICE *is heard, off camera, shouting, "Shut up up there.")* What are you trying to do? Get him sick again?

MALE VOICE: *(Off camera.)* Shut that goddamned radio off!

JESSIE MAE: *(Screaming back.)* You shut up. *(To* MRS. WATTS.*)* You're going too far with me one of these days, old lady.

LUDIE: *(Off camera.)* Jessie Mae.

(JESSIE MAE *walks into the bedroom.*)

JESSIE MAE: I can't stand it, Ludie. I'm at the end of my rope. I will not take being insulted by your mama or anyone else. You hear that?

(MRS. WATTS *is on the sofa, crying.* LUDIE *enters.* MRS. WATTS *gets up and goes to pick up the recipe.* LUDIE *sees what she is doing and tries to get there first. He is not able to. She hands the recipe to him. He stands there for a moment looking at it. He turns to his mother.*)

LUDIE: Mama. Will you give this recipe to Jessie Mae?

MRS. WATTS: All right, Son. *(She takes the recipe. She starts out of the living room toward the bedroom.*)

LUDIE: Mama, will you please tell Jessie Mae that you're sorry?

MRS. WATTS: Oh, Ludie . . .

LUDIE: Please, Mama.

MRS. WATTS: All right, Son. *(She goes into the bedroom. Through the bedroom door* JESSIE MAE *is seen sitting at the vanity.*)

LUDIE: *(Calling.)* Jessie Mae.

JESSIE MAE: What do you want, Ludie?

LUDIE: Mama has something to say to you.

(MRS. WATTS *turns and looks at* LUDIE, *then walks over to* JESSIE MAE.*)

JESSIE MAE: What is it?

MRS. WATTS: Jessie Mae, I am sorry for throwing the recipe on the floor. *(She hands her the recipe.*)

JESSIE MAE: I accept your apology.

(*As* MRS. WATTS *goes out,* JESSIE MAE *crumples up the recipe and throws it away.*)

INTERIOR: Bedroom.

JESSIE MAE *is still at dressing table.* LUDIE *enters.*

LUDIE: Jessie Mae. I know it's hard and all, but for your own sake, I sometimes think if you could ignore certain things . . .

JESSIE MAE: Ignore? Well, how can you ignore something when it is done right under your very nose?

LUDIE: Jessie Mae, nobody . . .

JESSIE MAE: I know her Ludie.

INTERIOR: Living room.
MRS. WATTS *listens as she turns out the lights.*

JESSIE MAE: *(Off camera.)* She does things just to aggravate me. Now, you take her hymn singing. She never starts until I come into a room. And her pouting!

INTERIOR: Bedroom.

JESSIE MAE: Why, sometimes she goes a whole day just sitting there and staring out the window. How would you like to spend twenty-four hours a day shut up with a woman who either sang hymns or looked out the window and pouted?

LUDIE: I'm not saying it's easy, Jessie Mae. I'm only saying . . .

JESSIE MAE: She just keeps me so nervous never knowing when I leave whether she is going to run off to that old town or not.

INTERIOR: Living room.

LUDIE: *(Off camera.)* Well, she's not going to run off again, Jessie Mae. She promised she wouldn't.
(MRS. WATTS *goes to the edge of the rug, lifts it up, and takes the pension check.)*

JESSIE MAE: *(Off camera.)* Sometimes I think she hides that check and I tell you right now, if it is not here tomorrow I am going to search this house from top to bottom.

INTERIOR: Bedroom.
LUDIE *sits down on the bed.*

JESSIE MAE: Rosella asked me if I realized it would be fifteen years this August since we were married.

INTERIOR: Living room.
MRS. WATTS *walks over to the closed bedroom doors.*

JESSIE MAE: *(Off camera.)* I never will forget the night I came home and told Rosella you had proposed.

INTERIOR: Bedroom.

JESSIE MAE: I thought you were the handsomest man alive.
LUDIE: And I thought you were the prettiest girl.
JESSIE MAE: Did you, Ludie?
    (A pause. LUDIE sighs.)
LUDIE: Jessie Mae, I've got to start making some more money. I'm thinking about asking for a raise.

INTERIOR: Living room.
MRS. WATTS *turns away from the doors and hides the check in her gown.*

LUDIE: *(Off camera.)* I'm entitled to it. I've been there six months now. I haven't been late or sick once. I am walking into Mr. Douglas's office the first thing in the morning and I'm saying . . .

INTERIOR: Bedroom.

LUDIE: . . . Mr. Douglas, I have got to have a raise starting as of right now. We can't live on what you pay us.
JESSIE MAE: Well! I would.
LUDIE: I don't understand it, Jessie Mae. I try not to be bitter. I try not to . . . I don't know.

INTERIOR: Living room.
MRS. WATTS *sits in her rocking chair.*

LUDIE: *(Off camera.)* All I know is that a man works for a company for eight years . . .

INTERIOR: Bedroom.
JESSIE MAE *takes off her robe.*

LUDIE: He saves a little money. He gets sick and he has to spend two years in bed watching his savings all go, and then start all over with a new company. Of course, the doctor says not to worry about it. He says you have to take things like they come. And that's what I do, every day.

(JESSIE MAE *gets up from the vanity.* LUDIE *is sitting on his bed thumbing through his book.* JESSIE MAE *sits on her bed, facing him, and looks at his book.*)

JESSIE MAE: What's this book?

LUDIE: It's mine. I bought it at the drugstore coming from the office.

JESSIE MAE: "How to Become an Executive"? (*She lies back on the bed and pulls up the covers.*)

LUDIE: My boss likes me. Billy Davis told me he did. He was positive he did. Today he told me. Billy Davis has been there ten years now, you know. (*A pause.*) You getting sleepy now?

JESSIE MAE: Yes. Are you?

LUDIE: Yes, I am. Good night. (*He kisses her.*)

JESSIE MAE: Good night.

(LUDIE *goes over to the doors to the living room.*)

INTERIOR: Living room.

MRS. WATTS *is sitting in the rocking chair.* LUDIE *enters. He turns off the radio.*

LUDIE: Mama.

MRS. WATTS: I'm all right, Sonny. I'm just still not sleepy.

LUDIE: Good night. (*He kisses her. As he turns away,* MRS. WATTS *grabs the lapels of his robe and pulls him back.*)

MRS. WATTS: (*Tearfully.*) Oh Ludie, please, Son, I want to go home.

LUDIE: Mama, you know I can't make a living there. We have to live in Houston.

MRS. WATTS: Son, Ludie, I cannot stay here any longer. I want to go home!

LUDIE: I beg you not to ask me this again. There is nothing I can do about it.

(MRS. WATTS, *hurt and angry, turns away and looks out the window.* LUDIE *goes out.*)

EXTERIOR: Outside the apartment.
The next morning. A woman walks a dog. A man puts trash on top of a pile by the street. Early morning traffic has begun.

INTERIOR: Living room.
MRS. WATTS is asleep in her rocking chair. She awakens with a start. She is still holding the check in her hand. She hides it under the cushion of the sofa. She turns toward the kitchen and sees the clock.

MRS. WATTS: Oh! Ludie! It's eight-fifteen!

INTERIOR: Bathroom.
LUDIE is shaving.

INTERIOR: Kitchen.
MRS. WATTS prepares breakfast and sings.

INTERIOR: Bedroom.
JESSIE MAE has gotten out of bed and is at the vanity.

JESSIE MAE: *(Calling.)* It's too early for hymn singing.

INTERIOR: Kitchen.
MRS. WATTS stops singing.

INTERIOR: Living room.
JESSIE MAE comes in from the bedroom. MRS. WATTS comes in from the kitchen.

JESSIE MAE: Walk. Don't run.

INTERIOR: Bedroom.
LUDIE finishes dressing.

INTERIOR: Kitchen.
MRS. WATTS works on breakfast.

INTERIOR: Living room.
LUDIE enters and goes to dining area where JESSIE MAE is drinking coffee.

LUDIE: Good morning, Mama.

MRS. WATTS: Morning, Son. I'll have your toast ready for you in a minute.

LUDIE: Why don't we have an early supper tonight? Six-thirty if that's all right with you and Mama. And after supper I'll take you both to the picture show.

JESSIE MAE: Oh. Do you want to go downtown or to one of the neighborhood movies?

LUDIE: Whatever you want to do, Jessie Mae.

JESSIE MAE: Maybe it would do us good to go downtown.

(She gets up. MRS. WATTS *brings* LUDIE *his toast and kisses him.)*

LUDIE: *(Half to himself.)* Billy's picking me up. I want to get in early. Mr. Douglas is usually in before nine. I think I'm doing the right thing, asking for a raise. Don't you?

JESSIE MAE: Sure.

*(*LUDIE *eats breakfast.* JESSIE MAE *goes to the phone on the desk.)*

JESSIE MAE: Oh, Rita. This is Jessie Mae Watts. Can I have an appointment for my hair? *(A pause; she laughs.)* Two o'clock.

INTERIOR: Bedroom.

MRS. WATTS *is making the beds, listening to the conversation.*

JESSIE MAE: *(Off camera.)* Nothing earlier? See you then. Bye.

(A car horn honks outside. Through the bedroom door we see LUDIE *kiss* JESSIE MAE *on the cheek.)*

LUDIE: *(Calling.)* Good-bye, Mama.

MRS. WATTS: Bye, Son.

INTERIOR: Living room.

LUDIE *puts on his hat as he goes out the door.*

JESSIE MAE: Holler if there's any mail down there.

LUDIE: *(Calling back.)* I will.

EXTERIOR: Apartment house.

LUDIE: No mail for us.

JESSIE MAE: *(Off camera.)* All right.

EXTERIOR: Upstairs porch.
JESSIE MAE *sees him off.*

INTERIOR: Living room.
JESSIE MAE *enters.*

JESSIE MAE: *(Calling.)* I can't understand about that pension check, can you?

INTERIOR: Bedroom.

MRS. WATTS: No, Ma'am.
JESSIE MAE: *(Off camera.)* You know, you are so absent-minded, you don't think that you put it around the room someplace, by mistake.
MRS. WATTS: I don't believe so.

INTERIOR: Living room.
JESSIE MAE *searches* MRS. WATTS*'s purse.*

INTERIOR: Bedroom.
JESSIE MAE *enters, takes dresses out of her closet, and tries to decide what to wear.* MRS. WATTS *passes her on the way to the living room.* JESSIE MAE *goes into the bathroom and shuts the door.*

INTERIOR: Living room.
MRS. WATTS *goes to the sofa and looks at the hidden check.*

INTERIOR: Billy Davis's car.
BILLY DAVIS *is driving.* LUDIE *is a passenger.*

BILLY DAVIS: Bus wasn't fast enough for you this morning, huh, Ludie?
LUDIE: No. I was hoping to get a chance to speak to the boss before we started our work this morning. How is everything with your family?
BILLY DAVIS: Oh, fine. The kids were full of life this morning, as usual. I said to Myrtle Sue, "My Lord have mercy, we have a lot of live-wires around here, don't we?" How is your wife?

LUDIE: She's fine.

BILLY DAVIS: Your mother lives with you, too, doesn't she?

LUDIE: She sure does.

INTERIOR: Living room.

MRS. WATTS *is folding sheets.* JESSIE MAE *enters.*

JESSIE MAE: I'm going to call Rosella and tell her to meet me at the drugstore for a Coke.

(JESSIE MAE *puts on perfume.* MRS. WATTS *is singing quietly to herself as she finishes making up her bed.*)

JESSIE MAE: Would you stop that hymn singing? Do you want me to jump right out of my skin? You know what hymns do to my nerves.

(MRS. WATTS *stops her singing.* JESSIE MAE *dials the phone number.*)

JESSIE MAE: Oh. And don't pout. You know I can't stand pouting.

MRS. WATTS: I didn't mean to pout, Jessie Mae. I just meant to be silent.

JESSIE MAE: *(Hangs up phone.)* She's not home. I bet she's at the drugstore right now. *(She begins to put her hat on.)* I can't make up my mind what movie I want to see tonight. Well, I'll ask Rosella.

(MRS. WATTS *turns on the vacuum cleaner.*)

JESSIE MAE: Would you stop that noise for a minute! I'm nervous.

(MRS. WATTS *stops vacuuming and gets a dust rag from the kitchen. She begins to dust the room.* JESSIE MAE *continues putting on her hat and arranging her dress in front of the mirror.*)

JESSIE MAE: You know, when I first came to Houston, I went to three picture shows in one day. I went to the Kirby in the morning, and the Metropolitan in the afternoon, and the Majestic that night.

(MRS. WATTS *has done her best to continue dusting the furniture, but she has been getting physically weaker. She sways, grabs hold of the sweeper trying to support herself, and gasps for breath.*)

JESSIE MAE: Mother Watts . . . Mother Watts . . .

(JESSIE MAE *runs to her.*)

MRS. WATTS: I'm all right . . .

JESSIE MAE: Is it your heart?

MRS. WATTS: No, no, no, no. It's just a little sinking spell. Just let me lie down on the sofa for a minute and I'll be all right.

(JESSE MAE *helps her over to the sofa.*)
JESSIE MAE: Can I get you some water?
MRS. WATTS: Oh, thank you.
(JESSIE MAE *runs into the kitchen for water.*)

INTERIOR: Kitchen.

JESSIE MAE: Do you want me to call a doctor?

INTERIOR: Living room.

MRS. WATTS: No, Ma'am.
JESSIE MAE: Do you want me to call Ludie?
MRS. WATTS: No, Ma'am.
(JESSIE MAE *comes back with a glass of water.* MRS. WATTS *drinks it.*)
JESSIE MAE: Are you feeling better now?
MRS. WATTS: Yes, I am, Jessie Mae. (*She gets up off the sofa.*)
JESSIE MAE: Do you think you ought to get up so soon?
MRS. WATTS: Yes, Ma'am. I'm feeling better already. I think I'll just sit here in this chair.
(MRS. WATTS *sits in an overstuffed chair.* JESSIE MAE *sits in another chair nearby.*)
JESSIE MAE: All right. I'll just sit here for a while and keep you company. (*A pause.*) It always scares the daylights out of me when you get one of those sinking spells.

EXTERIOR: Parking lot.
BILLY DAVIS *and* LUDIE *get out of the car and cross the street.*

LUDIE: Well, what do you think of the Buffs' chances in the Dixie Series?
BILLY DAVIS: I think they've gotta take the Texas League first.
LUDIE: That's right.
BILLY DAVIS: Myrtle Sue and I are going out to Buff Stadium Friday night if you'd like to go.
LUDIE: That's nice.
BILLY DAVIS: You can bring your wife, and bring your mom if you want to.
LUDIE: Sounds like fun.

INTERIOR: Living room.

MRS. WATTS *is still resting.* JESSIE MAE *is smoking a cigarette. The phone rings and* JESSIE MAE *answers it.*

JESSIE MAE: Hello? Oh, hello, Rosella. I tried to call you earlier. Oh. You're at the drugstore. That's what I just figured. Well, I would like to, Rosella, but Mother Watts has had another sinking spell and . . .

MRS. WATTS: You go on, Jessie Mae. I'm going to be all right. I'll just rest here. There's nothing you can do for me.

JESSIE MAE: Are you sure?

MRS. WATTS: Yes, I'm sure, Jessie Mae.

JESSIE MAE: Well. All right then. Rosella, Mother Watts says she won't be needing me here. So I think I will come over for just a little while. All right. I'll see you then. Bye. *(She hangs up the phone.)* Now, are you sure you're gonna be all right?

MRS. WATTS: Oh, yes, Jessie Mae.

JESSIE MAE: Well, I'll go on over then. Now, you call me over at the drugstore if you need me. You hear?

MRS. WATTS: Oh, yes, Ma'am.

*(*JESSIE MAE *leaves.)*

EXTERIOR: Apartment house.

MRS. WATTS *comes out on the porch and watches* JESSIE MAE *go down the street.* MRS. WATTS *goes back inside.*

INTERIOR: Living room.

MRS. WATTS *gets the check from under the sofa cushion and then gets a pen out of the desk. She goes to the table to endorse the check.* JESSIE MAE *comes back in.* MRS. WATTS *lays her handkerchief over the check.*

JESSIE MAE: I forgot to take any money.

*(*JESSIE MAE *is in such a hurry she pays no attention to* MRS. WATTS *and goes out to the bedroom.* MRS. WATTS *gets writing paper out of the desk, hides the check in her dress, and begins to write.* JESSIE MAE *comes back in.)*

JESSIE MAE: Who are you writing to?

MRS. WATTS: I just thought I'd drop a line to Callie Davis and let her know I'm still alive.

JESSIE MAE: Well, why did you decide to do that all of a sudden?

MRS. WATTS: No reason. The notion just struck me.

JESSIE MAE: All right. *(She starts out.)* But if you are trying to put something over on me with that pension check, I have told Mr. Reynolds at the grocery store never to cash anything for you. (JESSIE MAE *leaves.* MRS. WATTS *looks out the window and sees* JESSIE MAE *walking down the street. She takes some clothes from the dresser and wardrobe and puts them in a suitcase. She looks at some family pictures on top of the dresser and puts some of them in the suitcase. She takes her hat and coat, picks up the suitcase, and goes hurrying out.)*

EXTERIOR: Apartment stairs.

MRS. WATTS *hurries down the stairs.*

EXTERIOR: Apartment house.

MRS. WATTS *comes out the door leading to her apartment as her downstairs neighbor comes out of her front door.*

NEIGHBOR: Morning, Mrs. Watts.

MRS. WATTS: Oh! Good morning.

NEIGHBOR: How are you doing?

MRS. WATTS: Just fine.

EXTERIOR: Street.

MRS. WATTS *walks along the street past the grocery store.*

EXTERIOR: Drugstore.

JESSIE MAE *enters the drugstore.*

EXTERIOR: Street.

MRS. WATTS *walks down the street to the bus stop. It is a street of old mansions.*

INTERIOR: Drugstore.

JESSIE MAE *and* ROSELLA *finish their drinks.* JESSIE MAE *looks up at the clock.*

JESSIE MAE: Oh, child, look at that clock. It's ten-fifteen. Maybe I'd better get back up to Mother Watts. She wasn't feeling so well this morning.

EXTERIOR: Bus stop.
MRS. WATTS *gets on a bus.*

INTERIOR: Dress shop.
JESSIE MAE *and* ROSELLA *are looking at dresses.*

INTERIOR: Train station.
MRS. WATTS *enters. She crosses the waiting room and goes up to the* TICKET AGENT.

MRS. WATTS: Ticket to Bountiful, please?
TICKET AGENT: Where?
MRS. WATTS: Bountiful. It's between Harrison and Cotton.
TICKET AGENT: Oh, no trains go there anymore.
MRS. WATTS: Are you sure?
TICKET AGENT: Yes, I'm sure.
MRS. WATTS: Well, there used to be excursions between Bountiful and Houston, you know. I remember . . . because I had . . . well, I was . . .
TICKET AGENT: No trains go there now.

EXTERIOR: City street.
MRS. WATTS *walks down the street.*

INTERIOR: Bus station.
MRS. WATTS *enters. Over the loudspeaker we hear destinations being called: "Bus now boarding for Shinango, Argola, Rosharon, Angleton, Clute, and Velasco."* MRS. WATTS *gets in line for a ticket.* THELMA *is in the line in front of her.*

INTERIOR: Living room.
JESSIE MAE *comes in.*

JESSIE MAE: Mother Watts, I'm home.
(When there is no answer, she goes through the apartment calling: "Mother Watts.")

INTERIOR: Bus station.

TICKET MAN: *(Calling.)* Lady.

(MRS. WATTS *is absorbed in watching the doors and doesn't hear him.)*

TICKET MAN: Lady. It's your turn.

(MRS. WATTS *turns and sees she is next in line. She moves up to the counter.)*

MRS. WATTS: Oh, yes. Excuse me. I would like a ticket to Bountiful, please.

TICKET MAN: Where?

MRS. WATTS: To Bountiful.

TICKET MAN: What's it near?

MRS. WATTS: It's between Harrison and Cotton.

(He takes a book from behind the window on a shelf. He looks inside it. MRS. WATTS *is again watching the doors. He looks up.)*

TICKET MAN: Lady.

MRS. WATTS: Oh. Yessir.

TICKET MAN: I can sell you a ticket to Harrison or to Cotton. But there's no Bountiful.

MRS. WATTS: Oh, yes there is, it's between Harrison and Cotton.

TICKET MAN: I'm sorry, lady. You say there is, but the book says there isn't. And the book don't lie.

MRS. WATTS: But . . . I . . .

TICKET MAN: *(Impatiently.)* Make up your mind, lady. Cotton or Harrison. There are other people waiting.

MRS. WATTS: Well . . . let me see . . . How much is a ticket to Harrison?

TICKET MAN: Three-fifty.

MRS. WATTS: Cotton?

TICKET MAN: Four-twenty.

MRS. WATTS: Oh, yes. Well, give me the ticket to Harrison, please.

TICKET MAN: All right. That'll be three-fifty, please.

MRS. WATTS: Yessir. *(She reaches for her pocketbook and is about to open it. She turns to the* TICKET MAN.) Oh, could you cash a pension check? You see, I decided to come at the last minute and I didn't have time to go by the grocery store.

TICKET MAN: I can't cash any checks.

MRS. WATTS: It's perfectly good. It is a government check!

TICKET MAN: I'm sorry. It's against the rules to cash checks.

MRS. WATTS: Oh, is that so? Well, I can understand that. A rule is a rule. How much was that again?

TICKET MAN: Three-fifty.

MRS. WATTS: Oh. Hmmm. Three-fifty. *(She puts her coin purse back in her purse and takes a handkerchief, which has money tied up in it, out of her pocket.)* Just a minute. It's all in here, in nickels and dimes and quarters. *(She unties the handkerchief, places it on the counter, and begins to count out the amount for the ticket. She shoves a pile of silver toward the* TICKET MAN.*)*

MRS. WATTS: There. Now. I believe that is three-fifty.

TICKET MAN: Thank you. *(He rakes the money into his hand.* MRS. WATTS *ties her handkerchief back up.)*

MRS. WATTS: That's quite all right. I'm sorry to have taken up so much of your time. *(She picks up her suitcase and starts off.)*

TICKET MAN: Here, lady. Don't forget your ticket.

(She comes running back.)

MRS. WATTS: Oh, good heavens. I'd forget my head if it wasn't on my neck.

*(*MRS. WATTS *takes the ticket and goes to a bench where* THELMA *is seated, reading. There is an empty space behind her.* MRS. WATTS *sits with her back to* THELMA, *looks around, and* THELMA *sees her.)*

THELMA: Good afternoon.

MRS. WATTS: Good afternoon. *(She picks up the suitcase and puts it down along the side of the bench where* THELMA *is sitting.)*

MRS. WATTS: Honey, would you watch this suitcase? I'll be right back.

THELMA: Yes, Ma'am.

*(*MRS. WATTS *goes running toward the door to the street.* THELMA *watches her for a minute and then goes back to reading her magazine.* MRS. WATTS *comes back to the bench.)*

MRS. WATTS: Is this seat taken?

THELMA: No, Ma'am.

*(*MRS. WATTS *sits down.)*

MRS. WATTS: Warm, isn't it, when you're running around?

THELMA: Yes'm.

MRS. WATTS: I had to get myself ready in the biggest kind of a hurry, and I'm trying to get to a town nobody here has heard of.

THELMA: What town is that?

MRS. WATTS: Bountiful.

THELMA: Oh.

MRS. WATTS: Did you ever hear of it?

THELMA: No.

MRS. WATTS: That's what I mean. Nobody's heard of it. Not much
of a town left, I guess. I haven't seen it myself in almost twenty
years. It used to be quite prosperous. But all they had left was a
post office and a filling station and a general store, at least
when I left it.

THELMA: Do your people live there?

MRS. WATTS: No, my people are all dead. Except for my son and his
wife, Jessie Mae. They live here in the city. *(A pause.)* You know,
I'm hurrying to go to see Bountiful before I die. Do you know,
I had a sinking spell this morning. I had to get down on the
bed and rest. It was my heart.

THELMA: Do you have a bad heart?

MRS. WATTS: Well, it's not what you call a good one. *(Laughs.)* Doctor says it'll last me as long as I need it if I could just cut out
worrying. But I can't seem to do that . . . lately.

*(MRS. WATTS looks around the bus station again. She gets up out of her
seat. She moves her coat over onto the suitcase, and we see her handkerchief lying on the seat.)*

MRS. WATTS: Would you keep your eye on that suitcase again?

THELMA: Of course.

(MRS. WATTS hurries over to the window and peers out at the street.)

THELMA: Lady? Is there something wrong?

MRS. WATTS: Oh, no, honey. I'm just a little nervous. That's all.

*(The city bus stops outside the window behind MRS. WATTS. LUDIE and
JESSIE MAE get off the bus and start for the station. MRS. WATTS turns
and sees them just outside the window. She runs over to the seat and
picks up the suitcase, leaving her handkerchief on the seat.)*

MRS. WATTS: Say a prayer for me, honey. Good luck.

THELMA: Good luck to you.

*(MRS. WATTS goes running toward the cafe. LUDIE and JESSIE MAE
come into the waiting room.)*

JESSIE MAE: Ludie, she always tries to go by train. But no. We wait
at one railroad station for five minutes and because she isn't
there right then, you drag me on over here. We've always found
her there.

(LUDIE goes over to the schedule board.)

JESSIE MAE: Why, she won't believe them at the depot when they
tell her there is not a train to Bountiful. She says there is and

you watch, as far as she's concerned that is how it'll have to be.
(LUDIE *goes into the cafe.* JESSIE MAE *follows.*)

INTERIOR: Bus station cafe.

JESSIE MAE: I think we ought to just turn this whole thing over to
the police. That would scare her once and for all.
LUDIE: We are not going to call any police.

INTERIOR: Bus station.
LUDIE *goes up to the* TICKET MAN.

LUDIE: Excuse me. Did a lady come here and buy a ticket to a
town named Bountiful?
(We see he is a different ticket man.)
SECOND TICKET MAN: Not since I've been on duty.
LUDIE: Well, how long have you been on duty?
SECOND TICKET MAN: About fifteen minutes.
*(*JESSIE MAE *goes over to where* THELMA *is sitting.)*
JESSIE MAE: *(To* THELMA.*)* Oh! Excuse me. Do you have a match?
My lighter's out of fluid.
*(*THELMA *reaches in her purse. She finds matches and gives them to her.)*
JESSIE MAE: Thank you. *(She sits down next to* THELMA *and lights her
cigarette.)* I hope you're lucky enough not to have to fool around
with any in-laws. I've got a mother-in-law about to drive me
crazy. She's always trying to run off to this place called Bountiful. Of course, there has not been a train to that old town in I
don't know when. But you try and tell her that and she just
looks at you like you're making it up. *(While* JESSIE MAE *is talking
we see a shot of* LUDIE *at the magazine stand.)* But I was too trusting
today. I gave her every chance in the world to get away. People
ask me why I don't have any children. I say I've got Ludie and
Mother Watts. That's all the children I need.
*(*LUDIE *comes up to* JESSIE MAE.*)*
JESSIE MAE: What did you bring me? *(He shows her a magazine.)* I've
seen that one.
*(*LUDIE *offers her a piece of candy. She takes it. He sits beside her.)*
JESSIE MAE: I think we are wasting our time sitting here.
LUDIE: Do you want to go to the other train station?
*(*THELMA *is watching them.)*

JESSIE MAE: I don't care what you do. It is your mother. *(JESSIE MAE walks away.* LUDIE *looks over at* THELMA.*)*

LUDIE: Would you like this? *(He offers her the magazine.)* I never read them and my wife has already seen it.

THELMA: Thank you.

*(*LUDIE *looks on the bench and sees the handkerchief left by* MRS. WATTS *earlier. He picks it up and goes over to the magazine stand.)*

LUDIE: By any chance did you see a woman about . . .

(He sees THELMA *leaving. He goes to her.)*

LUDIE: Excuse me, Miss. Oh, Miss, Miss. I just found this handkerchief there, and it belongs, I think, to my mother. She has a serious heart condition and it might be real serious for her to be left alone. I don't think she has any money, and I'd like to find her. Do you remember having seen her? She'd be on her way to a town called Bountiful.

THELMA: Yes, I did see her. She was here talking to me. She left all of a sudden.

LUDIE: Oh. *(A pause.)* Thank you so much.

*(*JESSIE MAE *comes back in as* THELMA *walks away.)*

JESSIE MAE: Ludie.

LUDIE: I was right. She was here. That lady there saw her. *(He points to* THELMA *at the magazine stand.)*

JESSIE MAE: Well, we're not going to wait.

LUDIE: That lady there was talking to her.

JESSIE MAE: We are not going to wait. I talked it all over with the police.

LUDIE: You didn't really call them!

JESSIE MAE: I did, and they said in their opinion she's just trying to get our attention this way and that we should just go home and pay her no mind at all. They say such things are very common among young people and old people and they're positive . . .

INTERIOR: Bus station cafe.

MRS. WATTS *looks out through the glass door of the cafe and sees* LUDIE *and* JESSIE MAE.

JESSIE MAE: *(Off camera.)* . . . that if we just go home and show her that we don't care if she goes or stays, she'll come home of her own free will.

INTERIOR. Bus station.

LUDIE: Jessie Mae . . .

JESSIE MAE: We are going to do what the police tell us to. Now, Ludie, I wish you'd think of me for a change. I am not gonna spend the rest of my life running after your mother.

LUDIE: All right, Jessie Mae. *(He stands there, thinking.)*

JESSIE MAE: Come on, let's go. *(She starts out, then turns back to him.)* Come on.

(LUDIE pauses for a moment, then follows JESSIE MAE.)

LUDIE: All right. But if Mama isn't home in an hour I'm going after her.

JESSIE MAE: All right.

INTERIOR: Bus station cafe.

MRS. WATTS *opens the door and comes out. Through the bus station window we see* LUDIE *and* JESSIE MAE *getting on a city bus.* MRS. WATTS *gets on a bus.* THELMA *is in the line behind her.* MRS. WATTS *sits down, and a man sits beside her.* THELMA *gets on the bus, and* MRS. WATTS *smiles at her as she passes by in the aisle.*

EXTERIOR: Bus.

MRS. WATTS *is looking out the window as the bus pulls out of the station. We see the streets of Houston from* MRS. WATTS'S *point of view. The bus goes through a tunnel. We see the outskirts of Houston, pasture land, and* MRS. WATTS *looking out the window of the bus.*

INTERIOR: Bus.

MRS. WATTS *closes her eyes.*

EXTERIOR: Bus.

The bus continues down the highway.

EXTERIOR: Bus station, Gerard.

It is night. The bus pulls up. THELMA *gets out.* MAN *helps her with luggage.*

STATION MASTER: Is this one yours? I'll get it.

(BLACK WOMAN walks over to STATION MASTER.)

BLACK WOMAN: How long a wait do we have?

STATION MASTER: I'd say about an hour.

BLACK WOMAN: Mercy.

STATION MASTER: Well, it can't be helped.

BLACK WOMAN: Oh, no, sir. I know . . . I know it can't be helped. Well, we have to take what comes.

(The bus pulls out. STATION MASTER *and* PASSENGERS *including* THELMA, MRS. WATTS, BLACK WOMAN, *and* MEXICAN MAN *sit in front of the station.* THELMA *enters the station.* MRS. WATTS *looks at* BLACK WOMAN.)

MRS. WATTS: Do you have far to go?

BLACK WOMAN: Right far, Corpus.

STATION MASTER: Do you know what Corpus Christi means in Spanish?

MRS. WATTS: Why no, I don't.

STATION MASTER: The body of Christ.

MRS. WATTS: Oh is that so. I'd never heard that. *(To* BLACK WOMAN.) Had you?

BLACK WOMAN: No, I sure hadn't. Body of Christ. Is that right?

*(*STATION MASTER *turns to* MEXICAN MAN.)

STATION MASTER: Isn't that right?

*(*MEXICAN MAN *answers in Spanish that he doesn't understand English.* STATION MASTER *laughs. The sound of the bus.)*

BLACK WOMAN: I see it coming. *(Everyone turns to look.)* I sure am glad to see it.

(The bus pulls up. They get on the bus. We see the bus leaving Gerard and turning onto the highway. STATION MASTER *goes inside terminal.)*

EXTERIOR: Bus.

The bus continues down the highway.

INTERIOR: Bus.

MRS. WATTS *and* THELMA *are sitting together.*

MRS. WATTS: The bus is nice to ride, isn't it?

THELMA: Yes. It is.

MRS. WATTS: Excuse me for getting personal, but what is a pretty girl like you doing traveling alone?

THELMA: My husband has just been sent overseas. I'm going to stay with my family.

MRS. WATTS: Oh, I'm sorry to hear it. Well, you just say the Ninety-first Psalm over and over to yourself. It will be a bower of strength and protection to him. *(She begins to recite with closed eyes.)* "He that dwelleth in the secret place of the most high, shall abide under the shadow of the Almighty. I will say of my Lord, He is my refuge and my fortress."

*(*THELMA *covers her face with her hands. She is crying.* MRS. WATTS *looks up and sees her.)*

MRS. WATTS: Oh, I'm sorry. I'm sorry, honey.

THELMA: That's all right. I'm just lonesome for him is all.

MRS. WATTS: You keep him under the Lord's wing and he'll be safe.

THELMA: Yes, Ma'am. I'm sorry. I don't know what gets into me.

MRS. WATTS: Nobody needs to be ashamed of crying. I guess we've all dampened a pillow sometime or other. I know I have.

THELMA: If only I could learn not to worry.

MRS. WATTS: I know. I guess we all ask that. Jessie Mae, my daughter-in-law, don't worry. "What for?" she says. Well, like I tell her, that's a fine attitude if you can cultivate it. Trouble is, I can't any longer.

THELMA: It is hard.

MRS. WATTS: I didn't used to worry. When I was a girl, I was so carefree. I had lots to worry me, too. Everybody was so poor back in Bountiful. But we got along. I said to my papa once after our third crop failure in a row, whoever named this place Bountiful? He said his papa did, because in those days it was a land of plenty. You'd just drop seeds in the ground and the crops would spring up. We had cotton and corn and sugar cane. I think it's the prettiest place I ever heard of. Jessie Mae says it's the ugliest. But she only says that to bother me. She only saw it once, and that was on a rainy day at that. She says it's nothing but an old swamp. That may be, I said, but it's a mighty pretty swamp to me.

EXTERIOR: Highway.
The bus passes a tenant farmer's shack.

INTERIOR: Bus.
THELMA *is reading a magazine,* MRS. WATTS *her Bible.* THELMA *puts her magazine down.*

THELMA: Mrs. Watts . . .

MRS. WATTS: Yes?

THELMA: I think I ought to tell you this. I don't want you to think I'm interfering in your business, but well, you see, your son and daughter-in-law came in just after you left . . .

MRS. WATTS: I know. I saw them coming, that's why I left so fast.

THELMA: Your son seemed very concerned.

MRS. WATTS: Oh, bless his heart.

THELMA: He found a handkerchief that you dropped.

MRS. WATTS: Oh, mercy. That's right, I did.

THELMA: He asked me if I had seen you. I felt I had to say yes. Now, I wouldn't have said a thing if he hadn't asked me.

MRS. WATTS: Oh, that's all right. I would have done the same thing in your place. Did you talk to Jessie Mae?

THELMA: Well, yes, I . . .

MRS. WATTS: *(Laughs.)* Isn't she a sight? I bet she told you I was crazy.

THELMA: Well . . .

MRS. WATTS: Oh, you needn't worry about it hurting my feelings. Poor Jessie Mae thinks everybody's crazy who don't want to sit in the beauty parlor all day and drink Coca-Colas. *(A pause.)* You know, I think Ludie knows how I feel about getting back to Bountiful, because once when we were talkin' about something that happened way back there in the old days, he burst out crying. He was so overcome he had to leave the room.

EXTERIOR. Highway.
The bus goes through a very small town.

INTERIOR: Bus.
Most of the passengers are sleeping. MRS. WATTS *has her eyes closed and is humming "Softly and Tenderly."* THELMA *is eating a sandwich.*

THELMA: That's a pretty hymn. What's the name of that?

MRS. WATTS: "Softly and Tenderly, Jesus Is Calling." Do you like hymns?

THELMA: Yes, I do.

MRS. WATTS: So do I. Jessie Mae says they're going out of style, but I don't agree. What's your favorite hymn?

THELMA: I don't know.

MRS. WATTS: The one I was just singing is mine. I bet I sing that a hundred times a day. When Jessie Mae isn't home. Hymns make Jessie Mae nervous. (THELMA *laughs.*) Jessie Mae hates me. I don't know why, she just hates me. *(A pause.)* I gotta get back and smell that salt air and work that dirt. Callie said I could always come back and visit her. And she meant it, too. That's who I'm going to see now. Callie Davis. The whole first month of my visit I am going to work in Callie's garden. I haven't had my hands in dirt in twenty years. My hands just feel the need of dirt. Do you like to work the ground?

THELMA: I never have.

MRS. WATTS: Try it sometimes. It'll do wonders for you. I bet I live to be . . . I bet I live to be a hundred if I can just get outdoors again.

EXTERIOR: Bus.

The bus continues down the highway.

INTERIOR: Bus.

MRS. WATTS: It was being cooped up in those two rooms that was killing me. I used to work that land like a man. I had to, when Papa died . . . And I got two little babies buried there. Renee Sue and Douglas. Diphtheria got Renee Sue, and I never knew what carried Douglas away. He was just weak from the start. I know that Callie has kept up their graves. Oh! If only my heart holds out till I get there! *(A pause.)* Now, where do you go, after Harrison?

THELMA: Old Gulf. My family just moved there from Louisiana. I'll stay there with them till my husband comes home again.

MRS. WATTS: Oh, isn't that nice?

THELMA: It'll be funny living at home again.

MRS. WATTS: How long have you been married?

THELMA: A year. My husband was anxious for me to go. He said he'd worry about my being alone. I'm the only child, and my parents and I are very close.

MRS. WATTS: Isn't that nice?

THELMA: I so hoped my mother and daddy would like my husband and he'd like them. I needn't have worried. They hit it off from the very first. Mother and Daddy say they feel like they got two children now. A son and a daughter.

MRS. WATTS: Oh . . . Isn't that nice? I've heard people say that if your son marries you lose a son, but when your daughter marries you get a son. What's your husband's name?

THELMA: Robert.

MRS. WATTS: Ah . . . That's a nice name.

THELMA: I think so. But I guess any name he had I'd think was nice. I love my husband very much. Lots of girls I know think I'm silly about him, but I can't help it.
(A pause.)

MRS. WATTS: I wasn't in love with my husband. *(A pause.)* Do you believe we are punished for the things we do wrong? I sometimes think that's why I've had all my trouble. I've talked to many a preacher about it, and all but one said he didn't think so. But I can't see any other reason. Of course, I didn't lie to my husband. I told him I didn't love him, that I admired him, which I did, but I didn't love him. *(A pause.)* That I'd never love anybody but Ray John Murray as long as I lived, and I didn't, and I couldn't help it. Even when my husband died and I went . . . moved back with Mama and Papa, I used to sit on our front gallery every morning and every evening just to nod hello to Ray John Murray as he went by the house to work at the store. He went a mile out of his way to pass the house. He never loved nobody but me.

THELMA: Why didn't you marry *him*?

MRS. WATTS: 'Cause his papa and my papa didn't speak. And my papa forced me to write a letter saying I never wanted to see him again . . . *(She is crying.)* . . . and he got drunk and he married out of *spite!* *(A pause;* MRS. WATTS *shows* THELMA *her locket.)* I felt sorry for his wife. She knew he never loved her. *(A pause.)* Well, I don't think about those things now. But they're all part of Bountiful. I think that's why I started thinking about it again. *(A pause.)* You are lucky to be married to the man you love.

THELMA: I know I am.

MRS. WATTS: Awful lucky.

EXTERIOR: Bus station, Harrison.
Later that night. The bus pulls up.

INTERIOR: Bus station.
TICKET MAN *is asleep. He wakes up.*

EXTERIOR: Bus station.

MRS. WATTS *and* THELMA *have gotten off the bus.* THELMA *is carrying their suitcases.*

TICKET MAN: *(Seeing* THELMA *at the door.)* Want any help with those bags?

THELMA: No, thank you.

INTERIOR: Bus station.

TICKET MAN *wheels out a dolly.*

THELMA: Oh . . . Excuse me.

TICKET MAN: Yes?

THELMA: Is the bus to Old Gulf going to be on time?

TICKET MAN: Always is.

EXTERIOR: Bus station.

MRS. WATTS *goes into the station as the* TICKET MAN *is wheeling the dolly outside. We can see* MRS. WATTS *and* THELMA *through the window of the bus station as the* TICKET MAN *loads the dolly.*

MRS. WATTS: *(To* THELMA.) What time is it?

THELMA: Ten o'clock.

MRS. WATTS: Ten o'clock! Oh, I bet Callie will be surprised to see me walk in at ten o'clock.

THELMA: Did you tell her you were coming today?

INTERIOR: Bus station.

MRS. WATTS *and* THELMA *are sitting on a bench.*

MRS. WATTS: No. I couldn't. Because I didn't know. I had to wait for Jessie Mae to go to the drugstore.

THELMA: My bus leaves in half an hour.

MRS. WATTS: Oh, I see. Well, I'd better be finding out how I'm going to get on out to Bountiful. *(She starts to get up.)*

THELMA: No, you sit down. Sit down. I'll find the man.

(THELMA goes outside to the TICKET MAN in front of the store. MRS. WATTS follows her and stands in the doorway.)

THELMA: Excuse me again.

TICKET MAN: Yes?

THELMA: My friend here would like to know how to get to Bountiful?

TICKET MAN: Bountiful?

THELMA: Yes.

TICKET MAN: What's she going there for?

(MRS. WATTS *comes up to the* TICKET MAN.)

MRS. WATTS: I'm going to go visit my girlhood friend.

TICKET MAN: Well, I don't know who that's gonna be. The last person in Bountiful was Mrs. Callie Davis, and she died day before yesterday. That is, they found her day before yesterday. She lived all alone so they don't know exactly when she died. Excuse me. *(He pushes the dolly toward the door.)*

MRS. WATTS: Callie Davis!

TICKET MAN: Yes, Ma'am. They had the funeral this morning. Was she the one you were going to visit?

MRS. WATTS: Yessir, that's the one. She was my friend. My girlhood friend.

(TICKET MAN *goes inside.* MRS. WATTS *stands for a moment. Then she sits on the bench.* THELMA *goes inside to* TICKET MAN.)

THELMA: Is there a hotel here?

TICKET MAN: Yes'm. The Riverview.

THELMA: How far is it?

TICKET MAN: About three blocks.

(THELMA *goes out to* MRS. WATTS *at the bench.*)

THELMA: What'll you do now, Mrs. Watts?

MRS. WATTS: I'm thinking, honey. I'm thinking. *(A pause.* THELMA *sits down beside her.)* It's come to me what to do. I'll go on. That much has come to me. I'll go on. I feel my strength and my purpose strong within me. I will go to Bountiful. I will walk the twelve miles, if I have to.

THELMA: Now, Mrs. Watts, what are you gonna do if there's no one out there this time of night?

MRS. WATTS: Oh, yes. I guess you're right.

THELMA: I think you should wait until morning.

MRS. WATTS: Yes. I guess I should. And then . . . I can hire somebody to drive me out. You know what I'll do? I will stay at my own house, or what's left of it. You put me in a garden and I'll get along just fine . . . with the help of my government checks.

THELMA: Mrs. Watts, the man here says there's a hotel not too far from here. I think you'd better let me take you there.

MRS. WATTS: Oh, no thank you. I'm not going to waste my money on hotels. They're high as cats' backs, you know? I'll just sleep right here on this bench.

(They go inside; we see them through the window.)

MRS. WATTS: I'll put my coat under my head, and my purse under my arm . . . *(She puts the coat down on the bench like a pillow. She begins to look around for her purse. She has lost it.)* My purse! *(She begins to search frantically.)* Oh, honey, did you see my purse?

THELMA: Why, no.

INTERIOR: Bus station.

THELMA *and* MRS. WATTS *rush up to the ticket window. The* TICKET MAN *is drowsing.*

THELMA: Excuse me. Excuse me.

TICKET MAN: Huh?

THELMA: This lady left her purse on the bus.

TICKET MAN: All right. I'll call ahead about it. How can you identify it?

MRS. WATTS: It's a plain brown purse.

TICKET MAN: How much money?

MRS. WATTS: Thirty-five cents and a pension check.

TICKET MAN: Who was the check made out to?

MRS. WATTS: To me. Mrs. Carrie Watts.

TICKET MAN: All right. I'll call up about it.

MRS. WATTS: Oh, thank you. You're most kind.

THELMA: How long will it take to get it back?

TICKET MAN: Well . . . depends. If I can get ahead of the bus at Don Tarle, they can send it back on the Victoria bus and it should be here in a couple of hours.

MRS. WATTS: That's awfully kind of you.

*(THELMA *and* MRS. WATTS *go back to the bench.)*

THELMA: Try not to worry about the purse.

MRS. WATTS: Oh, I won't. I'm too tired to worry. Be time enough to worry when I get up in the morning.

THELMA: Why don't you see if you can go on to sleep now.

*(MRS. WATTS *sits on the bench.)*

MRS. WATTS: Oh, no, I thought I'd stay up and see you off.

THELMA: No. You go on to sleep.

MRS. WATTS: Oh, I can't go right off to sleep now. I'm too wound up. You know, I don't go on a trip every day of my life. *(TICKET MAN calls to them from the window.)*

TICKET MAN: You're lucky. The bus hadn't gotten to Don Tarle yet. Now, if they can find the purse, it'll be here around . . . *(A pause; he looks at his watch as THELMA and MRS. WATTS wait anxiously.)* . . . around twelve.

THELMA: Make you feel better?

MRS. WATTS: *(Laughs.)* Yes. It does. Of course, everything has seemed to work out today. Why is it that some days everything works out, and then other days nothing works out. What I mean is, I have been trying to get to Bountiful for over five years. Now, usually Jessie Mae and Ludie come and they find me even before I got inside the railroad station good. Today, I got inside both the railroad station and the bus station. I bought a ticket, I seen Ludie and Jessie Mae before they saw me. I hid out, and I met a pretty friend like you. I lost my purse, and now I have somebody finding it for me. I guess the Lord is just with me today. *(Laughs. A pause.)* I wonder why the Lord's not with us every day? Sure would be nice if He was. *(A pause.)* Well, maybe then we wouldn't appreciate it so much on those days when He is with us. Or maybe He's with us always and we just don't know it. Maybe I had to wait twenty years cooped up in a city before I could appreciate getting back here. *(She begins to sing a hymn.)*

Blessed assurance, Jesus is mine.
Oh, what a foretaste of glory divine.
Heir of salvation, purchase of God
Born of His Spirit, washed in His blood.

(She pauses.) Ah, isn't it nice to be able to sing a hymn when you want to? *(She continues her hymn.)*

This is my story, this is my song,
Praising my Savior, all the day long.
This is my story . . .

(THELMA *joins in and they finish the song together.*)

. . . this is my song,
Praising my Savior, all the day long.

MRS. WATTS: Oh! I am a happy woman, young lady. I am a very happy woman.

THELMA: I still have a sandwich left. Will you have one?

MRS. WATTS: Well, you sure you don't want it?

THELMA: No. I'm full.

MRS. WATTS: Well . . . I'll just take a half.

(THELMA *gets the sandwich from her suitcase and unwraps it.*)

THELMA: Take the whole thing.

MRS. WATTS: No, no, just a half, thank you. You know, I don't eat much. Particularly if I'm excited.

(*She rises and stands nibbling on the sandwich. She goes out on the porch.* THELMA *follows.*)

EXTERIOR: Bus station.

MRS. WATTS: You know, I came to my first dance in this town.

THELMA: Did you?

(*They move out into the street.*)

MRS. WATTS: Yes, Ma'am. It was the summertime. And my father couldn't decide whether he thought dancing was right or not. But my mother said that she danced when she was a girl and so I was gonna dance. And so I went. Oh! The girls from all over the county came for this dance. And it was at the Opera House. I can't remember what the occasion was, but it was something special. (*A pause. She looks at* THELMA.) You know something, young lady? If my daughter had lived I would have wanted her to be just like you.

THELMA: Why, thank you.

MRS. WATTS: Yes! Sweet and considerate and thoughtful and . . . and pretty.

THELMA: Thank you.

(TICKET MAN *comes out on the porch checking his watch.*)

TICKET MAN: (*To* THELMA.) You'd better get your suitcase, Miss. The bus will be up the road. He won't wait this time of night.

(THELMA *goes inside.*)

MRS. WATTS: I was just telling my little friend here. I came to my first dance in this town.

TICKET MAN: That right?

MRS. WATTS: Yes. I've been to Harrison quite a few times in my life. Shopping.

(Bus rounds corner. MRS. WATTS *waves it down.* THELMA *runs back with her suitcase. She hugs* MRS. WATTS.*)*

THELMA: Good-bye, Mrs. Watts.

MRS. WATTS: Good-bye, honey. Good luck to you.

THELMA: Good luck to *you.*

*(*MRS. WATTS *kisses her.* THELMA *gets on the bus. The* TICKET MAN *and* MRS. WATTS *wave as the bus pulls away.)*

TICKET MAN: Are you gonna stay here all night?

MRS. WATTS: I have to. Everything I have is on the bus. We can't go anywhere without money.

TICKET MAN: I guess that's right.

(She goes inside and he follows.)

INTERIOR: Bus station.

MRS. WATTS: Do they still have dances over at Borden's Opera House?

TICKET MAN: No, Ma'am. It's torn down. They condemned it, you know. *(A pause.)* Did you ever know anybody in Harrison?

MRS. WATTS: I knew a few people when I was a girl. Priscilla Nytelle. Did you know her?

TICKET MAN: No, Ma'am.

MRS. WATTS: Nancy Lee Goodhue?

TICKET MAN: No, Ma'am.

MRS. WATTS: The Fay girls?

TICKET MAN: No, Ma'am.

MRS. WATTS: I used to trade in Mr. Ewing's store. I knew him to speak to.

TICKET MAN: Which Ewing was that?

MRS. WATTS: George White Ewing.

TICKET MAN: He's dead.

MRS. WATTS: That so?

TICKET MAN: Been dead twelve years.

MRS. WATTS: Is that so?

TICKET MAN: He left quite a bit of money, but his son took over his store and lost it all. Drank.

MRS. WATTS: Oh. That so? One thing I can say about my boy, he never gave me any trouble that way.

TICKET MAN: Well, that's good. I've got one boy that drinks and one boy that doesn't. Can't understand it. I raised them the same way.

MRS. WATTS: I know. I've known of other cases like that. One drinks. The other doesn't.

TICKET MAN: A friend of mine has a girl that drinks.

MRS. WATTS: Ah.

TICKET MAN: I think that's the saddest thing in the world.

MRS. WATTS: Isn't it?

(A pause.)

TICKET MAN: Well. Good night.

MRS. WATTS: Good night.

EXTERIOR: Bus station.
The lights go out.

INTERIOR: Bus station.
MRS. WATTS *is lying on the bench. She thumbs through her Bible, then closes it and hums quietly to herself.*

INTERIOR: Sheriff's car.
The SHERIFF *drives down the street. He parks in front of the bus station and gets out of the car.*

INTERIOR: Bus station.
The SHERIFF *comes into the bus station and stoops to pet a cat just inside the door. He looks around and sees* MRS. WATTS *lying on the bench asleep. The* SHERIFF *picks up the cat and goes over to the* TICKET MAN.

SHERIFF: Roy. Come on, Roy, wake up.

(The SHERIFF *drops the cat on the* TICKET MAN*'s chest. The* TICKET MAN *knocks the cat off and it runs away howling.)*

TICKET MAN: *(Startled awake.)* Jesus! *(He sees the* SHERIFF.) Oh, hello, Sheriff.

SHERIFF: You're working too hard, Roy. How long has this old woman been here?

TICKET MAN: *(Looks at his watch.)* About six hours.

SHERIFF: Did she get off the bus from Houston?

TICKET MAN: Yessir. I know her name. It's Watts. She left her purse on the bus and I had to call up to Don Tarle about it.

SHERIFF: You have her purse?

TICKET MAN: Yessir. It just came. *(He hands the purse to the* SHERIFF*).*

SHERIFF: *(Looks in the purse.)* She's the one, all right. I've had a call from the Houston Police to hold her until her son can come for her.

TICKET MAN: She said she used to live in Bountiful.

(The SHERIFF *goes over to her to wake her up. He bends over her, looking at her for a moment. He comes back to the* TICKET MAN.*)*

SHERIFF: The poor thing's sleeping so sound, I don't have the heart to wake her up. Tell you what. I'm gonna go over to my office and call Houston, tell them she's here. Her son's coming in his car. He should be here around seven-thirty. I'll be back in ten minutes. Now, Roy . . . Roy, if she gives you any trouble, you just call me. Now, you keep your eye on her.

TICKET MAN: All right.

(The SHERIFF *goes out and the screen door bangs. This wakens* MRS. WATTS.*)*

MRS. WATTS: *(Sits up, confused.)* Good morning.

TICKET MAN: Good morning.

*(*MRS. WATTS *looks around trying to remember where she is. Then she sees the* TICKET MAN.*)*

MRS. WATTS: Did my purse arrive?

TICKET MAN: Yes, Ma'am.

MRS. WATTS: Oh, thank you so much.

*(*TICKET MAN *gets the purse and hands it to her.)*

MRS. WATTS: I wonder if you could cash a check for me?

TICKET MAN: Oh, I'm sorry, Ma'am. I can't.

MRS. WATTS: Oh, it's a government check and I have identification.

TICKET MAN: I'm sorry, Ma'am. I can't.

MRS. WATTS: Well, do you know where I *could* get a check cashed?

TICKET MAN: Why?

MRS. WATTS: Why, I need money to get me started in Bountiful. I want to hire somebody to drive me out and look at my house and get a few groceries. Try to find a cot to sleep on.

TICKET MAN: I'm sorry, Lady, you're not going to Bountiful.

MRS. WATTS: Oh, yes I am. You see . . .

TICKET MAN: I have to hold you here for the Sheriff.

MRS. WATTS: You are joking with me!? Now don't you joke with me. I have come too far.

TICKET MAN: I need to keep you here until your son arrives in his car this morning.

MRS. WATTS: My son hasn't got a car, so I don't believe you.

TICKET MAN: He'll be here in a minute, and you can ask him your- self.

MRS. WATTS: All right. But I'm going, do you understand that? You'll see. This is a free country. And I'm gonna tell him that. And no sheriff or king or president is going to keep me from going back to Bountiful.

TICKET MAN: All right. Well, you tell him that.

(MRS. WATTS *sits on the bench.*)

MRS. WATTS: What time is my son expected?

TICKET MAN: Around seven-thirty.

MRS. WATTS: Where can I find me a driver? I can make it to Bountiful and back way before seven-thirty.

TICKET MAN: Look, lady . . .

MRS. WATTS: That's all I want. Just to see it. Just to stand on the porch of my own house again.

TICKET MAN: Lady . . . I don't have anything to . . .

MRS. WATTS: I thought last night I had to stay. I thought I'd just die if I couldn't stay. But now . . . I'll settle for less. An hour. Half an hour. Fifteen minutes.

TICKET MAN: Lady, it ain't up to me. I told you, the Sheriff . . .

MRS. WATTS: *(Screaming.)* Well, then get me the Sheriff!

TICKET MAN: Lady . . .

MRS. WATTS: Get me the Sheriff. The time is going. They're gonna have me locked up in those two rooms again soon. The time is going . . . the time is . . .

(*The* SHERIFF *comes in.*)

SHERIFF: Mrs. Watts?

MRS. WATTS: Yessir. Are you the Sheriff?

SHERIFF: Yes, Ma'am.

MRS. WATTS: I understand that my son is gonna be here at seven- thirty to take me back to Houston.

SHERIFF: Yes, Ma'am.

MRS. WATTS: Then listen to me, Sir. I have made myself one promise, to see my home again before I die.

SHERIFF: Lady . . .

MRS. WATTS: Now, I'm not asking that I not go back. I'm willing to go back. Just let me go these twelve miles now. I have money. I can pay.

SHERIFF: That's between you and your son, Ma'am.

MRS. WATTS: Ludie? Why, he's got to do whatever Jessie Mae tells him to do. And I know why she wants me back. For my government check.

SHERIFF: I don't know anything about that, Ma'am.

MRS. WATTS: Won't you let me go?

SHERIFF: Not unless your son takes you.

MRS. WATTS: All right, then. I've lost. *(Crying.)* I've come all this way only to lose. *(She drops her coat and purse on the bench and stands there, tired and defeated.)* I'm going to die . . . and Jessie Mae knows that . . . and she's willful, and it is her will that I die in those two rooms. Well, she's not going to have her way. It is my will to die in Bountiful.

(She starts to run out of the bus station. The SHERIFF *stops her.)*

MRS. WATTS: Let me go those twelve miles before it's too late! Understand me. Suffering I don't mind. Suffering I understand. I didn't protest once. Even though my heart was broken when those babies died. But these fifteen years of bickering . . . of endless, petty bickering . . . It's made me like Jessie Mae sees me. It's ugly, and I will not be that way. *(Crying.)* I want to go home. I want to go home. I want to go . . .

(She is unable to speak any more. She is on the verge of collapse. The SHERIFF *helps her over to the bench and settles her there. The* SHERIFF *calls to the* TICKET MAN.*)*

SHERIFF: Hey, Roy. Get a doctor. Hurry.

MRS. WATTS: I'm all right. No doctor . . .

(The SHERIFF *helps her lie down. She is still crying.)*

SHERIFF: Just lie down. It's all right . . .

INTERIOR: Bus station.

DR. WHITE *and the* SHERIFF *are on the porch of the station conferring. We can't hear what they're saying. The* DOCTOR *leaves and the* SHERIFF *comes back in.* MRS. WATTS *is sitting up now. The* SHERIFF *goes over to her and kneels down by the bench.*

SHERIFF: Mrs. Watts. *(She opens her eyes.)* How are you feeling?

MRS. WATTS: Stronger by the minute, thank you.

SHERIFF: Well, the doctor said we are to keep you calm and see that you rest until your son gets here.

MRS. WATTS: Thank you. I appreciate your interest.

SHERIFF: But he said he didn't think it would do any harm if I wanted to drive you out to your place, as long as you felt well enough to go.

MRS. WATTS: Yessir! Thank you. I feel well enough to go.

SHERIFF: All right. I'll take you.

EXTERIOR: Countryside.
The SHERIFF *and* MRS. WATTS *are in his car driving over a country road.*

INTERIOR: Sheriff's car.
The SHERIFF *is driving.* MRS. WATTS *gazes out the windows at the land as they ride.*

EXTERIOR: Countryside.
The car continues down the road.

INTERIOR: Sheriff's car.

MRS. WATTS: Oh . . .

SHERIFF: Does this look familiar?

MRS. WATTS: Oh, yes. It surely does.

EXTERIOR: Bus station, Harrison.
LUDIE *and* JESSIE MAE *drive up to the station. They get out.*

EXTERIOR: Countryside.
The sheriff's car continues down the road.

INTERIOR: Sheriff's car.
MRS. WATTS *looks out at what is left of the town of Bountiful.*

EXTERIOR: Bountiful.
We see an abandoned store as the car goes through the town.

INTERIOR: Sheriff's car.

MRS. WATTS: My Lord, look at Bountiful. There's nothing left.

EXTERIOR: Countryside.
They pass more abandoned buildings. The car leaves Bountiful, crosses an old wooden bridge, and continues along a country road.

INTERIOR: Sheriff's car.
MRS. WATTS *appears nervous and excited.*

EXTERIOR: Sheriff's car.
They have turned off the road onto a grassy lane. The SHERIFF *parks the car, gets out, and opens the car door for* MRS. WATTS. *She gets out and walks a few steps.*

MRS. WATTS: I'm home. I'm home.

EXTERIOR: The Watts house and yard.
The house is an old, ramshackle two-story country place that hasn't been painted for years. The SHERIFF *and* MRS. WATTS *walk toward the house. She turns to him.*

MRS. WATTS: Thank you.
   (They pause for a moment in the yard.)
SHERIFF: You'd better come over here and sit down and rest for a
   while. Let me get this. *(He pulls a wooden crate out from under the
   porch.)* There you go.
   *(*MRS. WATTS *sits on the crate.)*
SHERIFF: You don't want to overdo it.
MRS. WATTS: Yessir.
SHERIFF: Are you feeling all right now?
MRS. WATTS: Oh, yes, I am. I feel ever so much better.
SHERIFF: Well, you look better. I hope I'm doing the right thing in
   bringing you here. Well.
MRS. WATTS: Thank you. You've been very kind.
   (A bird calls. MRS. WATTS *and the* SHERIFF *sit listening to it.)*
MRS. WATTS: Oh . . . What kind of bird is that?
SHERIFF: That's an old redbird.
MRS. WATTS: I thought it was a redbird, but it's been so long since
   I heard one I just couldn't be sure. *(A pause.)* Do they still have
   scissortails around here?

SHERIFF: Yes, Ma'am. I still see one every once in a while when I'm driving around the country.

MRS. WATTS: I don't know of anything prettier than a scissortail flying through the sky. *(A pause.)* You know, my father was a good man in many ways. He was a peculiar man, but a good one. And one thing he never could stand was to see a bird shot on his land. If he saw men coming here hunting, he'd just go take his gun and chase them away. And I think the birds knew that they couldn't be touched here. Our land was always home to them. We had ducks and geese and finches and blue jays. Bluebirds and redbirds.

SHERIFF: Ricebirds are getting thicker every year. They seem to thrive out here on the coast.

MRS. WATTS: I think a mockingbird is my favorite of all.

SHERIFF: I think it's mine, too.

MRS. WATTS: *(Laughs.)* I don't know, though. I'm mighty partial to scissortail. I hope I see one soon.

SHERIFF: *(Laughs.)* I hope you can.

MRS. WATTS: You know, my father was born on this land and in this house. Did you know my father?

SHERIFF: No, Ma'am. Not that I can remember.

MRS. WATTS: Well, I guess there aren't many around here who remember my father. I do, of course, and my son. *(A pause.)* You know, it's funny, but ever since we got here I just . . . I've had half a feeling my father and my mother would come out of this house and greet me and welcome me home. *(She begins to cry.)* Well, I guess when you've lived longer than your house or your family, you've lived long enough. *(A pause.)* But what happened to the farms? For the last five miles I've seen nothing but empty fields . . .

SHERIFF: I know. The land around Bountiful just played out. People like you got discouraged and moved away.

MRS. WATTS: Callie Davis kept her farm going.

SHERIFF: Yes. She did. She learned how to treat her land right and it began paying off for her toward the end. I've heard she was out riding her tractor the day before she died. *(Laughs.)* Yeah, it was a lonely death she had. All by herself in that big old house.

MRS. WATTS: There are worse things.

SHERIFF: Well, looks to me like you're gonna have a pretty day.

MRS. WATTS: Oh, I hope so.

(*A pause. The* SHERIFF *looks at her.*)

SHERIFF: You feeling more rested now?

MRS. WATTS: Oh, yes, I am.

SHERIFF: Well, I'm gonna go on back down to my car. Now, you call me if you need anything. Anything.

MRS. WATTS: Thank you.

(*The* SHERIFF *walks toward the car.* MRS. WATTS *sits for a moment watching him go and then gets up and looks around the porch. She touches the wooden boards of the house.*)

INTERIOR: Watts house.

MRS. WATTS *comes into the house and looks around. The house is as run-down inside as out. There is a rusted child's tractor in a corner.* MRS. WATTS *goes slowly through the house. She pauses at the fireplace in what once was the parlor, puts her purse on the mantle, and then goes toward the stairs.*

INTERIOR: Upstairs bedroom.

MRS. WATTS *enters the room. An old iron bed without a mattress is in the room. She stands looking around.*

LUDIE: (*Off camera.*) Mama. (*A pause.*) Mama.

EXTERIOR: Watts house.

LUDIE *is walking toward the house.*

LUDIE: Mama.

(MRS. WATTS *is sitting in a chair on the front porch as he walks up.*)

LUDIE: Hello, Mama.

MRS. WATTS: Hello, Son.

LUDIE: How do you feel?

MRS. WATTS: I feel much better, Ludie.

LUDIE: Yes, Ma'am.

MRS. WATTS: I got my wish.

LUDIE: Yes, Ma'am.

MRS. WATTS: I hope I didn't worry you too much, Ludie. But I just felt that I had to . . .

LUDIE: I know, Mama.

MRS. WATTS: You see, Son, I know it's hard for you to understand and Jessie Mae to understand . . .

LUDIE: Yes, Ma'am. I understand, Mama. It's done now. So let's just forget about it.

MRS. WATTS: All right, Son. *(A pause.)* You did bring Jessie Mae, didn't you?

LUDIE: Yes, Ma'am.

MRS. WATTS: Well, now she's here isn't she going to get out of the car and look around a little?

LUDIE: Oh, well, she didn't seem to want to, Mama.

MRS. WATTS: You asked her?

LUDIE: Yes, Ma'am.

(A pause.)

MRS. WATTS: Did you ask about your raise, Son?

LUDIE: Yes, Ma'am. Mr. Douglas said that he liked my work and he'd be glad to recommend a raise for me.

MRS. WATTS: Oh. *(A pause.)* The sky's so blue, Ludie. Did you ever see a sky so blue?

LUDIE: No, Ma'am.

(A pause.)

MRS. WATTS: You know, Callie Davis *died!*

LUDIE: Is that so? When did that happen?

MRS. WATTS: Well, they don't rightly know. They found her dead. She'd been riding a tractor the day before they found her. They buried her yesterday.

(A pause.)

LUDIE: Mama . . . I should have made myself bring you out here sooner. I'm sorry. I just thought it would be easier if we didn't see the house again.

MRS. WATTS: I know, Ludie. *(A pause.)* But . . . now you're here, wouldn't you like to come inside, Son, and look around?

LUDIE: I don't think I'd better, Mama. I don't see any use in it. I'd rather remember it like it was.

(A pause. MRS. WATTS looks at the house. She chuckles.)

MRS. WATTS: The old house has gotten kind of run down, hasn't it? I don't think it's gonna last out the next Gulf storm. *(She steps off the porch into the yard.)*

LUDIE: It doesn't look like it would.

(MRS. WATTS turns and looks at him standing in the yard.)

MRS. WATTS: You know who you look like standing there?

LUDIE: Who?

MRS. WATTS: My papa.

LUDIE: I do?

MRS. WATTS: Just like him. Of course, I've been noticing as you been getting older that you look more and more like him. My papa was a good-looking man.

LUDIE: He was?

MRS. WATTS: Well, you've seen his pictures. Didn't you think so?

LUDIE: I don't remember. It's been so long since I looked at his pictures.

MRS. WATTS: Well, he was always considered a very nice-looking man. *(A pause.)* Do you remember my papa at all, Son?

LUDIE: No, Ma'am. Not too well. I was only ten when he died, Mama. I remember the day that he died. I heard about it as I was coming home from school. Lee Weems told me. I thought he was joking and I called him a liar. I remember you took me into the parlor there the day of the funeral to say good-bye to him. I remember the coffin and the people sitting in the room. Old man Lou . . . uh, Joe Weems . . . Joe Weems took me up on his knee and told me that Grandpapa was his best friend and that his life was a real example for me to follow. I remember Grandmama sitting by the coffin and crying and she made me promise that when I had a son of my own I would name him after Grandpapa. I would too. I've never forgotten that promise. *(A pause.)* Well, I didn't have a son. Or a daughter.

(A pause. MRS. WATTS sits on the edge of the porch.)

LUDIE: Billy Davis told me today that his wife is expecting her fourth child. They already have two girls and a son. Billy Davis doesn't make much more than I do, and they certainly seem to get along. Have their own house and a car. It does your heart good to hear them tell about how they all get along. Everybody has their own job, even the youngest child. She's only three. She puts the napkins on the table at mealtimes. That's her job. Billy says to me, Ludie, I don't know if I could get along without my kids. He says I don't know how you get along, Ludie. What you work for. I said, well, Billy . . . *(A pause.)* I haven't made any kind of life for you, Mama, either of you, and I try so hard. *(A pause.)* Mama, I lied to you. I do remember. I remember so much. This house, this life here. The night you woke me up and dressed me and took me for a walk when the moon was full and I cried because I was scared and you comforted me. Mama, I want to stop remembering . . . It doesn't do any good remembering.

(MRS. WATTS *takes* LUDIE's *hand and strokes it lovingly. The car horn is heard.*)

LUDIE: That's Jessie Mae.

EXTERIOR: Car.
JESSIE MAE *is sitting in the car.*

LUDIE: *(Off camera.)* We have to start back now, Mama.

EXTERIOR: House.
LUDIE *takes* MRS. WATTS *by the arm and starts to help her up from the porch, but she collapses crying.* LUDIE *sits down beside her.*

MRS. WATTS: Oh, Ludie, Ludie. What has happened to us? Why have we come to this?

LUDIE: I don't know, Mama.

MRS. WATTS: To have stayed and fought the land would have been better than this.

LUDIE: Yes'm.

MRS. WATTS: Pretty soon all this will be gone. Twenty years . . . ten . . . this house . . . me . . . you . . .

LUDIE: I know, Mama.

(A pause. She puts her arm around him and leans her head on his shoulder. She speaks with great tenderness.)

MRS. WATTS: But the river'll still be here. The fields. The trees. The smell of the Gulf. I always got my strength from that. Not from houses, not from people. *(A pause. We see the fields and trees from her point of view.)* It's so quiet. So eternally quiet. I had forgotten the peace, the quiet. *(She points out into the distance.)* Do you remember how my papa always had that field over there planted in cotton?

LUDIE: Yes, Ma'am.

MRS. WATTS: See, it's all woods now. But I expect someday people will come and cut down the trees and plant the cotton and maybe even wear out the land again and then their children will sell it and move to the cities and then the trees will come up again.

LUDIE: I expect so, Mama.

MRS. WATTS: And we're a part of all that. We left it, but we can never lose what it's given us.

LUDIE: I expect so, Mama.

JESSIE MAE: *(Off camera, calling.)* Ludie. Are you coming or not?

LUDIE: We are just startin', Jessie Mae.

MRS. WATTS: Hello . . . Jessie Mae.

JESSIE MAE: *(Walking toward the house.)* I am not speaking to you. I guess you're proud of the time you gave us, dragging us here at this time of the mornin'. If Ludie loses his job over this, I hope you are satisfied.

LUDIE: I'm not going to lose my job, Jessie Mae.

JESSIE MAE: Well, you could.

LUDIE: All right, Jessie Mae.

JESSIE MAE: And she should realize that. She's selfish. That's her trouble. Always has been, just puredee selfish. *(A pause. She comes closer to LUDIE and MRS. WATTS.)* Did you tell your mama what we were discussing in the car?

LUDIE: No. We can talk it all over driving back to Houston.

JESSIE MAE: I think we should have it all out right here. I would like everything understood right now. I have it all written down. Do you want to read it or do you want me to read it to you, Mother Watts?

MRS. WATTS: What is it, Jessie Mae?

JESSIE MAE: It's a few rules and regulations that are necessary to my peace of mind. And I think to Ludie's. *(A pause.)* First of all, I'd like to ask you a question.

MRS. WATTS: Yes, Ma'am.

JESSIE MAE: Didn't you know you'd be caught and have to come back?

MRS. WATTS: I had to come, Jessie Mae. Twenty years is a long time.

JESSIE MAE: Didn't you know you could have died?

MRS. WATTS: I knew.

JESSIE MAE: And you didn't care?

MRS. WATTS: I had to come, Jessie Mae.

JESSIE MAE: Well, I hope it's all out of your system now.

MRS. WATTS: It is. *(She gets up from where she has been sitting on the edge of the porch.)* I've had my trip, and that's more than enough to keep me happy the rest of my life.

JESSIE MAE: Well, I'm glad to hear it. That's the first thing on my list. *(She reads from the list.)* There'll be no more running away.

MRS. WATTS: There will be no more running away.

JESSIE MAE: Good. Number two. No more hymn singing, when I'm in the apartment. When I'm gone you can sing your lungs out. Agreed?

MRS. WATTS: Agreed.

JESSIE MAE: Number three.

LUDIE: *(Interrupting.)* Jessie Mae, can't this wait till we get home?

JESSIE MAE: Well, honey, we agreed that I was going to handle this! *(She goes back to the list.)* No more pouting. When I ask a question, I would like an answer. Otherwise I'll consider it pouting.

MRS. WATTS: All right.

JESSIE MAE: Number four. With your heart in the condition that it's in I feel you should not run around the apartment when you can walk.

MRS. WATTS: All right, Jessie Mae.

JESSIE MAE: Is there anything you want to say to me?

(MRS. WATTS leans over and kisses her on the cheek.)

MRS. WATTS: No, Jessie Mae.

JESSIE MAE: I might as well tell you right now, I'm not staying in the house and watching over you anymore. I'm joining a bridge club and I am going to town at least twice a week.

LUDIE: We also agreed to try to get along. Jessie Mae also realizes that sometimes she gets upset when she shouldn't.

(JESSIE MAE turns and looks at him. She is taking a cigarette and lighter from her purse.)

LUDIE: Don't you, Jessie Mae?

JESSIE MAE: *(Lighting her cigarette.)* Uh huh.

LUDIE: So let's start by trying to have a pleasant ride home.

JESSIE MAE: All rightie. Is there any water around here? I'm thirsty.

LUDIE: I don't think so, Jessie Mae. Is there any water around here, Mama?

MRS. WATTS: The cistern is gone.

(JESSIE MAE notices a scratch on her shoes. She is furious.)

JESSIE MAE: Oh, look at my shoes! They have scratches on them. They're my good pair. I ought to have my head examined for wearing my only good pair of shoes out here in this old swamp!

LUDIE: *(Looking out in the distance.)* When I was a boy, Jessie Mae, I used to drink in the creek over there.

JESSIE MAE: Well, you wouldn't catch me drinking out of any creek. I knew a man once who went on a hunting trip and drank out of a creek and caught something and died.

MRS. WATTS: Cistern water, there's nothing like it for washing your hair with.

JESSIE MAE: Well, come on. Let's get going. Do we go back by way of Harrison?

LUDIE: Uh huh.

JESSIE MAE: Good. We can stop at the drugstore. I'm so thirsty I could drink ten Coca-Colas. Are you ready?

MRS. WATTS: Yes'm.

JESSIE MAE: Where's your purse?

MRS. WATTS: Are you talking to me, Jessie Mae?

JESSIE MAE: Well, who else would I be talking to? Since when did Ludie start going around with a pocketbook under his arm?

MRS. WATTS: Oh, I guess I left it inside.

JESSIE MAE: Where?

MRS. WATTS: I'll go get it. *(She turns to go into the house.)*

JESSIE MAE: No. I want to go. You'll take all day. You wait here.

(She goes inside the house. LUDIE turns to his mother.)

LUDIE: Mama . . .

MRS. WATTS: It's all right, Ludie, Son.

(JESSIE MAE comes back out with the purse.)

JESSIE MAE: Here. Here's your purse. Now. Where is that money for that government check?

MRS. WATTS: I didn't cash it. It's right there in the purse.

(JESSIE MAE opens the purse and begins to search through it.)

JESSIE MAE: No, it isn't.

MRS. WATTS: Oh, here. Let me look.

(JESSIE MAE hands her the purse and MRS. WATTS, too, begins to rummage around. All of a sudden she bursts out laughing.)

JESSIE MAE: What . . . what is the matter with you?

MRS. WATTS: Oh, that's a good joke on me.

JESSIE MAE: Well, what is so *funny?*

MRS. WATTS: You know, I just remembered. I left this purse on the bus last night and I caused a man a lot of trouble because I thought the check was in it. And do you know that check wasn't in that purse all that time?

JESSIE MAE: Where was it?

MRS. WATTS: It was in here. *(She reaches inside her dress and takes it out.)* It's been in here since yesterday afternoon.

(JESSIE MAE reaches for the check.)

JESSIE MAE: Well, give it to me before you go and lose it again.

MRS. WATTS: I won't lose it.

JESSIE MAE: Now don't start that business again. Just give it to me.

LUDIE: *(Interrupting.)* Jessie Mae.

JESSIE MAE: *(Grabs the check.)* Look, I'm not gonna . . .

LUDIE: *(Angrily.)* We are gonna stop this wrangling once and for all. You've given me your word and I expect you to keep your word. We have to live together and we're going to live together in peace.

JESSIE MAE: *(Hands MRS. WATTS the check.)* Go ahead. You keep the check. But don't lose it before you get home. Come on. Let's go.

LUDIE: Mama, if I get the raise you won't . . .

MRS. WATTS: It's all right, Son. I've had my trip. You go ahead. I'll be right there.

LUDIE: *(Taking a last look at the house.)* The house used to look so big. *(LUDIE walks away to join JESSIE MAE, and they continue walking toward the car. MRS. WATTS sits down in the grass and feels the dirt with her hands. After a moment she gets up and begins to walk slowly toward the car. She pauses for a moment, taking one last look at the house, and speaks quietly.)*

MRS. WATTS: Good-bye, Bountiful, good-bye.

(She walks toward the car, where LUDIE and JESSIE MAE are waiting. LUDIE helps her into the backseat, then gets in and starts the car, and they drive away.)

INTERIOR: Car.

MRS. WATTS *is looking straight ahead. In the background we hear a woman's voice singing "Softly and Tenderly."*

Come home, come home,
Ye who are weary, come home.

> Earnestly, tenderly, Jesus is calling,
> Calling, O sinner, come home.

EXTERIOR: Countryside.
The car moves through the fields toward the road and disappears in the distance. The hymn "Softly and Tenderly" continues in the background as the credits roll.

> Time is now fleeting, the moments are passing,
> Passing from you and from me.
> Shadows are gathering, dense night is coming,
> Coming for you and for me.

> Come home, come home,
> Ye who are weary, come home.
> Earnestly, tenderly, Jesus is calling,
> Calling, O sinner, come home.

FADE OUT

❧ IV ❧

Interviews with
Key Figures
from the
Film Version

Sterling VanWagenen (*Courtesy of Leucadia Film Corporation*)

Horton Foote with Peter Masterson (*Courtesy of Sterling VanWagenen*)

Carlin Glynn (*Courtesy of Sterling VanWagenen*)

Interviews with Key Figures from the Film Version

S ince the television and the Broadway versions of *Boun-tiful* were produced in 1953, thirty-five years before the film, many of the participants have died and others who have had full careers since then remember little of the experience. We chose to concentrate on the creative team for the film—the writer, a producer, the director, and an actress. Unfortunately, Geraldine Page, who won an Oscar for her performance as Mrs. Watts in the film version of *Bountiful,* died in June 1987 before the editors could interview her for this book.

Horton Foote

Horton Foote began his career as an actor on Broadway (1936–44) and later managed a semiprofessional theater in Washington, D.C. (1945–49). During the 1950s, he wrote numerous scripts for television's live dramatic anthologies, including—in addition to *The Trip to Bountiful*—*The Old Man, The Old Beginning, The Tears of My Sister, The Night of the Storm, Expectant Relations, Flight, The Oil Well, Member of the Family, Death of an Old Man,* and *A Young Lady of Property.*

Other of his plays besides *Bountiful* were adapted into films: *The Traveling Lady,* which played on Broadway in 1954, became *Baby, the Rain Must Fall* in 1964 starring Steve McQueen and Lee Remick; *The Chase,* Foote's 1952 Broadway play (and novel of the same name, published in 1956),

became a film in 1966 starring Jane Fonda and Robert Redford; *Convicts* became a film in 1990 starring Robert Duvall
and James Earl Jones.

Foote's screen adaptation in 1962 of Harper Lee's novel, *To
Kill a Mockingbird,* won an Oscar for best screenplay, and his
original filmscript for *Tender Mercies* (1983) won another
Academy Award. He also wrote the screenplay for *Tomorrow*
(1973–74), an adaptation of a William Faulkner story. For the
PBS series "The American Short Story," he adapted Flannery
O'Connor's "The Displaced Person" (1977) and Faulkner's
"The Barn Burning" (1980).

Three of the nine plays in his *The Orphans' Home Cycle* were
made into films, *1918* (1984–85), *On Valentine's Day* (1986),
and *Courtship* (1986); the three scripts had been produced in
New York City by the HB Playwrights Foundation (1978–80)
and were later reedited to become *The Story of a Marriage* for
PBS's "American Playhouse" in 1987. Foote's 1991 screenplay
based on the John Steinbeck novel *Of Mice and Men* was cho-
sen to show in the film competition at Cannes in 1992. Gary
Sinise of Steppenwolf Theatre Company directs and acts in
the production, which also stars John Malkovich.

Foote is currently working on producing more of the plays
from *The Orphans' Home Cycle* for film and stage. He now
spends most of his time in Wharton, Texas, in the family
home.

The following interview was conducted in New York City in
July 1987.

MOORE: Where did you get the idea for *Bountiful?*
FOOTE: I write mostly about things I've heard about and
witnessed. I think the idea—a variation of something I use
often in my plays—comes from a story about a woman who
wanted to marry someone and her father wouldn't permit
it. She married somebody else, and both their lives were
ruined by this action, or at least she felt they were. That, I
think, is probably the germ of the idea—thinking about
this woman, a woman I knew, although I've disguised her
greatly and her circumstances are very different.

When I first started writing it, I tried to write from the point of view of the start—of the father breaking up the engagement, but that just didn't work; so I then decided to try it from the end of her life with her looking back at just the one incident. And that seemed to get the focus I needed. That's the form it finally took.

There is a Bountiful in Utah. I didn't know that. I made up the name. I just gave the name "Bountiful" to a place in Texas, although that, too, is based on a fairly specific place, but it's not called Bountiful.

MOORE: Has it too pretty much disappeared?

FOOTE: Oh, entirely, entirely.

MOORE: How did the Broadway play change from the television script?

FOOTE: It was expanded. I did much work on the part of Jessie Mae so that she figured largely in the first act. Really it was the first act that was expanded and more thought through, more investigated.

MOORE: Were there other changes as far as pacing or tone? Did you think about writing for a different audience?

FOOTE: Not really. That kind of thing never entered into my head. I've always written as well as I can write. In those days, television was very close to theater. You didn't have nearly as many sets as you do today. There was a fluidity that theater was beginning more and more to discourage for economic reasons; so *Bountiful,* in that sense, was considered a fairly difficult play to do in the theater because we had three different sets.

But it worked well in Westport. Many people were very taken with it. It got wonderful notices out of town; so there was no rush to make any changes. You rehearse and work on things, try things. You know there are things you always do. I don't remember that. It's been so long ago. But mainly it was a rather unharried, unhurried time.

As a matter of fact, all the time when we were in Philadelphia, I was working on another TV play for Fred [Coe] for next year. I had promised to do two or three things for him; so I had to get busy on my commitment. And as I said, there was no rewriting done—out of town,

you don't have all that much time because you have two
matinees and performances every night. Unless you want
to kill the actors, there's not a lot you can do. If you're in
desperate trouble, you just do it; everybody works around
the clock. But we felt we were in pretty good condition.

MOORE: For the movie, did you make changes in the characters?

FOOTE: I wouldn't have consciously done that. It may be
there. You'd have to point it out to me. I didn't try to do
that.

On the screen, you can do things that you couldn't do
either in theater or in television as it was then. Without
destroying the thrust of the piece, the core of the piece,
we tried to do certain things. Well, we could take the trip,
for instance, which we couldn't do those days in televison
and we certainly couldn't do in theater.

MOORE: Did you expand the Broadway play for the movie
version?

FOOTE: Not really. As a matter of fact, I had to make some
cuts to make room for what few visual things I did. But
other than that there was nothing I changed about any of
the characters. The scenes that I wrote fresh were when
[Mrs. Watts] was waiting, having to change buses, when
she talks to the black lady and they discuss Corpus Christi
and what that means; then her walking to get the bus; her
going to the railroad station and seeing Jessie Mae and
Ludie, and we can go with her and see how she hides,
which we couldn't do in any other medium; then the trip,
the ride out to Bountiful in the car, which we couldn't do
any other way.

MOORE: In the film, you were also a producer. How much
say did you have?

FOOTE: I have a lot of say. I have a lot of say. That's why I do
the kind of films I do. In Hollywood, you're a writer for
hire, which means that you write it and turn it over to
them. And that's not so in the films that I do. I'm in on
the casting, on the editing, on the rehearsals, on the set as
much as I can be. Of course, when we did *Bountiful*, I was
also doing *Valentine's Day* at the same time. I had to go

back and forth, but I was around as much as I could physically do it. The people I work with like Sterling and Pete,
they're just delighted. That's how you work in the theater.
It's so much more sensible than in Hollywood. But there
would be those who disagree with me, I'm sure.

MOORE: You wouldn't have gotten involved unless it was on
that basis?

FOOTE: No more. I won't do it any more.

MOORE: Bad experience in the past?

FOOTE: Not any worse than any other writer. It's just that, to
me, it's degrading to have no control. You don't do it in the
theater. You don't do it in a novel. I have my own theory
about it. Many years ago there were silent pictures, and
writers made subtitles. They felt they were slumming; they
didn't care anything about it; so they didn't retain their
copyright. They just gave it away. In Hollywood today, the
writer doesn't ever have his work copyrighted. The studio
does. And if you don't own the copyright, you don't own
anything. That's not so in Europe, I understand. The writers over there do own their copyrights. But in any case,
however it's happened, you turn in a script to a studio and
that's it.

There's grown up the legend that the script is not the
essential part, which I don't agree with, that the director is
king and I don't agree with that or that a certain star [is
essential]. That's a fact of life, a fact of economics, but I
don't think it's artistically sound, and I don't think anybody should be king. It should be a collaborative medium.
That should be the key.

Whatever power I have, I've worked hard to get, but I
certainly would be foolish to abuse it because that would
just defeat everything. Just to have a director subservient
to the writer would be no more purposeful than the other
way around. I think you need a collection of equals. I
think you have to agree on a vision and you have to be
willing to stand up for it.

MOORE: Whenever you read about changing from one
medium into film, you always read about the importance
of "opening up the work."

FOOTE: That's almost a film-school cliché, as far as I'm concerned. That is the director's ego, often. I think what happens is that the whole work gets dissipated, gets to be like a travelogue. Visual things can be exciting and interesting if they're effective and add to the dramatic thrust; they're very useful. If they dissipate that and are a kind of exercise in wandering, then they're very harmful.

MOORE: To open up the scene in the apartment, to lose the sense of claustrophobia?

FOOTE: No, no, that's the whole essence of it, and nobody would quarrel with that. You could be perverse the other way and refuse to open up, and that's silly. You just have to weigh the balances and be very thoughtful and not be rigid either way. Sometimes when you take scenes meant to be indoors, outdoors, it's very distracting because you get so involved in the physical detail all around you.

MOORE: As a writer, do you have a favorite medium—television, the stage, film?

FOOTE: I don't like writing for television. It's a very restrictive medium as far as I'm concerned. I think essentially I'm a theater writer. That's my natural bent, although I'd hate to give up films. I'm very devoted to them now. Just a different kind of music from theater, but they both are very important to me. I really wouldn't ever want to give up theater. I wouldn't want to give up film.

MOORE: Theater is where you feel most comfortable?

FOOTE: I wouldn't think so now. It's a question of apples and oranges really. Each has its comforts, each has its discomforts, but there was a time when I felt very strange in film, but mainly because I felt like an appendage, but now that I've found a way to function and be a part of it, I'm very happy with it.

MOORE: When you say television is too restrictive, do you mean technically or in the themes they allow?

FOOTE: Just the bureaucracy, the nonsense. I think it's a waste of time for me. I have to qualify that. With "American Playhouse," that's not so at all. But I would think that's something else again. I'm talking about commercial television. PBS is a very different cup of tea.

MOORE: So it's not the technical part?

FOOTE: No, because nowadays, television is very near film. I don't see much distinction. Mainly they do on television now the kind of grade-B movies they used to do in Hollywood. I wouldn't care about a series. First of all, I think they're mostly moronic.

MOORE: What do you enjoy about the theater?

FOOTE: I just enjoy it as a mode of expression. It seems to be my talent. If I were a prose writer or a poet or a novelist, I'm sure I would get just as much satisfaction. It isn't the form so much. It's the ability to express and to investigate certain things that is important to me. Theater is the form that seems to come naturally to me, that I gravitate toward.

MOORE: When you're watching one of your plays, do you notice the reaction of the audience?

FOOTE: You can't help that. You try not to pay much attention to that because it can be very deceiving. Sometimes when you think they're bored or restless, they're not at all. It's just their way of coping with something. Sometimes emotion is very upsetting or very difficult for an audience. They don't necessarily react the way you think they should react. You've just got to learn to let that go and just realize the audiences are very different, very varied—and welcome it really.

I don't like to see films with audiences as much. I don't know why that is. I get very nervous and I guess it's because it's a looser atmosphere in film. People can get up, and they can eat popcorn and do all those kinds of things. Also, I would hate for films to give up theaters entirely to just become part of a little box. That would be terrible. We didn't always have a place to meet and see something together. It is wonderful to see the energy that happens.

MOORE: Does being able to write well for one medium mean automatically that you can write for another?

FOOTE: I don't know. I really couldn't answer that. I don't know. One would assume that, but I'm not sure it's so. As a matter of fact, I think it could be argued for some people that one works against the other. And maybe if I had any real sense, I'd feel that way. I don't feel that.

MOORE: Can any material work in any medium?

FOOTE: No, I don't think that. I think there are certain things whose very nature says to leave it alone, keep it here, and don't take it there. Well, I'm sure any really inventive person could turn around and prove me a liar. If I gave you an example, ten years from now somebody might come out and do just a brilliant work. But I just have to tell you that at the present that's my perception, that there are certain things I wouldn't want to do as films and certain things I wouldn't want to do as plays.

MOORE: What different qualities did Lillian Gish and Geraldine Page bring to their roles as Carrie Watts?

FOOTE: Great actresses—and I think they are both wonderful actresses, great actresses—they essentially very early on develop a style. That doesn't mean they play only one thing, but inherent in all their work is a style. It's as though, I would think, Horowitz and Rubinstein took the same piece of music. You might prefer this or that, but essentially you would have two great soloists and what would be different is almost intangible. With Lillian, she brought much more sense of spirituality, I might say, and Geraldine brought a great earthiness, a kind of strength. Lillian brought strength, too. I can't deny that, but it was a different kind of strength. Hers was a more fragile strength, if that's not a contradictory phrase, but there was enormous strength there. A drive—they both had great drive. It's just wonderful to have the experience of seeing these two women play Mrs. Watts.

MOORE: Do you get upset when actors rewrite your lines?

FOOTE: Well, they don't do that. Yes, I would get very upset. I'm not a fool, and if something is not working or if they don't feel comfortable with something, I'll try to solve it, but I would never permit them to rewrite.

MOORE: Which of the versions of *Bountiful* do you find most satisfying?

FOOTE: That's very hard to say. That's like saying, "Which child do you like the best?" Obviously the play is a memory, although it's being done all the time around in amateur theaters, but it was a very moving time for me. I thought it was wonderfully conceived in many areas. I was very proud of the film and very satisfied with it and moved by it. So it would be very hard for me to say. But television, again, has its strengths. The television version was the least developed, of course. You can see it [on film] at the Museum of Modern Art. It was the first television show they ever took.

MOORE: Your work as a whole seems very concerned with people trying to find their homes, their families. Why does that theme interest you?

FOOTE: I don't know. It's one of those mysteries.

MOORE: It's not conscious?

FOOTE: No, not really. It's something I obviously return to a great deal.

MOORE: It seems to be a theme that has a lot of appeal today.

FOOTE: I don't know that. I get differing kinds of response to my works, and I guess that is a part of it. I'm not nostalgic about the past; I don't necessarily want my work to imply that I am nostalgic. I try to look at the past with a pretty jaundiced eye. I think it was Katherine Anne Porter who said, in essence, saying you can't go home again is just crazy. I know there are people who have had bitter times in their childhood, in their homes, and I'm very sympathetic to that; I understand. But I'm on neither side; let's put it that way. It's an enigma really.

If these things appear, I'm reporting what I see as best I can, not literally. I'm interpreting, I hope, as an artist. In other words, I don't think necessarily that going back home is going to satisfy you or is going to be something very different. I don't think it's unimportant that people want to remember it or try to reestablish something. That just happens. And some people spend their lives cursing where they were born and run from it. I just happen to like to go home a lot. I have the house I went to when I was a year old. It's mine now. I go often.

What I'm trying to say is that I don't think the past was any great . . . the past had its problems just as today has its problems and tomorrow is going to have its problems. You look back and the problems seem lessened or they seem more in perspective perhaps, but if you are honest, you know there were plenty of problems and always were.

MOORE: Everyone talks about your ear for dialect. How do you keep that fresh?

FOOTE: I hear it. I'm back in Texas all the time. It's a remembered thing. It's one of the gifts of a writer. A certain kind of writer would be most interested in describing the chaos in this room, the minutiae in this room. Now, I'd be more interested in remembering what you said to me or what I said to you. I spent my early life listening to people. I listen to them now. I never get bored. I can listen forever. When I go home, I love to listen. I love to talk; I love to listen. In the few times I taught writing, one of the things I feel I'm helpful with writers about is to try to get them to train their ear, just to listen, listen, listen. And I first listen, not even edit. There's a time when you've got to edit, of course, and take all you've heard and put it all together into something else. The basis of it is listening for me. And I think about all these things a lot.

MOORE: Most of your work is set in the South. Are you tempted to write about other people and other places?

FOOTE: I've tried and it just doesn't work because I don't know what the impulse to write comes from, but whatever it is—there is a theory, and I don't know whether it's just a theory, but certainly I've thought about it often—that your themes are kind of set by the time you're twelve. And I really think with the writers I like, you could pretty much say that's true. Again that's a mystery to me. It's like things choose you. I think things choose you more than you choose them. I really do. Saul Bellow writes mostly about Chicago and that's what he knows, and it isn't that he hasn't been other places. God knows I've lived out of the South a lot. My friend Alan Pakula [producer (*To Kill a Mockingbird* and other films) and director] says, "Well, if you went and lived there all the time, you'd probably then start writing about the New York theater." Maybe I would, but I'm not going to do that. I'm not going to take that chance.

MOORE: The distance maybe helps a little?

FOOTE: Well, it obviously does help. Certain writers like Joyce, people like that just have to get away—Gertrude Stein. I mean they wrote about America, but they had to get away. Now Eudora [Welty] lives down there and Reynolds Price is there. He's my great friend.

MOORE: I've talked to a lot of people who've seen *Bountiful* on videocassette. It's wonderful that they can see it even when they've missed it at the movie theater.

FOOTE: This is the final problem for nonstudio films. There are so many places that they don't go to; so in that sense, VCRs are just remarkable. I lecture often in the South in small colleges because I happen to like to go to small colleges. I happen to like small towns and to get to these little towns. And none of them have movie theaters anymore. And all of them have two or three VCR stores. In that sense, it's very helpful.

MOORE: How would you summarize the experience of working on *Bountiful*?

FOOTE: The play was done under the last days of the very old-fashioned Broadway system of doing a play and trying it out and taking it to towns and coming into towns. They rarely do that anymore. The television thing was done at a time of great experimentation when it was just defining itself as a medium. And as a film, it was done when the big studios were breaking up. And it was done at great sacrifice for everyone involved because I don't think Geraldine made a lot of money, and there were none of the accouterments that big productions have. We didn't have Winnebagos and we didn't have the first class tickets—all that kind of stuff. So in that sense it kind of got back to a more experimental, freer basis. And I think that helped it a great deal because the only expectation was that they make as good a film as they could.

MOORE: Not having a studio helped?

FOOTE: A big studio has built-in costs, which you have to understand. You can't criticize them for that. They have to carry a staff year in and year out. They like to try things out. We didn't try *Bountiful* out in a [movie] theater to see how the audience would like it. We liked it and that was it.

And that's a new way of approaching it. *Bountiful* was again a part of a new way of doing things, just as it had been in its first concept. Part of its vitality, part of what is interesting about it is that you can put it into so many different categories; there are so many ways of approach. And the thrust of the story just remains the same. But you always had to have major actresses in the part or else it would have been diminished terribly.

Sterling VanWagenen

Sterling VanWagenen was cofounder of the United States Film Festival in Park City, Utah. With Robert Redford, he established the Sundance Institute and became its first executive director. For the stage, he directed Sartre's *The Flies* and several Shakespearean tragedies. For PBS, he directed *Christmas Snows, Christmas Winds*. He directed the feature film *Alan and Naomi* starring Michael Gross and Lukas Haas. He coproduced the documentary *Yosemite: The Fate of Heaven* (1985) and was producer of the film *Convicts*. He is now head of Leucadia Film Corporation in Salt Lake City.

The following telephone interview was conducted in October 1987.

MOORE: How did you get involved in the filming of *Bountiful?*
VANWAGENEN: In the summer of 1984, I was the executive director of the Sundance Institute, and I was approached by Peter Masterson, who was one of the resource people that the Sundance Institute used for acting. Peter and I passed each other on the lawn one afternoon, and he said, "I have a play that I'd like you to look at." I said, "Sure." That afternoon he gave me a copy of *The Trip to Bountiful* by Horton Foote. I was immediately interested because I had been a Horton Foote fan for a very long time—*Tender Mercies, To Kill a Mockingbird*, just exquisite works. I've been such a fan of his for years; so I immediately read it and liked it very much.

I saw Peter the next day, and he said, "What do you think of the play?"

I said, "Oh, it was wonderful, a lovely piece."

Peter said, "Well, I'm going to try to make it as my first feature film. Would you like to be helpful?"

Carlin, Peter's wife, said, "Well, would you like to produce it?"

I said, "Yes, I'd love to."

Peter said, "Great, let's talk to Horton about it." He said, "I'll talk to Horton." So he called Horton. Horton said, "That's fine. I'd like to meet him." So I guess about forty-five days later Horton was down in Dallas, Texas, completing the editing on another film he had written called *1918*. I flew down there and met Peter. Together we went to Horton's hotel, knocked on the door, and a rather elegant southern gentleman with gray hair and a pink face with a broad smile opened the door. Horton! I'd never seen a picture of him before, but he looked exactly as I'd always imagined him, right to the way he dressed, in a blue blazer and no tie—just a very elegant southern gentleman.

To my surprise—I was really expecting a kind of interview, a sort of drilling to determine whether or not Horton and I appeared able to work together; I expected to give information about my background and what I'd done. Instead, Horton treated me as though he'd known me all of his life. He immediately started in on questions such as where we were going to get the funding, what were the first steps we were going to take. And I said, "Well, are there things you'd like to ask or explore in terms of me and my past history or things I've done?"

Horton said, "No, I don't think so. Let's just go to work." I was really quite astonished at his response. We just immediately went to work trying to raise money for the movie, based not really on the screenplay, but on the script of the play and on the involvement of the three of us and Geraldine Page. Peter and Horton wanted really from the beginning for her to play that role. So that's how I got involved.

MOORE: This may sound basic, but what does a producer do?

VANWAGENEN: Actually, that's not basic at all because it gets very confusing, because people who take producer's credit on pictures don't always do the same things. Some people who get producer credits are brothers-in-law of the director, and other producers actually do the work. Let me try to clarify this. There are usually two kinds of producers. One is independent and the other is related to a major studio. An independent producer will generally, number one, find money for the films he or she wants to make, and number two, will develop material either from books, magazines, newspaper articles, or original ideas from someplace and will develop that material with the writer. Then he will go out to find the money to make the picture, then supervise it, then supervise the other creative process—putting a cast together, hiring a director, the crews. But he also manages the production to make sure it's on budget and on schedule and makes the deals with the actors. He also makes the deals at the back end to distribute the picture, to make sure it goes out to the public properly and at the right time with the right public relations campaign and so forth; so actually what a really good producer is, is a kind of combination of a strong, creative type, who understands the creative process and the creative team, with a businessman and a good manager. You don't normally find all those qualities in one person, but in your best producers you do.

MOORE: How did you go about raising money for *Bountiful?*

VANWAGENEN: Well, there was an acquaintance of mine, a fellow named Sam Grogg, whom I had known at the American Film Institute when I was working with Sundance Institute. Sam had recently left the AFI and left running the film festival in Dallas and had started a motion picture investment company with some partners in Dallas, Texas. And having known that they had just recently gotten some money, I called him. And it happens they were looking around for a first project to invest some money in and to get into production. So I sent Sam the play, which he liked very much. Obviously, he knew Horton's other works like *Tender Mercies.* And he got very excited about it. There was no doubt they would put up the money initially for Horton to write the screenplay and then they committed the first production capital to the project. Our second piece of money actually came from an acquaintance of Peter Masterson's, a man [George Yaneff] who used to be director of an American branch of the Swiss bank. He had various connections in London. He had known Peter Masterson because he also had an interest in theater. Of course, Peter was an actor and director of the Broadway theater. And at one time he [Yaneff] had approached Peter and said, "If there's ever a project you want to do, please give me a chance to see if I can get the money." So Peter and I flew to New York. Peter introduced me to this gentleman and we described the project. He agreed to find other pieces of money for us, which he did.

The interesting thing, the deceptive thing, about this whole process was that very, very quickly we had gotten commitments for two-thirds of the budget of the film. So we were feeling rather relaxed and rather positive about how quickly that amount of money had come together. The real excruciating part, it turned out, was finding the last third of the producing money, which turned out to be very, very difficult. We took the script to a number of Hollywood agencies and production companies. I took it to dozens of people and we got turned down by everyone with the argument that nothing really happens in the story; it's too light; it's too soft. After all these turndowns, the Dallas people managed to find one other individual investor in Dallas, and I found another individual investor from Austin, Texas. Then Peter, Horton, myself, and one other friend borrowed the last piece of money from a New York bank ourselves and put up the collateral to finish the picture. It's like putting together pieces of a very complicated puzzle.

MOORE: Then how did you arrange for distribution of it?

VANWAGENEN: Sam Grogg of Dallas had made a previous deal with a company called Island Alive, which is a distribution company in Los Angeles. They put up some money to finance the advertising campaign for a picture called *Choose Me,* and so Sam Grogg had a relationship with the head of Island Alive Pictures, a man named Cary Brokaw. In turn, I had a relationship with a distributor in New York called Orion Classics. And so when the time came, when the pieces of our puzzle came together—and by that, I mean not just the money but also the cast—we went simultaneously to both distributors. And both companies very much liked the idea of the picture and both companies made us an offer. The Orion Classics' offer collapsed because of politics within the company. The people in Orion Classics were terribly, terribly disappointed; so we then went with Island and they distributed the picture for us.

MOORE: During the actual filming, what was your role? Talking to the people involved, I get a feeling of a team effort.

VANWAGENEN: Yes, that's right. I always worked very closely with Peter and with Horton. My objective as a producer was to support responsibly the director in finding ways to accomplish what he wanted to accomplish. I was responsible for hiring the key people on the crew, including the cameraman, the costume designer, the production designer, the production manager, first assistant director, the really key people—the editor—who make the movie work. I was responsible basically for trying to match the right talent, the right personality with the director's. Then, while the picture was actually shooting, I spent time on the set monitoring the budget, being certain we were shooting on schedule through the entire production, dealing with frustrated actors and actresses, generally trying to solve problems.

MOORE: Did you get involved in the creative aspects of the film?

VANWAGENEN: I actually had less to do with the script. That was pretty much a matter between Peter and Horton though I gave Peter some notes and made some suggestions about cuts in the script. I was heavily involved in casting and editing for Peter. Everybody did their jobs and did their jobs well, but obviously there were some areas of aggravation. Peter, Horton, and I got along well.

MOORE: That's much different than you usually hear about egos on the set.

VANWAGENEN: That certainly happens, but it didn't happen to the three of us. There were disagreements, I'll admit, but they were never a matter of ego; they were always about work.

MOORE: What did you see in the script that made you think it would transfer well into film?

VANWAGENEN: I was moved at the end. I was deeply moved by the end of the play, by the accumulation of the pain and emotion. For me in terms of basic criteria, it certainly had a narrative line with Mrs. Watts's journey. The script seemed to me very strong and capable of turning into a film plot.

MOORE: What is the major difference between working in the theater and in film?

VANWAGENEN: To me, the principal difference, and there are many differences, but creatively the principal difference is in the process of rehearsing and mounting. A play is in many ways a more organic process than making a film. One has much more latitude in terms of experimenting and trying different possibilities. The process of mounting a play is often sensed by the actors and directors as more of a whole, whereas a movie tends to be a very fragmented enterprise. Even for the actors, it's very fragmented because they do a little piece here, a little piece there, not necessarily in sequence. And so it's the difference really between in theater a painter who paints with very large brushes and very broad strokes and in film a painter who is rather a pointillist, who uses small bits and pieces of paint that will gradually build into a whole picture. That's probably the major difference between the two.

MOORE: I've talked to a number of people who enjoyed the videocassette. They missed seeing it at the theater.

VANWAGENEN: Yes, the picture was actually very successful in the videocassette market for an independent film. And that market also counts for a significant number of dollars coming back to the investors. It's a very crucial part.

MOORE: How would you summarize the experience of working on *Bountiful*?

VANWAGENEN: Obviously, I'm very proud of what we did on
the picture. We certainly got a lot of really lovely response
about the film. It moved a lot of people profoundly. What
more can one ask for than a picture that moves people,
brings out questions about their families and lives?

Peter Masterson

Peter Masterson has had experience as both an actor and a
director. He starred in *The Trial of Lee Harvey Oswald* on
Broadway (1967) and had major roles in *The Great White Hope*
and *That Championship Season*. As a film actor he has appeared in *The Exorcist, Man on a Swing,* and *The Stepford Wives.*
His directing experience began with an off-Broadway play,
A Nice Spring for Humans. In 1979, he won the Drama Desk
Award as best director for *The Best Little Whorehouse in Texas*
and was nominated for a Tony Award as director and as co-
author of the book. He wrote and served as executive producer of the made-for-television movie *City in Fear* (1980)
and directed the off-Broadway production of *The Last of the
Knuckle Men* (1983) with Dennis Quaid. His latest projects
include the films *Night Game* with Roy Scheider and *Convicts*
with Robert Duvall.

The following telephone interview was conducted in February 1988.

YELLIN: How did you get involved with *Bountiful*?

MASTERSON: I asked Horton to come see *Best Little Whorehouse* when we were doing it at the Actors Studio, the first
time we had gotten back together in a while. I was in [the
film] *Tomorrow,* which he did, but that was before this.
When they did the movie of *Best Little Whorehouse,* they
hired me to write the screenplay, which I did. They liked it
and hired me to direct it. I did all the preproduction work
for about a year. Then Burt Reynolds wanted somebody he

could boss around, I think, and so he got rid of me. They did the movie without me. I thought, well, I didn't want to do a twenty-five-million-dollar musical anyway as my first movie. I'd done a lot of films myself as an actor.

It was a couple of years after that that I was talking to Robert Redford. He said, "You ought to do something you really care deeply about, a small thing." It started that way. [My wife, Carlin Glynn, and I] were up at the Sundance Film Institute, just visiting friends. We were up there riding horses in the mountains. And so I thought, right, that would be a good idea. I had seen Horton's play off-Broadway, a revival of it. I never saw the original.

YELLIN: *Bountiful?*

MASTERSON: Yes, it had moved me very much.

We were at the Sundance Institute that year [1984] in June when I decided, well, let me just put a package together and do my thing, just to get a movie done. So I called Horton to start with and told him I wanted to do it. I told him, "It's about time somebody did *Bountiful,* and I'd like to direct it."

Horton said, "Well, I think that would be a fine idea. Who do you want to play Mrs. Watts?"

I said, "Who do you want?"

He said, "Geraldine [Page]."

And I said, "I don't think we can do any better than that. I'm with you."

He said, "Will Carlin play Jessie Mae?"

I said, "I don't know. She's right here. I'll ask." He had tried to get Carlin to do a couple of things, which never did work out quite.

And I asked her. And she said, "Gosh, I don't know. That's a tough one. That's a tough part. Sure, I'll do it."

Then we were off and running. So I went over to the office of the Sundance Institute. Sterling VanWagenen was running it then. And I told him what I wanted to do. I explained that we wanted to do it ourselves and we wanted to see if the Sundance Institute could help do it. I gave him a script of the play. We got it out of the Salt Lake City Library, a very historic library. He read it, and I had a meeting with him late that night. He started mumbling around a little bit. I said, "Do you think you can be of some help to us?"

"Well, of course, it's a beautiful, beautiful play."

And Carlin said, "Do you want to produce it?"

He said, "I wouldn't be presumptuous enough to put myself in that position."

I said, "Why not? I never directed anything before and you never produced anything before. Might as well make it a hundred percent."

He said, "I'd love to. What about Horton?"

I said, "Oh, I think you and Horton will like each other."

I checked it out with Horton. He said, "That would be lovely." And so we had a producer.

I went back to New York and had somebody set up a dinner with George Yaneff. George had never been involved in anything theatrically or on film, but he had been an insurance man for oil factories off Bermuda. He had come to New York and was looking for something to do. It wasn't his money. He just collected it from a lot of people who had money. He wanted to raise money for theatrical and film projects and he did, just made a call and got money to do a play with. At the dinner, George said, "I want to back anything you do. I've seen your work and I admire it. And I'd like to put some money into whatever."

I said, "I just happen to have this play I want to do as a film." I gave him the script.

He called back and said, "I like it. I'll put up the money." So he was made an executive producer. Then it got a little complicated because Sterling thought it might be a good idea to get Filmdallas involved, which I think it probably was. Yaneff didn't put up all the money, but he put up almost half of it.

YELLIN: How much did the film cost?

MASTERSON: A million six.

YELLIN: And who was Filmdallas?

MASTERSON: They have a fund that they invest, like five hundred thousand dollars in a film. And for that they get half of the money spent in the Dallas area. It's a Dallas organization. They try to promote film in the Dallas area.

YELLIN: And somebody decides where they'll put it?

MASTERSON: Sam Grogg. He was a friend of Sterling, too. They went along with it. They were the general partners. We are, too. They are the managing general partners.

YELLIN: Who are "we"?

MASTERSON: Sterling, Horton, myself, and George Yaneff are the Bountiful Film Partners. I guess that's what we're called.

YELLIN: Did Island Pictures, Filmdallas, and Bountiful Film Partners account for all the people sharing in the profit?

MASTERSON: Yes.

YELLIN: When you thought about it as a film, what did you think had to be done? What did Horton have to do as writer? Or as a director, what did you think about the translation into a film?

MASTERSON: Well, I just thought like a lot of stage plays, it had a movement to it. It had that narrative story. In fact, I thought it would be a better film than a play because it started out in a confined space and ended up in an expanded space. It was originally a television play.

[The stage director] had to do things that were fake although they worked. They weren't done in any kind of reality. I mean the bus ride had to be imagined. You couldn't have any sense of the expanding space with Mrs. Watts as she first got out of the house. I always thought of that as a moment of freedom—when the bus pulls away from the Houston bus station and moves out to the country. I always thought of that as a musical sequence. In the rehearsal, I told Geraldine, "When we do it, this is flight. This is a bird who's escaped and who's enjoying the flight." That made sense to her. I thought that as acted out, this became one of a series of coming-back-to-earth scenes, I guess, coming-home scenes.

I didn't think that we had to worry about writing too much extra. I followed Ludie a little bit more away from the house. There was more we shot. Some of it we didn't use because it got a little long. We had Jessie Mae and Ludie going away from the bus station, coming toward the bus station, going away, coming back to look for her and all kinds of things. It actually worked pretty well, but we needed to lose something; so I thought we could cut that and get on with the story.

YELLIN: That scene where she gets on the bus—that's very sensitive.

MASTERSON: Yes, it is. Kind of a lyrical music, don't you think?

YELLIN: Why color?

MASTERSON: It was hard for me to see it in color, if you want to know the truth. I kept seeing it in black and white. I'm glad we used color, but there really was no option. Nobody wants to make a black-and-white film. It's commercial death. It's also, strangely enough, more expensive to do black and white. Everything is geared to color now, the labs and everything else, so that you have to have special runs for black-and-white film. It's more difficult. So that really wasn't an option. But you're right. I did have to strain some. Even in my mind, I saw it in black and white.

YELLIN: But the colors other than the field of flowers were generally subdued anyway. They weren't colorful colors.

MASTERSON: Well, we used particular colors—like the greens and reds in the apartment taken from Edward Hopper's paintings. And the colors we used in a lot of ways for clothing and all were based on that.

The reason is—I discussed it with Horton and the designer—Horton's writing is very much what's not said, much of it. The actors get it and they understand it, but the people who read Horton, the producers, the studio people have a hard time. They say, "What happened?" They don't like that. They'll say, "Well, what?" You give it to an actor, and she just lights up. She knows what to do with it. She knows who's going to let her perform. Anyway, it seemed to me that in a Hopper painting, it looks like a realistic painting, but then you look closer, closer, and it's not at all. There are no eyes much of the time; they're in deep shadows. I think he's very American. I like his style.

Also, the loneliness of his paintings was just right for this film. I used that for a basis for ideas. That was the formula for color and design.

YELLIN: That's fascinating because Horton is that kind of writer.

MASTERSON: Now, Horton was wondering what we were doing. He'd look at the set and say, "There's too much of this and not enough of that. No, that's okay." His mind is all realistic, naturalistic. I think the film has a sharper focus than that. So he was a little nervous about that, but he got past it.

YELLIN: He let you alone?

MASTERSON: Yes, he did.

YELLIN: But it took a little persuading?

MASTERSON: A little bit, but he trusted me a lot. I really appreciate that. When we were rehearsing, he came around a little bit. A couple of times, he came to the readings. Very easily, the play could have been a sweet old lady and a wimpy son and a horrible, mean daughter[-in-law]. And I didn't want that. I wanted all those things that are there. "That woman is tough," I told Geraldine the first day.

She said, "Oh, thank God." They are both fighting for the favor of the son. Mrs. Watts lives right next to the bedroom. We put glass doors up there with curtains over them to make it as unpleasant a situation as possible for people living in the same place.

YELLIN: You're touching on the theme of the story; could you amplify that?

MASTERSON: I just thought it was about a situation that probably wouldn't exist today. And that was why it was interesting to me, and that's why it had to be in the forties.

YELLIN: It's somewhere between '46 and '50. Did you have a date in mind?

MASTERSON: Yes, 1947. That was my favorite year. That's why we picked that one. Horton said—I asked him when it was—and he said, "I don't know."

I said, "When did you write it?"

He said, " '51 or '52."

I said, "How about '47?" The design stuff was more interesting then and that was my favorite year.

YELLIN: It had to be then because you mentioned Truman.

MASTERSON: That was me, as a matter of fact, on the radio.
But the sensibilities of it had to be, it seemed to me, in a
period when a man really had to take care of his family
and women didn't go to work. We had to create a situation
where Jessie Mae wouldn't be expected to go to work. Her
father took care of her and now her husband takes care of
her. She might want some more clothes and that sort of
thing, but she wouldn't work to provide them.

So they had been living there with the mother for fifteen years; they've been living in the same situation. Jessie
Mae and Ludie had no private life. And it was perfectly
understandable that they were sticky. They were in a difficult situation for all of them. Today they would have put
her in an old folks' home, and that's too bad, too.

YELLIN: What is the story about? The story revolves around
her need to get some dignity in her life through seeing
what her memory created as a wonderful time in her life.

MASTERSON: Well, I guess so. Also, I think you make a great
deal out of something that's in the past when you haven't
been there and seen it in a long time. It becomes much
more glamorous, mythological. I think Mrs. Watts had to
go there to find her strength to go on with life rather than
to die. At least that's the way I read it. And I think her son,
Ludie, needed to see it to take from her strength so that
he could go on with his life. And I think the key scene in
the play is when they sit down together on the porch at the
end before Jessie Mae comes up from the car.

YELLIN: I think in the film more than in the other two versions, this permeates to Ludie, and he gets the feeling so
that he can finally call a halt to the two of them quarrel-
ing, and it gives him strength.

MASTERSON: Well, I think we worked that out very well. And
I think John [Heard] was quite good in that. You have to
be very careful with Horton's things that you don't just
passively play through something. You have to attack it
sometimes, and John certainly did in that scene. When he

exploded, when he tried to tell about the time when her father died, she asked him, "Do you remember my father?"

And he said, "No, ma'am, I don't, but I remember the day he died. I remember I came home from school and everybody was sitting around and uncle somebody took me on his lap."

Then, he started to get angry. He got very angry when he was telling that story because it was the thing that had been haunting him. When Ludie said he couldn't take Mrs. Watts back because it was too hard to get there, Heard asked me a good question, "Why couldn't he do that? Why is he so mean? He won't borrow a car and take his mother back to her house. She's been begging for fifteen years to go. It's not much to do for her."

I said, "Because he can't stand to go. It's too painful." That's what came out of that moment. I didn't tell him he should get angry, but that's the way it came out.

YELLIN: Did you feel or did he as an actor feel that also what sustained him was his love for his Mom?

MASTERSON: I think so. I think he certainly loves her, yes. I think he loves Jessie Mae. I think he loves both of them. He's a man who has to deal with two women. I had that in my life. I understand it. My mother—she's tough to deal with, but I love her. I'd take her home. I'd chase her if she ran away.

YELLIN: Can we talk more about your directing style? Did you take a lot of shots?

MASTERSON: No, not many. I don't go to a lot of takes unless I haven't gotten what I want. And I've been lucky enough to have good actors. I think I've gotten really good performances, even in the other movies I've done since. I continue to do the same kind of thing; so I guess that's what I do. I don't plan it that way. I get satisfied very soon if an actor does what he wants, what I think is good. If I think I can get a little more, I'll go again.

YELLIN: Do you prepare ahead of time?

MASTERSON: I prefer to rehearse more before we do the take. If you have action scenes, you don't have to rehearse except technically. If you have two- or three-page scenes where the actors interact with each other in dialogue, that's very difficult to do without a rehearsal period.

YELLIN: You rehearse whole bits at a time, regardless of how you would be filming it? You do it before you shoot in sequence?

MASTERSON: I like to rehearse ahead of time. What I like to do in rehearsal is to get out of the way certain things that take time on the set like the circumstances, the place and time, the characters, relationships with the characters and what they're doing in a scene—get all of that stuff done so that we don't do that on the set because it's a labor-intensive period.

YELLIN: Do you tell the actors how you're filming the scene, where the angle is going to be and so on?

MASTERSON: No, I won't discuss it with them when we're rehearsing. I try not to talk a lot. I try not to talk any more than necessary. I think the actors respond better to that. I talked a lot the first time I directed anything, and I think I just confused the actors to the point that they didn't know what the hell was going on. But I've kind of gotten to the point where I can let them know where I'm going without telling them what to do. Then I don't talk much, and we do the scene. We'll discuss some; we'll talk about it. I let them talk about it. I try to create a dialogue.

YELLIN: Do you see the scene when they do it with your naked eye or do you have to see it in the rushes? How do you know a scene is good?

MASTERSON: If it's functioning between the characters, I think. I don't stage it in a certain way right away for the camera. I just get the scene functioning. Once the actors are functioning in the scene, then you can tell them to go here or there, but when you start directing actors to go here or there before they're comfortable, then they'll fight you. And it'll also hurt them.

I don't like to get the final result in a rehearsal. I don't want to push it to that in rehearsal for a film. That's like telling the actor, "Show me you know how to do it." I just want to see if they're prepared. It's almost like a football team. You kind of make sure they know what the paces are, where the holes are going to be, where the blocking is going to develop, but you don't want them to go full out. I kind of wait until we get on the set for that. But I know that they know. I try to make sure I know what they're going for, what the tensions of the scene are. When we get on the set, then they can do it for the first time for the camera. There are a lot of actors who like to do it that way, most of them do—film actors. If they want to rehearse over and over, I'll let them.

YELLIN: Sometimes the camera does something special. Can you see that with the naked eye? Do you understand what I'm talking about?

MASTERSON: Yes, I do. Most of the time you can, but sometimes not. I know what you mean. Some actors you see it, and some actors are more subtle in a way than that. I was usually not fooled on the set in that film; I wasn't surprised at the dailies is what I mean. The most surprising thing in dailies to me was when I saw Rebecca DeMornay [who played Thelma] and what the camera did for her. She really lights up. The camera really loves her. What seemed the simplest thing was more interesting on film. The reason I wanted Rebecca was that I thought she had a kind of sexuality that was not written in the part, but that might make it interesting, just a little bit.

YELLIN: Now, we're talking about actors. Your wife is splendid, different than Eileen Heckart [Jessie Mae in the television version], who was kind of shrewish.

MASTERSON: I would imagine.

YELLIN: If I may, your wife had a sexiness about her.

MASTERSON: Yes, that was one of the things that Horton was a little bit—I don't know. Carlin and I talked about it. We said here she is living with John; they probably haven't had any kind of sexual relations in a long time. That's what she came up with. She loves him.

YELLIN: Why did you take away her Hollywood syndrome that was in both other versions? Horton made a little bit more of it in the beginning.

MASTERSON: I think we cut some of that stuff. I don't know whether we cut some of that after production or before

production. I remember we cut all of that scene, Jessie
Mae's talking with her friend. It seemed to go on a little
too long. So we lost some of that. I can usually tell when it's
going to be too long; so I asked Horton to cut some stuff.
And he cut some things, but then he said, "I don't know
how to cut it; you want to cut it? What would you cut?"

I said, "I don't know. I like it all. I just know it's going to
be too long." What we ended up doing was losing some
stuff after we shot it.

YELLIN: The film ran 107 minutes, and I guess you didn't
want to go too much more.

MASTERSON: I don't know how many hours we had when we
went to the editing room. When we showed the first cut, it
was getting close to three hours. It was rambling. We obviously lost some things we really liked.

YELLIN: Do you remember anything in particular?

MASTERSON: Yes, one of my favorite scenes. It was so good,
but it killed the next scene; it overshadowed it. At the end
of the movie, the sheriff says he's going to go out by his
car. In the script he comes back. [Mrs. Watts] goes in the
house, goes looking through the house, goes upstairs, and
sees—well, we put that in there—sees an old, broken-down
bed there. Then the sheriff calls her. He comes up to the
house, walks around, doesn't know where she is, calls her,
and she comes out the window the way we did it, and looks
out the window, almost like a Romeo and Juliet sequence.
And the sheriff, this big old fellow, says, "Your son's here,
says he wants to see you."

And she says, "Oh, have him come in."

"No ma'am," he says. "He wants you to come on out.
He's in a hurry to get back to Houston."

And she says, "Ask him if he can't come in."

And the sheriff says, "He thought you might have died
out here." And he says, "Well, I got to get back to town,
ma'am."

She says, "All right," and keeps flirting with him. And he
left. Then Ludie comes in and has a scene. And that scene
was so well played by the sheriff and Geraldine that it
just—

YELLIN: I must confess I wondered what happened to the sheriff. The assumption is that he's decided it's private and he should go away.

MASTERSON: That's the thing you count on. Nobody would be too worried about something like that—if the play's working. And I kept the scene to the very last cut, screening after screening. I realized as good as it was—nobody really suggested cutting it; it's just something that became clear to me. He's also one of my best friends. I didn't want to cut his scene.

YELLIN: Richard Bradford as the sheriff, why is he good?

MASTERSON: I've known Richard for years, and I just talked to him. He was out in California. He has, I think, maybe more integrity than any man I know. He is the most honest and straightforward.

YELLIN: Both as an actor and a person or can they be separated?

MASTERSON: Well, as a person, and I think that permeates the art. Nothing is ever good enough for Richard. I think that's probably his biggest problem. He wants everything to be perfect.

YELLIN: The scene that bears out what you said is the one where she is asleep, and he goes over there to wake her up. I think another person playing the sheriff might have done it a little more sternly or not done it as tenderly as he did, without being oversentimental and hammy. That was a beautiful scene.

MASTERSON: Yes, he's also very formidable, his voice, so I thought he was the perfect person. I told [Geraldine Page] that maybe he looked a little bit like the man who walked by her house, she wasn't quite sure. Maybe he could be a cousin or something; so that's what she was working with there. But she loved Richard. She'd known him from before. I thought it was really important to cast someone like him. He looks like he could be a big old Texas sheriff. He's from Houston, and he played football at Texas A & M.

YELLIN: Talk about Geraldine Page. Comparing her with Lillian Gish—it's a different quality.

MASTERSON: I never saw Lillian Gish play this part, but I would imagine that there was more delicacy to her than to Geraldine, because Geraldine was a much more full-boned, strong woman, and I thought that Geraldine was much more believable as a person who could work the land. And so in that way, I just don't see how anybody could have done any better. Geraldine also would not play a sweet little old lady. She just wouldn't do it. She's tough. She confronted everybody. She confronted that little guy in front of the bus station. She gave him a hard time. I thought she was at the peak of her talent at the time she worked with us. And it's just a shame she's not around because she was having such a good time working.

YELLIN: Is there anything you can say about how you worked with her in particular?

MASTERSON: I just tried to set it up properly. I tried to set the stage to make it easy for the actor to work, to make the set the right environment, I guess is what I mean by setting the stage.

YELLIN: You mean psychological or emotional environment? Not just the staging itself?

MASTERSON: No, the set itself, the atmosphere around the set. Actually, in the house we had the set designer ask the actresses what they wanted in the drawers. He put whatever they asked for including some of their personal things; so if someone opened a drawer, it looked like they lived there. That kind of thing—we tried to make sure it worked. Geraldine and I talked about the fact that she has a little tendency to have mannerisms and tended to—well, she said, "I get hammy sometimes." She said, "Just watch me and tell me if I do it." Sometimes, she would ask me after a take.

YELLIN: Is that where she does things with hands on her face and things of that sort?

MASTERSON: Yes. See, sometimes it's in character, and sometimes it's not; so I would try to make the call between whether it was in Mrs. Watts's character or whether it was that she was nervous and uncomfortable in the scene. And I think you can tell the difference. Actors try to keep going whether or not they're perfectly right on, most of the time. When you have an actor who's a little uncomfortable, sometimes they start to fidget, and they start to do things with their face or their hands that they wouldn't do if they were relaxed and comfortable. I think sometimes she would do that. And yet that was also part of her nature, too; so you had to see the difference. There was a difference between the two things.

YELLIN: When you talked to her, did you do it privately?

MASTERSON: Yes, usually, yes. Sometimes she'd shout across the room at me, "Was that too hammy?"

And I'd say, "Yes, a little bit." We were doing the bus sequence, which was a long sequence and took eighteen hours of shooting in one day. We started it in the wrong sequence. I broke it down in five different parts so we wouldn't try to do ten pages in a take because I was going to cut away anyway. We rehearsed it, and it was really bad. So I went over and said, "Geraldine, if you would think of this as the beginning of a symphony, the allegro part. Take it twice."

She said, "You want me to get more active."

I said, "Yes, but I wouldn't insist on it."

She said, "I know. It's a long scene. It would be boring if I did it like that at that pace." There were a few times, but I didn't have to remind her much. She got most of the things after the rehearsal period. She thanked me all day one day because I reminded her of her friend Callie Davis when she was doing the scene up on the porch. I said, "Don't forget about Callie."

She said, "Oh, thank you very much."

YELLIN: The relationship on the set with your wife?

MASTERSON: That was okay. We've worked together before. It was good. I'd try not to show favoritism. Actually, you get a lot of work done at home. She can do things better than most actors I know. I like working with Carlin. Not only does she deliver as an actress, she helps keep everybody else straight on the set. She's a good teacher. She teaches at Columbia now. She teaches directors acting. It's a good course, by the way. It's a new idea.

YELLIN: Now, talk about Fred Murphy, the cinematographer. He helped you a great deal?

MASTERSON: He was a wonder. The first day, when we were talking about lenses, he said a number. I said, "Look, I don't know what that means. Draw me a picture of what it would look like." He said, "There's no reason why you would have to know the number. That's my job. Just tell me what you think, what you want to see." I learned it during the shooting, but it doesn't take you long, just one set of dailies.

YELLIN: Whose decision was it—there were all cuts in this film, no fades, no dissolves?

MASTERSON: There was a dissolve in the musical section when she's going from one place to another. Basically, in a story like this, you want to stay away from anything that attracts attention to the technical. Anytime you use an optical, the audience knows you're doing film. That's fine in certain films that are technically oriented. You do a zoom or you do this or that. What we tried to do is keep the camera unobtrusive and let people look at beautiful shots, which I set up as shots that tell us something, just the shot itself.

YELLIN: Now, the opening credits—

MASTERSON: I'll tell you about that. That was an idea I had before we even started shooting, and Fred Murphy was in Dallas and I was in New York. He was scouting locations; so I said, "Why don't we shoot something of Geraldine as a young girl, a little boy and a dog, and all that?" I didn't know quite what I was going to do with it. It might work in the credits, but I didn't know exactly how it was going to work or what it would mean.

So Fred called me and said, "I think the bluebonnets are dying out here. You're going to lose them pretty soon." Sterling was there, too.

I said, "Why don't you go out there and go do it? Do it tomorrow." And I said, "Do it in slow motion. Do it in regular speed."

He said, "Okay," so I got on the phone with the casting guy. I told him what kind of people to get and the costumes; so they called back after they had done it.

Fred said, "Well, I think we got most of it. The only thing is it got a little late on us."

I said, "Did you get it in slow motion?"

And he said, "No, I couldn't do it in slow motion because it was too late."

And I said, "Oh, no!"

YELLIN: Too late because of the light?

MASTERSON: Yes, you need more light with high-speed cameras; so anyway he just miscalculated. We got the footage and Fred said, "This looks terrible, not beautiful." We got back to the lab and they said, "What can we do?" We printed the frames. "Let's go over to the optical house." So we went over and talked to the guy from the optical house. And he said, "We can do a lot of things. We can slow it down by printing each frame three times, four times, six times."

I said, "Can you make it closer?"

He said, "Sure, we can blow it up, move in closer on this piece of this, that piece of that."

I said, "What will happen?"

He told me, "Well, it will break up. As you adjust it more, it will break up into dots of color, grainy." So anyway, he gave me several different versions of it so I could look at it.

And I said, "Hey, this is really looking right. It's starting to look like a painting, like a Seurat painting." I said, "That's interesting." I saw this as a romantic piece anyway.

YELLIN: The whole film?

MASTERSON: Yes. And this opening would be Mrs. Watts's memories of the time; so I wanted to make it a romantic kind of version of what it was. Then when I got the girl to sing the opening piece, I told them I wanted a soprano because I think that has almost a thrilling sound, just so moving a sound—soprano. So when Horton heard it, he said, "That's terrible. Mrs. Watts would never have sung like that."

And I said, "No, but she thinks she did."

Then he said, "Well, okay." And we put it all together, and it really worked for that title sequence. It led you right into her old, cracking voice speaking.

YELLIN: There was some family in the casting, wasn't there?

MASTERSON: Yes, my daughter was in the drugstore. And Geraldine's kids were behind her in the bus line. And the VanWagenens—on the bus, they're his wife and his kids.

YELLIN: Can I ask you, has the film made money?

MASTERSON: Yes, everybody got their money back, and we made a little profit.

YELLIN: Of course, the Oscar didn't hurt?

MASTERSON: No, it didn't. That was the big thing, I think, to everybody. It was a delight to make. Horton is such a wonderful person. I owe him so much for having the faith in me to make a picture.

Carlin Glynn

Carlin Glynn won a Tony Award for her performance as the madam in the Broadway version of *The Best Little Whorehouse in Texas* and a Lawrence Olivier Award for best actress in a musical in the London version. Her films include *Three Days of the Condor, Sixteen Candles, Continental Divide,* and *Gardens of Stone.* On television, she costarred with George C. Scott on the Fox Television series "Mr. President" (1987) and cohosted "Good Morning New York" for WABC. She is a professor in the graduate film division at Columbia University.

The following telephone interview was conducted in August 1987.

MOORE: Have you seen any of the previous versions of Jessie Mae?

GLYNN: No, I didn't purposefully because I didn't want to be affected by the work of the actor who had done the part before.

MOORE: It must have been a bit daunting to take on the role that Jo Van Fleet won a Tony for. How did you make Jessie Mae your own character?

GLYNN: When Horton asked me to do it, I said, "Oh, no," because it was a very difficult part, but a wonderful part. I thought the trap in the part was caricature. I had to make her be abrasive enough to act as a catalyst, the force in the screenplay that would make Mother Watts want to leave home. But I truly thought that the character had her own hidden agenda. To make her just strident and shrewish would be to deny the boldness and richness of the character that Horton had written.

I worked on the areas of the character in terms of making it my own. What were Jessie Mae's problems? It's so easy to read *Bountiful* and see the mother's problems, but I think Jessie Mae is a woman who truly loves her husband, who has no privacy. She's living in very cramped quarters with her mother-in-law. And this woman, her mother-in-law, dotes on her son, Jessie Mae's husband; so I see Jessie Mae's role as childlike, trying to be pretty, trying very hard not to be like her mother-in-law. Interestingly enough, it's a role women truly understand. They may not like her, but they understand the character. And for me, I felt that was a victory.

One of the strengths of Horton as a writer is that he doesn't answer all the questions for the actors. He lets you delve into questions of background. For example, the relationship between husband and wife is not clearly defined in the writing. I chose to add the sexuality, the fact that she was an orphan, thinking that her class was better though it probably wasn't. I thought of her as looking forward to a modern, convenient world rather than a woman wanting to go back in time. As far as the final results, Jessie Mae was much more verbal in the beginning of the film than in the final cut, which meant that you could get it very clear what type of speech patterns she had, how she filled the empty air with verbiage. To go back to my work on it: I worked very hard on my relationship with Ludie. It's a thwarted relationship because of the mother-in-law's presence. Now, Horton doesn't tell us why Ludie was sick; he doesn't answer why we don't have children; so John and I had the fun of answering those questions—privately, not together necessarily.

MOORE: According to Horton, *Bountiful* was much more a team project than most films. Would you agree?

GLYNN: It was definitely a team project. The whole thing
about the way this happened was [that] Pete was fired off
the film *Best Little Whorehouse in Texas,* which was a play he
had conceived, coauthored, and codirected. And he was
asked to direct the film, then fired. After that experience,
we were talking with Robert Redford, who is a friend, and
we were very involved with Sundance Institute. And Redford said, "Why don't you do a film you feel very deeply
about?"

And we were going back to our cabin, and I said, "Pete,
what about *The Trip to Bountiful?* You've always loved that
play."

And Pete said, "Horton would never let anyone do that."

I said, "It doesn't hurt to ask. Why don't you call him
up?" And he did.

Horton said, "Yes." They agreed on Geraldine Page, and
I would play Jessie Mae. Things just all seemed to fall into
place. We were all involved. For producer, we got someone
who had never produced, Sterling VanWagenen, who had
been involved with Sundance. In a sense, yes, it was a team
project. That's how we worked. We collaborated. Within a
year, the film was done. Pete did the casting. Everybody
had the same goal. Everyone felt the same way about the
experience, about the veracity of the material. They believed in Horton's writing. We agreed it was a play about
three people, not just one downtrodden old lady.

And then, I would say Geraldine and I were trained in
the same way. We worked the same in rehearsal and when
we shot. John Heard had a different method of acting, but
he was very easy to work with. Pete cast an old friend as
sheriff, Richard Bradford. It all comes down to the casting. This is performance material, not special effects, not
cartoons, not commercial films. All of us were stage actors.
Pete could make the film very quickly because we were all
stage actors. He could shoot six to eight to ten pages in a
master. He was allowed to cut into it because our stage
training had allowed us as film actors to rehearse the
whole scene, retain the whole scene, then break it up.
That's how we got it done in twenty-seven days.

MOORE: Is rehearsal unusual for a film?

GLYNN: Pete insisted on rehearsal. That's very unusual in a commercial film, but not so unusual in a performance film. The actors will do it for nothing. Maybe one day that will change and we'll get paid for rehearsing, but we were all actors eager to rehearse.

MOORE: As an actress who has been on stage and in films, do you prepare differently for each medium?

GLYNN: There's no difference in preparation. The only difference is that with plays, you have six weeks of rehearsal. In film, you do it on your own time. And with film, you can't shoot in sequence. The actor has to be sure he or she knows where the character is at all times. When I do a role like Jessie Mae, I write down scene by scene what the character is doing. The film takes place over only thirty-six hours. In terms of character development, it's the same process on film and in the theater. It's just in film, you have to know the character well enough to shoot out of sequence and to be prepared well enough to know what that character is feeling at all times.

MOORE: The cliché is that the actress has to underplay for film. Is that true?

GLYNN: In film acting, you don't have to project. You don't have to reach an audience at the back of an auditorium, but the central core is the same. The intimacy with the audience is different. In film, you work intimately with the camera, but the intensity is the same whether you're on stage or film.

MOORE: As a performer, are you more of a collaborator with the writer and director onstage or with the movies?

GLYNN: I would say I'm a collaborator whenever I can be. I think it's easier in the theater. In my role as the madam in *Whorehouse,* I collaborated because of the way it came about. It was Peter's idea. He wrote it with Larry L. King. We collaborated in rehearsal in the studio. The composer came down and wrote the songs. I had never been intended to take the role of the madam. They used me in rehearsal because I had a facility with the dialect. As I worked on it, it became my own. And so in that sense, I was very involved in the collaboration. That was such a luxury. We worked together on the creative process. That was a tremendous opportunity.

There are all different kinds of actors. There are actors who are wonderful actors, who are stars. And there are actors who are personalities and, therefore, stars. And then there are actors who care about the whole project. Personally, I'm not a celebrity. I like my privacy. In *Bountiful*, I worked with people who had a very flattering regard for my work. We had agreed at the start, before we even began rehearsal, about the characters. We never had any arguments. Our version of *Bountiful* was to be different from the others. Our concept was that it was a triadic relationship. I would guess the stage version was different. Lillian Gish is so fragile. And Jo Van Fleet is so strong. When they said Geraldine Page was going to play Mrs. Watts, I was glad. This was not going to be a film about a poor little old woman. In the fight scene, she really goads me.

Anyway, the process of making the film was wonderful. Making the film, working with Pete, Geraldine, Horton, John—that was a delicious work experience. I mean very few times in a career do all the actors, the writing, the directorial concept work together so well.

I did have a surprising thing happen to me as an actor during the performance. I have always worked deeply within myself to get the character, but during the very last section of the film when we were shooting at the farmhouse, I felt very, very isolated while waiting to join the scene, very left out. I was interested in that reaction and used it for Jessie Mae.

MOORE: Why was the role so difficult for you?

GLYNN: I'm not like Jessie Mae. Quite the contrary. I'm very maternal, an outgoing person. She is almost all the other way. I have a mother-in-law. But to play a character that is basically the villain, to embrace her, to love her, to find parts of her that work, to create what is not you—it was the biggest architectural job that I've tried.

I tried to find the little girl in her even though I'm the mother of three adult children. I grew up in Texas and

lived in Houston. I could draw on many things from childhood. Her core was sixteen years old. I saw her tenacity. A
scene that was very important for me is where Mrs. Watts
has her spell. It was an opportunity to show I didn't want
her to die, just to quit singing.

   Old people now are farmed out. In 1947, you were expected to take care of your own. As poorly as Ludie and
Jessie Mae are dealing with the problem, they are trying.
And sociologically, that was interesting to me. I thought
that was very important. Nowadays, people just want to go
forward and to leave the past behind.

MOORE: You even had a different voice for her, a much
   higher pitched voice.

GLYNN: Oh, yes, definitely. I see her as about fourteen to
   sixteen years old. And the other thing—and I feel very
   strongly about this—is that she really does love Ludie. I
   would describe her as someone who has a lot of negative
   attitudes, whereas in my own life, I'm a doer, a problem-
   solver. There are many good things in my life, and I feel
   very comfortable with myself.

MOORE: Was there anything particularly memorable about
   making the film?

GLYNN: I guess the thing that was most interesting to me
   was—I'm married to the director, Peter Masterson. I was
   cooking for everybody, living with the director while he
   was under such tight budget restrictions and time restrictions. And I had to save enough energy to do the most difficult role for me in my career—with great joy, by the way.
   It was very taxing. Pete creates a family atmosphere. Everyone is respected equally, even the grips. It's a wonderful
   atmosphere.

❧ V ❧

Comparison Chart (Scene by Scene) of the Three Scripts

Comparison Chart (*Scene by Scene*) of the Three Scripts

TELEPLAY	STAGEPLAY	SCREENPLAY	EFFECTS OF THE CHANGES
Act I	**Act I**		
Mrs. Watts is rocking in a chair as Jessie Mae puts on makeup. J.M. tells Mrs. W. to look at the time and remind Ludie to get the clock fixed. J.M. tells Mrs. W. to stop hymn singing. Mrs. W. stops. J.M. says Mrs. W. is pouting. Mrs. W. says she's only being silent. J.M. sends her to get a Coke. J.M. asks if the check has arrived. Mrs. W. says no. J.M. says movie magazine has a contest for a trip to Hollywood and she wants to go there just as Mrs. W. wants to go to Bountiful. J.M. complains about the hymns again and wants Mrs. W. to prepare dinner. J.M. warns Mrs. W. not to run off to Bountiful and threatens to call the police if she does. J.M. leaves. Mrs. W. gets up and screams. She pulls out her check. J.M. returns and says Mrs. W. can't cash the check. J.M. leaves. Mrs. W. packs a suitcase.	Mrs. Watts rocks. We learn that Ludie was an accountant. His savings were depleted during his illness. He had to accept a new job at a lower salary.

*L. comes into the living room as Mrs. W. rocks. . . . .

They talk about the pretty night, the chance for a bad accident at the corner, and fast cars. | | The television version is much shorter than the others. For the Broadway play, the author chose to expand the first act by giving more background on the characters, adding the presence of Ludie, and painting a more detailed picture of the feud between the two women.

Theatrical version gives us more information about Ludie and his financial problems.

In the TV version, we don't meet Ludie until the bus station. In the other two versions, he comes in early in the first scene. As a result, the TV battle is essentially between the two women, while the latter versions picture a triangular struggle.

Discussion of cars reinforces the idea of an urban neighborhood to a theater audience seeing only an interior set. |

L. talks about his job and says he'll ask for a raise. He asks why she can't sleep. She says because of the full moon. Does he remember their walk in the moonlight? No. She comforted him about his fear of death. He asks about a song he remembers. She sings it and says the world can't be bought. She goes to get him warm milk.

J.M. is awakened by tires screeching. She turns on the lights. Her cigarette lighter is out of fluid. She says L. hasn't been sleeping well, but she never has any trouble sleeping except once at Bountiful.

J.M. asks about a recipe. Mrs. W. looks for it. . . . .

J.M. says Mrs. W. is getting forgetful.

J.M. wants to go out more and talks about Rosella. . . . .

J.M. says they can't go out because of Mrs. W. and says she insulted R. about her hair.

R. and J.M. made up. J.M. says she's plainspoken. R. can't have children.
J.M. tells Mrs. W. to walk, not run and comments on the check not arriving.

These scenes give the film and theater audience a better idea of the relationship between Ludie and his mother and introduce the contrast in their willingness to reminisce about Bountiful.

The play allows us to know more details about Jessie Mae.

The "recipe battle" dramatizes the conflict between the two women in all its pettiness and the role of Ludie as frustrated peacemaker.

In the stage version, Jessie Mae is more insulting, more vicious, more menacing than in the movie version.

Jessie Mae's selfishness and self-pity become more obvious.

The play and movie indicate that Jessie Mae is insensitive to Rosella also, but Rosella is like Jessie Mae—able to bounce back. We see that Jessie Mae is not alone in her values.

*Occurs in both stageplay and screenplay. Dots are used throughout the chart to extend a short line of type across more than one column, indicating that the scene occurs in more than one version.

Comparison Chart (*Scene by Scene*) of the Three Scripts (*continued*)

TELEPLAY	STAGEPLAY	SCREENPLAY	EFFECTS OF THE CHANGES
	J.M. says Mrs. W. is stubborn as she continues to search. J.M. sings with a song on the radio. The neighbors complain. She fusses, then talks about movie magazines, and says to count backward to get to sleep. L. says they could go to a baseball game. He used to play in Bountiful. J.M. talks about auto crashes, complains about Ludie's salary, and says he's too steady. J.M. says she doesn't want to see photos from the past.		This dialogue reinforces the image of Jessie Mae as uncaring about people's needs. The neighbors' complaints remind us that the Watts family is in an urban setting where privacy is rare.
	Mrs. W. returns with the recipe. She says she found it in J.M.'s dresser. J.M. is angry. Mrs. W. throws the recipe on the floor. They shout. L. tries to break up the argument. He leaves for bedroom. J.M. follows. He returns to living room to ask Mrs. W. for an apology and gets it. She returns recipe to J.M.		We see that Ludie is more likely to side with Jessie Mae than with his mother.
		J.M. throws away recipe.	A visual example of Jessie Mae's pettiness.
	Ludie asks J.M. to ignore some things.		This scene indicates that although Ludie chooses Jessie Mae over his mother, he is sympathetic to his mother's plight.

J.M. says she has to stay home because she's afraid Mrs. W. will run away.

L. says she can't because the check hasn't arrived. As they talk, Mrs. W. gets out the check but doesn't turn it over to her son and daughter-in-law.

The author gives a motive for Jessie Mae's irritation toward Mrs. Watts.

L. checks on Mrs. W. J.M. says she wants to go to a beauty parlor and to get a radio for the bedroom. J.M. says Mrs. W. is a good cook.

Jessie Mae's love of popular culture is underlined, and we see that she views Mrs. Watts as a sort of servant, but a good one. To keep the movie from running too long, much of Jessie Mae's chatter about Hollywood is cut out.

They talk about their marriage of 15 years and say they thought well of each other from the beginning.

J.M. looked like a cross between Joan Crawford and Clara Bow. She wants to be good company and a good sport like Sue Carol, who can afford children.

These scenes help us understand why the couple married and how their marriage survives. Ludie's disappointment in his failing to support his family adequately becomes clear.

L. wants to ask for a raise. He talks about his illness and a book on success.

J.M. wants ice cream and a movie magazine, but doesn't want to disturb Mrs. W. She says R. cried when she found out she couldn't have kids, but J.M. doesn't worry since it's the Lord's will. She can't afford to see doctors. He wants to buy her a dress when his salary is increased. J.M. says *(cont. next page)*

We see the battle from Jessie Mae's point of view. We find out more about the couple's childlessness, which neither consciously blames on Mrs. Watts, but Jessie Mae's prudishness hints at a possible problem. Ludie again sides with Jessie Mae, this time on the advantages of the *(cont. next page)*

Comparison Chart (*Scene by Scene*) of the Three Scripts (*Continued*)

TELEPLAY	STAGEPLAY	SCREENPLAY	EFFECTS OF THE CHANGES
	(*cont.*) she wants to live in the city and Mrs. W. in the country. L. says he doesn't think about the past. J.M. says the past is too morbid. J.M. tells L. not to look at her as she goes to bed.		(*cont.*) city over the country and of the present over the past.
	L. goes out to living room. Mrs. W. wants to go to Bountiful. He says he can't make a living there. L. leaves.	Mrs. W. wants to go to Bountiful. He says he	Mrs. Watts's desperation is emphasized.
	Mrs. W. starts packing.	Mrs. W. rocks.	
	Alarm goes off. Mrs. W. fixes breakfast. J.M. complains about hymn singing, turns on radio, and asks L. to turn it down. J.M. complains about Mrs. W.'s running in the apartment.		The morning scenes parallel the themes of the night scenes, but Mrs. Watts seems more hopeful.
	J.M. says she has to get out, maybe to a beauty parlor. She sends Mrs. W. to see if the check has arrived. J.M. says Mrs. W. is too silent and is thinking about running away. Mrs. W. says no mail yet.		Jessie Mae's suspicion builds suspense.
	L. offers to take them to the movies. J.M. makes a hair appointment. L. leaves. He looks to see if the check has arrived, but it hasn't. J.M. looks around for the check.		The importance of the check to the family's income is indicated by their concern over its late appearance.

Mrs. W. says she'll clean today while J.M. does sewing or cleans out a drawer. J.M. fusses about running, gets Mrs. W. to check a hem, then says she wants to win a trip to Hollywood.	L. is in car with Billy.	The car scenes take the movie away from the cramped apartment and allow the film to open up some.
J.M. gets ready to go to a drugstore. She wants a Coke and fusses about Mrs. W.'s hymns and pouting. She talks about the movies they could see. Mrs. W. has a sinking spell while cleaning. R. calls and J.M. leaves. Mrs. W. pulls out suitcase and goes to endorse the check. J.M. returns. Mrs. W. says she's writing to Callie. J.M. leaves with warning that Mrs. W. can't cash check.		The scene reinforces the servant role of Mrs. Watts and the shallowness of Jessie Mae. The sinking spell adds another layer of suspense and shows Jessie Mae's concern. Jessie Mae's unexpected return adds to the suspense.
	L. and Billy talk about going to a baseball game.	Billy's "normal" family life is a contrast to Ludie's.
	Exterior shot of house. Mrs. W. goes downstairs. A neighbor greets her. She walks down the street. J.M. enters the drugstore. Mrs. W. waits for the bus. J.M. is at drugstore. Mrs. W. gets on the bus. J.M. and Rosella look at dresses.	Exterior shots open up film. Cross cutting creates visual interest
Mrs. W. goes to train station but no train goes to Bountiful. The next train that goes near Bountiful leaves the next morning.	Mrs. W. goes to train station, but there are no trains to Bountiful. Mrs. W. goes to bus station. J.M. goes through apartment calling for Mrs. W.	The train station would be an additional set that would have to stay on stage for the duration despite its brief use. Television and film allow Mrs. Watts the visual freedom to go more places.

Comparison Chart (*Scene by Scene*) of the Three Scripts (*Continued*)

TELEPLAY	STAGEPLAY	SCREENPLAY	EFFECTS OF THE CHANGES
	Act II		
Thelma buys a bus ticket. Mrs. W. tries to buy a bus ticket to Bountiful, but no buses go there. She settles for a ticket to Harrison. Mrs. W. wants the ticket seller to cash her pension check, but he won't. She uses coins to buy her ticket, then almost forgets it. Mrs. W. sits by Thelma and says she's going to Bountiful. Mrs. W. talks about J.M. and her heart problems. Mrs. W. jumps up to look for L. and J.M. She sees them, drops her handkerchief and runs off.			
L. offers to get J.M. a movie magazine.		L. looks for Mrs. W. He asks the ticket agent.	Adds movement to the film.
	J.M. sits next to Thelma and complains about Mrs. W.; L. returns with a magazine. The couple argues about what to do next. J.M. leaves. L. offers movie magazine to T. L. sees the handkerchief. He goes to ticket man for information, but he's just gone on duty. L. asks T. and she says she has seen Mrs. W. J.M. returns. She says she called the police. The couple walks away.		
Mrs. W. sits next to T. on the bus.		Mrs. W. in the cafe sees them leave. She gets on the bus.	Adds movement to the film
		We see city and country from Mrs. W.'s point of view. The bus arrives at Gerard. The passengers get off. They wait and chat. Then they get on the bus.	Film allows us to see the countryside go by. Scene at Gerard suggests the alienation of the passengers from each other, from their past, and from God.
L. asks if the bus has left. He's told yes. He and J.M. argue loudly about getting the police. Mrs. W. hums.			Forms a strong ending for act one of the TV play.

Act II

Mrs. W. talks to T. about Bountiful. T. says her husband's away. Mrs. W. recites a Psalm. They discuss worrying. T. says she told L. about seeing Mrs. W.

They talk about the hymn "There's Not a Friend like the Lowly Jesus."   ("Softly and Tenderly")

Mrs. W. says L.'s nerves gave out, which wouldn't have happened in Bountiful. She explains that she sold off land to get L. an education.   More background information about Mrs. Watts.

She talks about her friend Callie and Mrs. W.'s dead babies. T. explains about her husband. Mrs. W. says she never loved her husband and tells of her lost love. Mrs. W. says she now has her wish—going to Bountiful. They arrive at Harrison. T. checks on the bus to Bountiful. They learn Callie is dead. T. asks about going to a hotel. Mrs. W. says she's going to Bountiful somehow. Mrs. W. realizes her purse is gone. The ticket man calls to get purse back. Mrs. W. wonders why things work out well sometimes.

Thelma and Mrs. W. share a sandwich. Mrs. W. talks about dances of the past and says she wants a daughter like T. Ticket man joins them.   Illustrates the relationship between Thelma and Mrs. Watts.

T. leaves when her bus arrives...............................

Mrs. W. asks ticket man about her friends from the past. He knows no one. They discuss children who drink.   The ticket man's failure to remember her friends is an example of the effects of passing time.

Mrs. W. sleeps. Sheriff arrives and wakes up the ticket man. Sheriff has come for Mrs. W.; L. will arrive soon, he says. Sheriff can't awaken her and leaves. Mrs. W. wakes up and asks about her purse. It's there. She wants to cash her check in order to go to Bountiful. Ticket man says sheriff wants her to stay. Sheriff arrives. Mrs. W. begs to go to Bountiful. She almost faints. Sheriff calls for the doctor.

Comparison Chart (*Scene by Scene*) of the Three Scripts (*Continued*)

TELEPLAY	STAGEPLAY	SCREENPLAY	EFFECTS OF THE CHANGES
Act III	Act III		
		Sheriff offers to take her after she's seen doctor. We see the countryside from the sheriff's car. L. and J.M. arrive at Harrison. Mrs. W. is driven up to the house.	Film lets us see the countryside and the house.
Mrs. W. is overjoyed to be at Bountiful..........			
	They discuss birds.		The conversation on birds indicates the sheriff's sympathy for Mrs. Watts and gives an insight into her father's personality.
She asks what happened to the countryside. It's deserted. Sheriff says land played out, but Callie took care of hers. He leaves for the car.		Mrs. W. tours the house.	The film camera can go inside the house and show Mrs. Watt's reaction to it.
Sheriff announces L. has arrived. Sheriff leaves. L. asks Mrs. W. about her health. She tells him about Callie's death.			

Ludie's explanation for not bringing her home sooner reveals his own feelings about the past.

She explains she had to go back and wants to know if J.M. will come out. L. apologizes for not bringing Mrs. W. back sooner. He thought it would be hard. He refuses to look inside the house. Mrs. W. says L. looks like her Papa. L. describes the day his grandfather died. He promised to name a son for his grandfather, but has no children. He confesses he does remember everything, but he doesn't want to.

L. says they'll have to leave now. She breaks down. Why did they leave the land? She says the land has brought her peace.

She says she won't fight J.M. again. . . . .

She says cotton fields have turned to woods and may turn to cotton fields again. J.M. calls out. She fusses at Mrs. W. about running away.

J.M. goes over her list of demands. L. says J.M. will try to improve too. She wants a drink of water, but not creek water. She wants a Coke.

J.M. wants to know where Mrs. W.'s purse is. J.M. retrieves it from the house. Where is the check? Mrs. W. remembers it's in her bosom. They wrangle over the check.

Mrs. W. tears up the check. L. sends J.M. to the car. Mrs. W. apologizes. L. cries. He says he's being pulled apart by J.M. and Mrs. W. Mrs. W. says she won't fight again.

The television scene is more emotional.

Comparison Chart (*Scene by Scene*) of the Three Scripts (*Continued*)

TELEPLAY	STAGEPLAY	SCREENPLAY	EFFECTS OF THE CHANGES
	L. tells them to stop arguing. J.M. allows Mrs. W. to keep check. J.M. leaves.		This scene indicates a small degree of reconciliation between the two women with Ludie sticking up for his mother. Still, it's clear Jessie Mae does not share the same values as Mrs. Watts.
			The last two versions underline the reconciliation rather than the conflict.
Mrs. W. pauses as L. leaves. She lets the dirt sift through her fingers.			
Mrs. W. starts crying again but says no more. She's had her trip.			The teleplay is more emotional.
She says goodbye to Bountiful.			

Afterword

I AM indebted to Barbara Moore and David Yellin for taking a work of mine through its various stages.

Their thoughtful introductions and insightful interviews set me to thinking back again to the writing of *The Trip to Bountiful* and its earliest productions.

It was the late winter of 1952 that I first began thinking of *The Trip to Bountiful*. Fred Coe asked me if I would write another television play for his "Philco/Goodyear Playhouse" (he had previously commissioned and produced two other of my plays, *The Travelers* and *The Old Beginning*). I began working on *The Trip to Bountiful* by dramatizing the scene where Carrie Watts's father forces her to stop seeing the young man she's in love with, but I was not satisfied at all with the result. I put it aside and began searching in my mind for another play idea, when I suddenly thought why not investigate the woman at the end of her life. The television play was written very quickly after that. That was forty years ago. Is it possible? It seems almost like yesterday—the writing of the play and taking the finished play to Fred Coe and his calling back the next day to say he was scheduling it as soon as it could be properly cast.

Vincent J. Donehue, my longtime friend, was to direct, and we began at once to cast Carrie Watts. Shirley Booth was our first choice, but she turned the role down saying she wasn't ready to play an old woman. Then Fred Coe suggested Lillian Gish. He had directed her in television in, I believe, Sidney Howard's *The Late Christopher Bean*. Lillian Gish was, of course, a household word because of her film work, but I

253

had only seen her some years earlier onstage in Maxwell Anderson's *Star Wagon* and as Ophelia in John Gielgud's *Hamlet*. Fred assured me that now she was playing character parts. Fred gave her the play, and she sent back word that she was interested but would like first to meet the director and the author. Vincent and I went to her Fifty-seventh Street apartment, and she greeted us at the door. She was dressed in a handsome black dress and was still a very great beauty. She said she thought it was a very daring piece to do, but she would be happy to play Carrie Watts if we wanted her. We began our rehearsals soon after.

We had a wonderful cast: Eileen Heckart as Jessie Mae, John Beal as Ludie, Eva Marie Saint as Thelma, William Hansen as the station master, and Frank Overton as the sheriff. At the first reading we saw how fortunate we were in having Lillian Gish, for from the beginning it was obvious that this great international beauty, a film and theater star for many, many years (since she was fifteen, she was now fifty-five), felt a real kinship with the country woman Carrie Watts.

Lillian Gish in many of her film roles played fragile and helpless women. There was none of this in her Carrie Watts. It was apparent at once that she realized this woman's strength, her willfulness and her determination. You believed absolutely that this was a woman who had worked in the fields with her hands for many years.

Fred Coe and the Theatre Guild asked me then to expand the television play. This expanded version was produced first at the Westport Playhouse in the summer of 1953, and then in the fall went on the road for a pre-Broadway tour.

Jo Van Fleet was cast as Jessie Mae for this production, and she was wonderful, shrewd, willful, coquettish. One felt in her performance the influence of the movie stars, the Flapper of the silent era and early talkies, that she so incessantly talked about and constantly compared herself to as she looked in the mirror. This was a comic Jessie Mae, but underneath her chatter and smugness, a heartbreaking one.

Eva Marie Saint as Thelma in both the television and play production brought great sensitivity to the part. She and

Lillian Gish had a special rapport in their scenes together, and you felt they might have been, or should have been, mother and daughter.

While we were playing *The Trip to Bountiful* in New York, Elia Kazan came to see the play and offered Eva Marie Saint the lead in *On the Waterfront*. She would only consent to take the part if he would allow her to continue performing in the play for the evening performances.

When the play closed in New York, Lillian Gish took it on the road, this time with Kim Stanley as Jessie Mae. Whatever Kim Stanley did was always special and impressive.

The play was done a few years later in England and Ireland, directed by Alan Schneider. I never got to see that production, and the only person I know who did was Geraldine Page, who was playing in London in *The Rainmaker* at the time.

A few years later the play was done off Broadway in a production directed by Adrian Hall; it was this production that Pete Masterson saw.

Through the years there continued to be stage productions of *The Trip to Bountiful*, and every few years or so a producer would inquire about the movie rights, but we could never agree on the casting of Mrs. Watts.

In December 1984 when Geraldine Page came to pick up the screenplay for *The Trip to Bountiful* she left me a note saying "Thank you for my Christmas present." Of course it was the other way around—she was the one making the gift.

When F. Murray Abrams was asked to announce the name of the actress winning the Oscar that night in Los Angeles, he said, "If her name hadn't been on that slip of paper I would have called it out anyway, because she is our greatest living actress."

It was her eighth nomination for an Academy Award [she was nominated four times for best supporting actress and four for best actress]. She deserved it, in my opinion, all eight times, but never more than for her performance in *The Trip to Bountiful*.

Pete, Sterling, and Carlin have spoken so eloquently about their contributions to the film that there is little for me to add, except that it was a most happy and satisfying time for me.

In the hands of a talented director and actors, a play or a screenplay is given a new life and meaning. That is the greatest gift, I feel, actors and directors can give a writer, and that gift Pete, Geraldine Page, Carlin Glynn, John Heard, Richard Bradford, and the other actors gave me in abundance.

Horton Foote
Wharton, Texas

Bibliography

Barbera, Jack. "Tomorrow and Tomorrow and Tomorrow." *Southern Quarterly* 19, no. 3, 4 (Spring–Summer 1981). 183–97.

Barr, George Terry. "The Ordinary World of Horton Foote." Ph.D. diss., University of Tennessee, 1986.

Bluestone, George. *Novels into Film.* Baltimore: The Johns Hopkins Press, 1957.

Blumenthal, Eileen. "Deftly Footed." *Village Voice,* April 13, 1982.

Broughton, Irv. *The Writer's Mind: Interviews with American Authors.* Vol. 2. Fayetteville: University of Arkansas Press, 1989.

Burkhart, Marian. "Horton Foote's Many Roads Home." *Commonweal,* February 26, 1988, 110–15.

Canby, Vincent. "Film: Geraldine Page in *A Trip to Bountiful.*" *New York Times,* December 20, 1985, sec. C-10.

" 'Christianity Today' Talks to Horton Foote." *Christianity Today,* April 4, 1986, 30.

Clurman, Harold. "Theater." *Nation,* November 21, 1953, 43.

Darnton, Nina. "Horton Foote Celebrates a Bygone America in *1918.*" *New York Times,* April 21, 1985.

Davis, Ronald L. "Roots in Parched Ground: An Interview with Horton Foote." *Southwest Review* 73, no. 3 (Summer 1988): 298–318.

DeVries, Hilary. "Geraldine Page." *Christian Science Monitor,* March 25, 1988, 18, 21.

"Dialogue on Film: Horton Foote." *American Film,* October 1986, 13–16.

Edgerton, Gary. "A Visit to the Imaginary Landscape of Harrison Texas: Sketching the Film Career of Horton Foote." *Literature/Film Quarterly* 17, no. 1 (Winter 1989): 2–12.

Fein, Esther B. "The Women behind *The Trip to Bountiful.*" *New York Times,* January 6, 1986.

Foote, Horton. "Dialogue on Film: Horton Foote." *American Film,* October 1986, 13–16.

———. "On First Dramatizing Faulkner" and "Tomorrow: The Genesis of a Screenplay." In *Faulkner, Modernism, and Film: Faulkner and Yoknapatawpha,* edited by Evans Harrington and Ann J. Abadie. Jackson: University Press of Mississippi, 1979.

———. "Writing for Film." In *Film and Literature: A Comparative Approach to Adaptation,* edited by Wendell Aycock and Michael Schoenecke. Lubbock: Texas Tech University Press, 1988.

Forsberg, Myra. "Southern Memories Shadow the Makers of 'Convicts.'" *New York Times,* December 3, 1989, sec. C-15.

Freedman, Samuel G. "From the Heart of Texas." *New York Times Magazine,* February 9, 1986, 30, 50, 61–63, 73.

Fulton, Mary Lou. "Stardom Reached in Her Own Way." *Los Angeles Times,* June 15, 1987, 20.

Hachem, Samir. "Foote-Work." *Horizon,* April 1986, 39–41.

Hey, Kenneth. "*Marty:* Aesthetics vs. Medium in Early Television Drama." In *American History/American Television: Interpreting the Video Past,* edited by John E. O'Connor. New York: Frederick Ungar, 1983.

Manvell, Roger. *Theater and Film: A Comparative Study of the Two Forms of Dramatic Art, and of the Problems of Adaptation of Stage Plays into Films.* Rutherford, N.J.: Fairleigh Dickinson University Press, 1979.

Martin, William B., ed. *Texas Plays.* Dallas: Southern Methodist University Press, 1990.

Neff, David. "Going Home to the Hidden God." *Christianity Today,* April 4, 1986, 30–31.

Nicoll, Allardyce. *Film and Theatre.* New York: Arno Press, 1972.

Price, Reynolds. Introduction to *Courtship, Valentine's Day, 1918,* by Horton Foote. New York: Grove Press, 1986.

Reinert, Al. "Tender Foote." *Texas Monthly,* July 1991, 110, 132–37.

Richardson, Robert. *Literature and Film.* Bloomington: Indiana University Press, 1969.

Sinyard, Neil. *Filming Literature: The Art of Screen Adaptation.* London: Croom Helm, 1986.

Skaggs, Calvin. *The American Short Story.* New York: Dell Publishing Co., 1977.

Sterrit, David. "Horton Foote: Filmmaking Radical with a Tender Touch." *Christian Science Monitor,* May 15, 1986, 1.

Toles, George, ed. *Film/Literature.* Winnipeg: University of Manitoba

Press, 1983.

"The Trip to Paradise." *Texas Monthly*, December 1987, 140–49.

Walker, Beverly, and Leonard Klady. "Cinema Sanctuaries." *Film Comment*, June 1986, 61–66.

Weales, Gerald. *American Drama since World War II*. New York: Harcourt, Brace & World, 1962.

Wilk, Max. *The Golden Age of Television: Notes from the Survivors*. New York: Delacorte Press, 1976.

Wood, Gerald C. Introduction to *Selected One-Act Plays of Horton Foote*. Dallas: Southern Methodist University Press, 1989.

Wood, Gerald C., and Terry Barr. "A Certain Kind of Writer: An Interview with Horton Foote." *Literature/Film Quarterly* 14 (Winter 1986): 226–37.

Yellin, David G., and Marie Connors, eds. *Tomorrow and Tomorrow and Tomorrow*. Jackson: University of Mississippi Press, 1985.

Young, Stark. Introduction to *The Traveling Lady*, by Horton Foote. New York: Dramatists Play Service, 1955.